The Tempest and New World-Utopian Politics

The Tempest and New World-Utopian Politics

Frank W. Brevik

Chapter 1 of this book appeared in the online journal *This Rough Magic* in Spring/Summer 2011.
Chapter 3 of this book appeared in print in *Authority of Expression* in 2009. It is used here with kind permission from Cambridge Scholars Publishing.

First published in 2012 by
PALGRAVE MACMILLAN®
in the United States—a division of St. Martin's Press LLC,
175 Fifth Avenue, New York, NY 10010.

Where this book is distributed in the UK, Europe and the rest of the World, this is by Palgrave Macmillan, a division of Macmillan Publishers Limited, registered in England, company number 785998, of Houndmills, Basingstoke, Hampshire RG21 6XS.

Palgrave Macmillan is the global academic imprint of the above companies and has companies and representatives throughout the world.

Palgrave® and Macmillan® are registered trademarks in the United States, the United Kingdom, Europe and other countries.

ISBN: 978–1–137–02179–3

Library of Congress Cataloging-in-Publication Data

Brevik, Frank W.
    The Tempest and new world-Utopian politics / Frank W. Brevik.
        p.   cm.
    Includes bibliographical references and index.
    ISBN 978–1–137–02179–3 (hardback)
    1. Shakespeare, William, 1564–1616. Tempest.
    2. Utopias in literature.   I. Title.
    PR2833.B66 2012
    822.3′3—dc23   2012005800

A catalogue record of the book is available from the British Library.

This book is printed on paper suitable for recycling and made from fully managed and sustained forest sources. Logging, pulping and manufacturing processes are expected to conform to the environmental regulations of the country of origin.

Design by Integra Software Services

First edition: August 2012

10 9 8 7 6 5 4 3 2 1

To my son, Oliver Anker Brevik

Contents

Acknowledgments   ix

Part I   The New World *Tempest* Orthodoxy as Multicultural Pedagogy

Introduction: The Rampant Politicization of *Tempest* Criticism—and Its Recent Discontents   3

1   Teaching *The Tempest* in an American-Adamic Context: The New World Orthodoxy as Multicultural Pedagogy   13

Part II   "Text" versus "Context" in Post-Second World War Criticism

2   Such Maps as Dreams Are Made On: Discourse, Utopian Geography, and *The Tempest*'s Island   35

3   Calibans Anonymous: The Journey from Text to Self in Modern Criticism   55

Part III   Subversive American Adams and Anarchic Utopists

4   *The Tempest* Beyond Post-Colonial Politics: Vargas Llosa's *The Storyteller* as Topical Retrotext   71

5   "Any Strange Beast There Makes a Man": New World Manliness as Old World Kingliness in *The Tempest*   91

6   "Thought Is Free": *The Tempest*, Freedom of Expression, and the New World   113

Part IV   Post-Communist Topicalities

7   Toward a Post-1989 Reading of *The Tempest*   131

Conclusion: Readers vs. Text in the Age of Democracy: *The
Formalist Tempest* or Presentist "*Tempests*"?   159

Notes   169

Works Cited   179

Index   189

Acknowledgments

The publication of this book marks the high point of a project that has been with me since I was a junior in college thirteen years ago, and my deeply felt thanks are due to a number of people whose help has been significant.

I wish first and foremost to thank Jessica White, who has co-written the first chapter and who deserves special thanks for her willingness to contribute to the book and for the quality and intelligence of her input.

Jennifer Vaught, who supervised the doctoral dissertation that forms the backbone of the research, was as tireless as she was insightful in her feedback.

I also wish to thank LaGrange College reference librarian Arthur Robinson, who has pulled several rabbits out of his hat toward this project. Jay Simmons and David Garrison deserve thanks for awarding me the LaGrange College Dean/Provost Summer Research Grant in 2009 and 2011.

At Palgrave Macmillan, I am grateful to Brigitte Shull, Jo Roberts, and Maia Woolner for believing in my book manuscript and for taking it on board.

Special thanks also go to the anonymous reviewer for invaluable comments and remarks on the manuscript.

Finally, my love and sincerest gratitude go to my family in Norway—my mother, Anne Lise Brevik, and my sisters Kristin Waage and Lena Brevik.

Part I

The New World *Tempest* Orthodoxy as Multicultural Pedagogy

Introduction: The Rampant Politicization of *Tempest* Criticism—and Its Recent Discontents

It has been 400 years since *The Tempest* was written. For about 340 years the play was enjoying a largely panegyric criticism laden with honorifics like "transcendent," "artistic," and "Shakespeare's farewell to the stage." By now, the play is without a doubt one of Shakespeare's most politicized plays. This book will trace and challenge the major recent political interpretations of *The Tempest*, especially where these readings draw on the very earliest suggestions by Edmond Malone and Sidney Lee that the play portrays or foreshadows the way in which the English/Americans would later dispossess the natives of America of their land and culture. Many *Tempest* critics have since sought to expand the applicability of the play to include historically more recent ideological issues particular to the "third world" as well as the more New World-specific slant found in Malone and Lee. The study on New World and Americanist utopian politics in *The Tempest* that follows focuses on how paradigm shifts in literary criticism over the past six decades have all but reinscribed the text of Shakespeare's last unassisted play into a fiercely political palimpsest grounded in historical events like colonialism or even prophetically envisioning post-colonial issues. In the following chapters, I problematize the by now hegemonic views that the play has a dominant New World dimension, reject the idea that Caliban can be seen as a Native American or African slave, and disprove textually the premise that the play unproblematically addresses a uniquely Western colonial history and post-colonial plight. My conclusions are not only drawn on the important basis of a method of holistic close readings that demonstrates how a textually derived, ultimately utopian setting at the same time enables and effaces discursively over-invested New World settings but also informed by intertextuality, sources, historical context, and presentist co-texts. To the extent that this hybrid methodology—hardly original in itself—yields original findings, it does so in this book's ensuing discussion of utopian politics, which posits the argument that *The Tempest* is a politically subversive play rather than a compliant and decorous one, drawing, as it does, on explosively radical passages that form a proto-Americanist discourse that displays and interrogates a power vacuum where nearly all authority has been suspended. The New World dimensions that this book sees at work in the play are in other words not the colonial or political relationship between Caliban and his master Prospero that fits into the narratives that post-colonial writers and scholars have so often rehearsed. Instead, the Americanist impulses of the play form a part of a larger utopian discourse that has so far been all but neglected in *Tempest* criticism. Such proto-Americanist discourse can be found not so much in the red herring of Caliban as an Indian or cannibal but rather in Ferdinand's New World masculinity, in the freedom of speech and movement that the setting's New World-topical space affords, in Gonzalo's utopian urges to start mankind all over again, all resonating with the (sometimes unrealistic) optimism that forms an important part of the discourse about the New World—as opposed to the bleak pessimism associated with Europe. This latter tension has been given almost no critical attention in *Tempest* scholarship, and, over several chapters, my book interprets the play's pastoral, utopian, and "American" tensions in light of its aporic setting as well as through a "presentist" post-1989 prism—unfathomably, almost totally neglected as a historical and political paradigm shift in Shakespeare criticism.

More specifically, this book seeks to answer the following questions relevant to understanding *The Tempest* and its myriad interpretations in the last sixty years: What led to the New World orthodoxy in terms of the play's themes? How can this interpretation be best discussed and understood in a pedagogical situation involving students unfamiliar with the play's considerable contextual resonances? Where is the play's island set, cartographically as well as metaphorically speaking? To what extent is literal text privileged over more fluid understandings of "texts" and "contexts" (or, lately, perhaps, vice versa) in *Tempest* criticism? How convincing—in terms of text, intertext, and context—is Caliban as a symbol of everything and everybody, especially as a suffering colonial subject oppressed by the European conqueror? Beside the much-touted (post-)colonialist parallels, what Americanist dimensions pervade the play otherwise? In what ways are these New World or "American" points of interest interpretable in terms of sex and gender? Can we speak of a New World masculinity that is different from European manliness? Can the play be said to be politically subversive in its advocacy of a sense of freedom of expression, of freedom of movement, of conscience, of thought, of belief, of religion, of spirit? And to what extent is this multifaceted freedom, then, a result of the play's setting, in how great measure reliant on vastness of space, on the New World in its literal topicality? Is American speech, therefore, freer than European utterance in early modern discourse? And what sort of political and social parallels does the play hold post-1989? And *why*, finally, have such possible post-communist and post-colonial parallels remained nearly *entirely* unarticulated in criticism of the play these last twenty-two years?

As the above questions intimate, this work addresses a black hole in *Tempest* criticism. I suffer no delusions that my work can somehow fill this critical gap, but, for its small part, the holistic, text-centered approach that follows in the next chapters yields a dramatically different interpretation than most of the last sixty years of scholarship. Previous criticism—for example by Mannoni (1950); Césaire (1955); Lamming (1960); Fernando Retamar (1972); Leslie Fiedler (1973); Peter Hulme and Francis Barker (1984); Paul Brown (1985); Thomas Cartelli (1987); and Ania Loomba (1988)—has been exceptionally successful in stressing the play's historical and (post-)colonial points of interest. Carolyn Ann Porter (1987) and Meredith Anne Skura (1989) were among the first to take issue with New Historicists and Cultural Materialists and have since been supported by a new camp of "discontents" whose concerns have been particularly well voiced by Ben Ross Schneider (1995), Jonathan Gil Harris (1999), Ivo Kamps (2004), and Tom McAlindon (2004). My own contribution to this debate aligns itself only in certain chapters, and admittedly not wholly without internal self-contradiction, with this most recent criticism that questions the ubiquitous politicization of *Tempest* readings—and then goes on to suggest a political interpretation of its own.

And toward the 1990s, *The Tempest* witnessed a more moderate (that is to say, *less*) political interpretation that found the methods, premises, and conclusions of previous anti-colonialist scholarship wanting. In the words of Meredith Anne Skura,

> it is assumed that the similarities [the play poses to colonialism] matter but the differences do not: thus Prospero's magic occupies "the space *really inhabited in colonial history* by gunpowder" [Skura's emphasis]; or, when Prospero has Caliban pinched by the spirits, he shows a "similar sadism" to that of the Haitian masters who "roasted slaves or buried them alive"; or, when Prospero and Ariel hunt Caliban with spirit dogs, they are equated to the Spaniards who hunted Native Americans with dogs. So long as there is a core of resemblance, the differences are irrelevant. The differences, in

fact, are themselves taken to be evidence of the colonialist ideology at work, rationalizing and euphemizing power—or else inadvertent slips. (49)

To the extent that Skura's scathing critique can be called political, it is so only insofar as it goes against what it perceives as an overpoliticized criticism that neglects the text in central places and that wishes to read only one side of the story, as it were. Skura's broadside stresses that cultural critics who otherwise tend to operate chiefly in the contextual and discursive realms of literary criticism readily point to textual detail whenever it may confirm some suspicion of a larger New World historical or cultural issue at work in *The Tempest* but tend not to acknowledge the text whenever it might challenge such politically motivated readings.

This revised criticism enjoys, perhaps surprisingly, much support in the Marxist critic Howard Felperin (1995), who finds great weaknesses in New World-specific discussions of *The Tempest*. Felperin points out that most of the readings dealing with colonialism in *The Tempest* tend to be partial and incomplete, ultimately shaped by political interest.[1] He suggests instead a much larger vision: whereas previous critics on the Left have been skeptical or downright dismissive of a humanist utopia, Felperin suggests that we see Prospero's epilogue as central in sketching, or at least alluding to, a utopian view that is fused with elements of a teleological Marxism as well as a theological Christianity, claiming that

> *The Tempest* is not an explicitly Christian play, nor is its "magic" the expression of a primitive pre-theological system; yet it is deeply compatible with both.... So much so, that we might be justified in viewing the play's representation of history as a kind of "missing link" between the historical schemes of Christianity and Marxism. (62)

My own interpretation is indebted to Felperin in both its pronouncements on current criticism and especially in its broadened understanding of utopias seen above that this book in turn links to numerous *benevolent* travel narratives from the New World.

In slight contrast, by calling attention to and emphasizing the Old World and Mediterranean dimensions of the play, some recent scholars have since tried to temper the predominantly dystopian New World angles—and thus, axiomatically, downplay the political castigations leveled at the play—that have been the staple of much recent criticism. Jerry Brotton (1998, 2000), David Scott Wilson-Okamura (2003), Ivo Kamps (2004), and Andrew Hess (2000) are recent examples of this "re-revisionist" tendency. Because of the admirable range of their work, Alden

T. Vaughan and Virginia Mason Vaughan could perhaps be placed in the same camp, but the Vaughans steer clear of polemics and controversy about the play or about Caliban yet nevertheless provide an enormously useful survey of reception, criticism, and cultural metaphors in their seminal book *Caliban: A Cultural History* (1991), to which this book is necessarily greatly indebted. Interesting works have also been written by Jonathan Hart (1996), Jeffrey Knapp (2000), Peter Hulme (2000), and Tom McAlindon (2004), who decries the New World angle as spurious by instead pursuing a similar discussion of the discourse of religion and prayer in the play in order to demonstrate and temper a critical generation's perhaps obsessive focus on the play's colonial aspects and New World-discursive references.

To return to the questions I listed at the outset, my own approach and answers suggest that lecturing to students about the play in this tremendously thorny critical-political climate is very, very easy—but it remains an extremely difficult undertaking to *teach* the play and its myriad contexts and themes in a way that allows student readers who are critically and contextually innocent (what I refer to as "Adamic" students in Chapter 1) to interpret the text with some degree of autonomy. Chapter 1 argues that in order to do so, one ought to start at the critical ground zero, the text of *The Tempest*, and accept the fact that since each student brings a unique background and prism to the reading experience, interpretations will differ greatly. Further, a reading, for example, that is colored by the professor's pronouncement that the play is heavily involved in colonialism (or that it is not, for that matter) can hardly be a fruitful pedagogical experience if student autonomy or freedom of interpretation are the articulated aims—which they nowadays so very often are, of course. Yet some common interpretative experiences will necessarily be shared by most (if not all) readers by virtue of the text's (in)ability to communicate its generic and thematic intent and content; hence the return to the text itself, to its genre and form, the return to lexical (as well as metaphorical) meaning is a useful first step toward appreciating not only the play itself but also, in due time, its legion contexts, intertexts, and co-texts.

Such a pragmatic pedagogy may well entail a time-tested method of thorough close reading, a familiar method that, in the case of Chapter 2, will result in unfamiliarly different conclusions than those drawn by a generation of *Tempest* critics influenced by "old historicism" and the New Criticism that preceded the current New Historicist orthodoxy. For a holistic close reading reveals that the play's setting is not so much a Caribbean colony but a "floating" island, a "hovering" Laputa of sorts that has no consistent geographical coordinates, thus rendering the island perpetually unstable and literally utopian—that is, *nowhere*. This interpretation, while original in its conclusions, is one that nevertheless draws on a distinctly uncartographical and purposely bewildering sense of geography previously described by David Baker as "hypertopical" (68) and by Geraldo de Sousa as an "alien habitat" (447). This geography, so seldom an issue taken seriously in *Tempest* criticism, is greatly at odds with the bulk of recent criticism's tendency to locate the play's island semi-metaphorically and semi-geographically—but wholeheartedly in terms of pathos—in the New World, as if its literal and/or geographical setting were an unimportant afterthought. This book criticizes the blithe convenience with which perhaps especially Marxist-influenced critics have done so—often with an eye to Caliban's presumed New World *topicality*—as highly paradoxical and indeed befuddling, since the axiom accepted by most Marxists posits that material forces (the basis; in this case either the play's setting or the immediate circumstances under which Shakespeare conceived this striking character) are the conditions that enable the superstructure such as culture, art, and language. Thus the play's setting, the very grounds and physical forces of which Caliban is presumably a result, would seem to wield a major influence on the characters and the themes—rather than the other way round. In myriad universally accepted ways, of course, Renaissance London around 1610–11 also shaped the play—but importantly also Caliban, which we witness on the one occasion when, for comedic purposes, he is likened to an Englishman (II.ii.27–30),[2] a point hardly mentioned by any *Tempest* scholar in the last thirty years. Hence there is an enormous inconsistency at work here for Marxist-inspired Cultural Materialist critics seeking to stress the importance of the shaping forces of the basis, the setting, the means of production, the nature, the geography, the climate, the weather, the trees, the rocks, the logs, and so on, while at the same time overtly, artificially, far-fetchedly privileging the setting in particular as New World on the strength of this one, this very European, perhaps even English and local, character's dubious Americanness alone.

I thus contend that many political readings of *The Tempest* rely on the textually highly shaky premise that the setting for the play is *de facto* New World. As I demonstrate in Chapter 2, a setting in the Virginia Colony, in Bermuda, or in America more generally is in many ways a clearly selective and anti-textual locus that enables critics to discuss the play's purported relevance to political problems particular to the New World. In other words, recent discussions over issues like racism and colonialism often rely on circular argumentation in the sense that some critics ostensibly seek to address a *textually* extant dimension from a political angle—the same political impetus that reads the text *against the grain* in order to produce such an otherwise textually unfounded angle in the first place.

Part of Chapter 3, devoted to Caliban, seeks to answer the question why so many New Historicist and Cultural Materialist *Tempest* critics seem to eschew materialism for an unstable culturalism that finds minimal support in the text but rather flimsy evidence in a "discourse" that can be traced back just as much to our own sensibilities as to the historical bases that produced it. Subsequently, Caliban, only recently symbol of nearly every body and every thing in criticism, ought to be interpreted outside of the false guiding premise that the play's setting is to be understood as New World. Caliban's disentanglement from this geographically predicated misreading, stripped of his phantom Indianness and textually ill-defined Africanness, reveals a decidedly mythological, Old World version of the wild man or savage. In contrast to the most dystopian readings that equate Caliban's savageness with the benign portrayals of the "noble" savagery of Native Americans so often found in Renaissance New World travel narratives, an Old World Caliban seems historically and empirically far more convincing. The strength of such a reading finds its root cause in a critical methodology that privileges close textual analysis over historical and contextual discourse. For while New Historicism, Cultural Materialism, and post-colonialist studies have in many ways provided valuable critical perspectives to perhaps especially *Tempest* scholarship, Caliban has been claimed by so many political factions that "his" views—whatever they are—rarely fit with those that appear in the text but rather with a projected set of views that shift attention away from Shakespearean text onto a politicized "context" that a brief survey of *Tempest* criticism after the Second World War strongly affirms is exclusively our own presentist co-text.

There are, precisely for this reason, some rather obvious ironies and problems attendant with reading the play along the lines of post-colonial works. My choosing to do so in the case of Mario Vargas Llosa's topically convergent novel *The Storyteller* in Chapter 4 runs no little risk of practicing the sort of extratextual criticism that my book criticizes post-colonial scholars for having got carried away with to the point of almost no primary-textual recognition or acknowledgment in their efforts to discuss works by, for example, Fanon, Césaire, or Brathwaite. Commentary on these post-colonial works are often passed on as Shakespearean criticism yet in many cases eclipse the Shakespearean play that gave their spin-offs life and fail to explicate and comment on the original. My own defense of the similar exercise that Chapter 4 calls for is first of all that its reaching outward toward Vargas Llosa's novel does not neglect or jar with the Shakespearean text but actually harmonizes with it—that the novel employs similar thematic and structural strategies to what *The Tempest* itself does. Furthermore, Chapter 4 seeks to demonstrate not that extratextual post-colonial readings necessarily display anachronistic fallacies but that there are far more fruitful examples to lean on than those that employ overt *Tempestian* language and characterization, perhaps especially as New World utopias are concerned.

There is no doubt that New World-thematic content infuses the play but most interestingly in ways that have seldom been precisely articulated in scholarship heretofore. My own interpretation in Chapter 5 of what these New World or Americanist dimensions are relies far less on the (metaphorically) geographical setting or on Caliban than on Ferdinand's topical battle with the natural and spiritual forces of a "brave new world" that Miranda understands in a pregnantly ironic way. For Ferdinand could well be seen as the proto-American—indeed, the proto-Puritan—pioneer whose pious display of traditional Roman-stoical *virtus* and contemporary Renaissance travel experience are engendered as a result of the space the island setting furnishes. Feminist criticism has so far shown no real interest in Ferdinand, and the reading I call for in Chapter 5 is one that seeks to understand the character's and indeed the whole play's project as one that is heavily tinged with the discourses of both traditionally European and more modern, often New World-inspired, ideals of masculine conduct. I argue that Ferdinand's masculine project is a quest for a *virtu* that owes at least as much to studies in Renaissance travels and derring-do as it does to a more theoretical Roman stoicism and that such qualities that Ferdinand learns are in fact a proto-American male formation.

Influential though Leo Marx's 1964 work *The Machine in the Garden* was in stressing the play's Americanness, its treatment of *The Tempest* leaves out any detailed discussion of utopian freedom of movement and freedom of speech, which are factors that Chapter 6 discusses with regard to characters like Gonzalo, Trinculo, Stephano, Caliban, and the Boatswain. An interesting common situation these characters share is the fact that they normally do not enjoy the right to speak or move freely but find that the physical, highly pastoral nature of the island presents them with a newfound freedom in this respect. Chapter 7 also links this freedom to post-1989 parallels that presentist *Tempest* scholars too preoccupied with the colonial past have failed to register these last twenty-two years. The post-1989 moments of interest that the chapter briefly sketches out not only deal with Eastern Europe and the Soviet Union but also mention the largely peaceful revolution that took place in South Africa, where Nelson Mandela finally enjoyed an ultimate Prosperian moment of forgiveness, honor, and empowerment. Even Martin Orkin's recent article "*Whose* Thing of Darkness? Reading/Representing *The Tempest* in South Africa after April 1994" fails entirely to reflect upon these striking parallels, which point well illustrates the need for the discussion I set out to invite.

The urgency for a revised criticism of the play is perhaps best illustrated by the outdated interpretation of Caliban as Cuban revolutionary suggested by Roberto Fernando Retamar. Instead of pandering to self-professed anti-colonial critics like Retamar, Castells suggests a politically more contemporary Cuban reading of *The Tempest* by drawing parallels between the play's motif of maritime escape and exile and poor boat refugees trying to flee from Cuba to Florida:

> In *The Tempest*, Shakespeare's monster lamented his inability to people the island with Calibans, but in 1980 the Revolution made up for this shortfall by creating 125,000 *lumpen* and *escoria*, faithful reproductions of the monster's abject state. Yet these people demonstrated—by voting with their feet, their relatives' boats, and ten years later with their own makeshift rafts and inner tubes, and occasionally with airplanes and helicopters—that the ultimate symbol of Prospero's tropical island is not Caliban or Ariel but rather Mariel, the relinquishment of the Caribbean paradise to seek for grace on foreign shores. (176–177)

Castells here manages to shift the entire political onus from the crimes of the colonizers to the crimes of its self-proclaimed post-colonial victims, a case that serves well to illustrate the inherent ironies that the vast majority of Western practitioners of post-colonial critique have—for political reasons, one suspects—so far failed to problematize in relation to escape, refuge, and exile in *The Tempest*. Again, such "re-revisionist" post-colonial insights on the play have nevertheless recently emerged not only from Castells relative to official Cuban excesses but also from several scholars from the Baltic states and from Eastern Europe who, unlike their erstwhile Cuban comrades, have gained a distinctly post-communist view of *The Tempest* as a result of the several related moments and revolutions that took place in 1989.[3]

There is every reason to hope that such parallels will not entirely eclipse the Shakespearean text that inspire them, that these readings will shape our conversations about the play in the years to come, and that conversations about Shakespeare and *The Tempest* will in fact find better, more credibly presentist parallels than has so far been the case. For political readings of *The Tempest* are here not so much to stay but to be *refined*, to be developed, to act as a vision of both art and life in a new manner that addresses both presentist concerns and the historical and artistic moments under which Shakespeare—whoever he was—wrote his plays. And if we can accept only grudgingly that literary criticism, and especially the criticism that addresses the holiest of the holy of canonical literature, is inherently conservative (whatever critical impulse one is driven to conserve), then a look at the incredible critical trajectory of *The Tempest* will give us both pause and encouragement. In the chapters that follow, I hope to invite scholars, teachers, students, thinkers, and readers to move this debate forward rather than backwards, to challenge established truths. As Chapter 1 will argue, the most important arena when so doing is the classroom.

I

Teaching *The Tempest* in an American-Adamic Context: The New World Orthodoxy as Multicultural Pedagogy

Part I

The Tempest has long been my favorite play, certainly the one whose criticism and background I know the best. It is also the play I consistently teach the worst, ten years on the trot and counting. What follows could be read as a poor excuse as to why the play has caused me so many pedagogical headaches in the past but more charitably, perhaps, as a contribution to a much-neglected debate over how to teach the play to a student body overwhelmingly unfamiliar with an erstwhile critical controversy that makes the text of *The Tempest* so disproportionately compelling to professors. One of the most central concerns of this chapter is to facilitate a discussion over how to approach *patiently* the textual matter of *The Tempest* without forcing biased contextual points of view on students who, in my experience, at least, are generally ill-prepared to fathom the play's enormous contextual richness. The following chapter is a collaboration with my student Jessica White, who took my latest Shakespeare course in autumn 2009. The chapter is divided into two main parts, the second forming a case study of her paper as a(n) (a)typical response to critical controversies over the play's purported New World relevance, its colonial resonances, and its significant sites of interest to post-colonial scholars and authors.

The paramount challenge now in *Tempest* scholarship should perhaps be how to transmit not only the play but also its criticism in a fashion that balances our own prejudice with the text itself and the students' own inter-pretations. Part of the pedagogical problem is that the text of the play has since ceased to be only one "text," and if we take seriously the critically well-founded question as to what "text" really is, then thousands of *Tem-pests* exist now that will hardly be the same tomorrow. For instance, what post-colonial writers did in the '60s via creative adaptation and political rewriting to alter and multiply the meanings of the 1623 First Folio text was followed up by New Historicist and Cultural Materialist readings that, even though obviously greatly influenced by reader-response criticism, deserve much credit for having managed to enrich our understanding of *The Tem-pest*'s hypertextuality. In fact, the historical-contextual camp has been so successful in stressing the play's indebtedness to myriad intertexts, obscure sources, countless travel tales, and New World-political pamphlets that, even though these connections still remain a fairly grateful topic to *lec-ture* about, it is by now extremely difficult to introduce and *teach* the play to critically inexperienced students and readers.

Pedagogical approaches being central to this chapter, I argue that there is a challenging discrepancy between "Adamic" students who do not imme-diately appreciate the finer points of the contextual forces at work in *The Tempest* and a critical multicultural orthodoxy that often struggles to see the "text itself" behind them. I will argue that in order to hope to explore the play in a student-centered manner, one ought to eschew criticism, political controversies, and historically relevant intertextual material until rather late in the discussion, ideally when these points are brought up organically. It is a sign of the times, perhaps, that this organic form of teaching is seen as a needlessly time-consuming exercise that does not yield the desired "truth," one that may lead the professor astray from the impor-tant knowledge he or she so wishes to impart. I am unfortunately entirely guilty of this tendency myself, as I have reasonably maximum two weeks to devote to the play in an undergraduate Shakespeare course.

For I am constantly torn between my own wish to provide unbiased information to students—insofar as it is at all possible to attain—and my very real wish to elicit their own true responses while also introducing them to the most influential criticism over the last fifty years. There is a right syntax in which to do this, perhaps, and Lev Vygotsky's Zone of Proximal Development stresses that at the early stage in a pedagogical sit-uation students understand for themselves with a sense of autonomous mastery and ownership, that which the pedagogue has not spoon-fed them. When teaching *The Tempest,* the traditionally understood "primary text" is not only the most useful *ground zero* but also a position that can later illu-minate its necessarily ancillary historical con-texts in a way that provides students with (or indeed provokes them to) a sense of Vygotskian independent mastery over both Shakespearean text and multicultural con-text as well as a maturer sense of meta-reflection. Especially important in this syntax is the dissemination of the play's New World and colonialist dimensions in a pedagogical climate that is as interesting as it is challenging: despite a college setting where multiculturalism is *the* accepted orthodoxy, precious few Shakespeare students in my own experience manage to reach independently the New World or colonial extratextual link *de rigeur* among critics. This chapter seeks to answer why this is so, as well as to explore interpretative and pedagogical strategies in which such angles can be introduced and understood without doing violence to the students' autonomy and sense of mastery of the subject.

But first a clarification and some musings: the phrases "Adamic students" or "Adamic readers," which I pilfer in part from R. W. B. Lewis's "American Adam" and here halfheartedly claim as my own, entail admittedly highly self-contradictory ideas. For even though one cannot assume an entirely utopian, *total* knowledge or ignorance on the part of students' or professors' contextual savvy, it seems a fair bet that professors are far more knowledgeable than their students, yet the modern *pedagogical* consensus seems to be that the learning experience should be theirs—nearly to a fault. For, what are, after all, the most "important" aspects of, for example, Shakespeare's last unassisted play? Has the professor any right to assume the stage as a *central* actor when interpreting *The Tempest*? Yet, is it not in fact part of the students' expectations that he or she do? But does that mean that it is simply understood that the professor has time and place and right (since *paid* by said students) to address extratextual issues at the cost of students' own perspectives? These are banal questions, perhaps, but pressingly relevant vis-à-vis a *Tempestian* criticism that has lately been both pedagogically conservative and politically radical. My own pedagogical position is simply that students need *more* than they already know, but I feel that most modern teacher-scholars have a tremendously difficult time articulating just that, as a culturally pervasive democratic relativism leads us toward a position where our own authority is undermined, to a frustrating position where we are simply running out of time, our "educated" perspectives potentially the victim of student-centered democracy and time constraints. I have never read any *Tempest* scholar address these concerns and will for that reason try to tackle them in this chapter with an emphasis on an "Adamic reading" that is a useful starting point as a relative concept that may facilitate discussion over pedagogical delivery that has hitherto been sadly under-researched and unacknowledged in *Tempest* scholarship.

Some of the myriad practical problems attendant with any "Adamic" response in general and certainly as it applies to my teaching *The Tempest*'s relation to post-colonial and New World-specific issues include first of all the introductions to various versions of the play that often give the premise away. Secondly, students from my previous classes who have heard me speak about specific textual or thematic issues in the past tend to anticipate my teaching strategy. Thirdly, as I assign readings such as William Strachey's account of 1609—which describes a tempestuous scene taking place near the Bermudas—or Montaigne's essay on the cannibals (published in English in 1605), the intertextual links more than hint away the New World-topical issue. Finally, some of my students then make an early educated and by all means "correct" guess in class that the play has indeed a relevance to the discourse of the New World or to the subaltern, perhaps also on the basis of previous conversations about Otherness in earlier plays like *Othello, The Merchant of Venice, Titus Andronicus,* et cetera.

All these significant problems aside, I suggest that an "Adamic" learning approach can provide a fruitful *ground zero* that can be an auspicious starting point to approach a densely layered text like *The Tempest.* Less is necessarily more in this sense, for when the students have learned to master and make sense of the primary-textual strategies that make the character Caliban so compelling, they can then move on to assess the myriad competing *inter*textual and political-symbolic claims to Third World *Calibanismo* and post-colonial *Tempest*-dom. In this pedagogical syntax, then, students may not only come to appreciate Caliban's considerably rich symbolic resonance outside of the text but might also begin to reflect introspectively and meta-pedagogically upon the implications of their previous (limited, strictly text-specific) responses that managed to make no such link. In other words, it is *later* rather than sooner we ought to ask ourselves why Caliban is such a potent symbol for previously colonized people in the Third World, why scholars rather than students generally appreciate the political significance of this popularity, and what prevents students in our own classroom situations from immediately apprehending this angle. This approach places an initial emphasis on *aesthetic* value as a first experiential premise, a technical, artistic, and personal dimension that also does well to show its own limitations but illustrates how the play succeeds in moving its content—via form—toward the ideological and political, thus fostering an understanding that "transcendence of politics" is a problematic phrase that in itself forms an unsatisfactory conclusion.

In this central respect, my pedagogical syntax is the diametric opposite of that expressed in much recent criticism, especially the methods and overtly political purposes set out by Lisa McNee, who, "in order to address the issues relevant to the text," urges "instructors [to] share their own emotional responses" while at the same time managing to "avoid the hostile atmosphere that leads students to claim that instructors are trying to indoctrinate them" (199). Since "students easily see through the instructors' supposedly 'neutral' stance," she encourages "the instructor of postcolonial literatures [to] ... use an explicit discussion of students' goals in coming to the university" (200), an "honesty" that must nevertheless be "tempered by courtesy and tact" (200).

Instead, I argue in favor of an approach inspired by Lev Vygotsky's idea of student-centered mastery, one that relies upon the professor's sense of self-discipline and restraint, the Zone of Proximal Development, or ZPD. According to Vygotsky, the ZPD is the level between those problems that can be solved with the help of an authority and those "assignments ... which can be solved independently" (61).[1] The key balance is found in the zone between the sphere of contact with the pedagogue and cooperation with other learners, for, what students can do today with the help of an authority, they "will supposedly accomplish independently tomorrow" (Danielsen 62). Problematically for my own purposes, though, Vygotsky also "warns about how easy it is to underestimate the abilities of children and teachers, when studied in isolation" (Danielsen 62). To assume, therefore, as I do here, that students' responses are relatively unmediated or "Adamic" is a seeming contradiction, yet one that owes more to the democratic impulses of reader-response criticism than to arrogance. For my initial hypothesis was precisely that such democratic and "Adamic" readings would yield dramatically different responses than those predictable post-colonial interpretations that result from classes where the professor insists on critical controversy from the get-go.

Another sign of the critical times is that some works that aim to deal with teaching the play are stingy with their reflection over pedagogical strategies. Maurice Hunt's *Approaches to Teaching Shakespeare's The Tempest and Other Later Romances,* an edited collection of essays from 1992, is a case in point where few contributors make a wholehearted attempt to tie in practical-pedagogical concerns with their own critical insights. For instance, for all of Donna Hamilton's paper's strengths, one finds scant reflection on the enormous pedagogical challenges associated with teaching new historicism in addition to the play itself. While it is supposedly the plural-organic classroom "we" who "examine the Parliament of 1610" and other "power relations" (66) and absolutist theories as a way to understand the play (67), it could be interesting to know how long Hamilton's students are allowed independently to ponder and digest the political significance of Caliban's rebellion and Prospero's magic before the professor assigns a relevant historical passage to read or how many class sessions the students are given to appreciate fully the absolutist political angles that Hamilton herself discusses with such seemingly effortless erudition.

Other scholars are not so much critically focused as ideologically (and therefore also pedagogically) bound by the moral and ethical dilemmas into which *Tempest* criticism these last sixty years has managed to navigate interpretations of the play itself. This tendency is clearly seen in Virginia La Grand and Craig E. Mattson's work, which is concerned with ethics as a supplement to aesthetic value in a pedagogical setting. This ethical focus is one that follows and refines George Lamming's fierce assertion that the practice of making post-colonial "parallels" that are "deeply felt" constitute "a *value* you *must* learn" (Lamming 95, italics mine). The problem with such readings is their tendency to move the play's purported colonialist discourse into a rhetorical space where considerations of ethics become predictably binary: Caliban is simply The Victim poised against Prospero, The Evil Dictator.

But while my own students' responses often show (certainly to me) a rather surprising degree of understanding for Prospero's callous conduct vis-à-vis his slave, La Grand and Mattson suggest that an emotional "discovery" of Edward Kamau Brathwaite's post-colonial sampling and reference use is necessary since "the literature . . . and other institutions of British culture operate as an Ideological State Apparatus that enforce a colonial domination no longer legally in force" (La Grand and Mattson 478). Their article's conclusion about adding "virtue" to "virtuosity" laments the "elitism" it claims to find in "rationalist and ironist pedagogies" that are preoccupied with "factual mastery" (491)—presumably one to be understood as an unhealthy attention to "the text itself." And one is led to believe that the text of the play—hardly mentioned at all in a 20-page article—cannot explicate itself, but La Grand and Mattson could have given "the text itself" more than a superficial analysis so as to avoid the oft-repeated red herring that Caliban lives on a "Caribbean island" (479). The still commonly heard claim that Caliban (because of his name) is a historically accurate native Caribbean islander (or Indian) is a brief but illustrative case in point, for significant problems of consistency arise to account for this native's *blue-eyed* African mother (I.ii.269), his father the *Judaeo-Christian* Devil himself (I.ii.319), and Caliban's "freckled" skin (I.ii.283). In fact, a close reading of the text's island setting also reveals a hyper-ludic geography that undercuts its own epistemological status, thus de-situating the island in any meaningful cartographic sense (Brevik 182). La Grand and Mattson also fail to defend properly, outside of appeals to pathos and ethics, why it is important to understand *The Tempest* primarily via *other* works but especially what "virtuous" and "ethical" responses and interpretations might look like—or whether such vaguely multicultural intertextual exercises are an undertaking that undergraduate student readers are equipped to assess with a sense of meta-critical distance.

By far the best reflections on the pedagogy of Shakespeare and *The Tempest* can be found in Gerald Graff and James Phelan's *William Shakespeare's The Tempest: A Case Study in Critical Controversy* (2000), which acknowledges that "[l]earning by controversy" (92) "is a good thing" (107) and that exposure to literary criticism is a necessity (103) since "all responses are mediated . . . [for] . . . it is not possible . . . to read Shakespeare today without the mediating filter of his reputation as the greatest writer" (102); hence, a "diversity of teaching theories and styles" are central in their attempt to "empower" students, whose privilege and responsibility it will be to "take control . . . over [their] own learning" (107). For all its honesty and considerable pedagogical strengths, though, also Graff and Phelan's book fails to reflect over just *how much* their students have read in their lives and *when* one should introduce whatever extratextual material recent scholarship deems relevant. Instead, they illustrate a rather conventional syntax for teaching the play when they sketch out a debate where the students are told about, persuaded into accepting, or even berated for entertaining the post-colonial link—seemingly *before* one has started talking about the play at all (93–97). The representations of post-colonialist and traditionalist professors that follow are entertaining yet seem somewhat caricatured,[2] but Graff and Phelan assure us that

> [o]ur premise is not that literary value and interpretive truth are merely arbitrary matters of opinion or that matters of debates should proliferate without ever reaching resolution. Our premise is that it is only through the process of reasoned and passionate debate about questions of value and truth that we can ever hope to resolve such questions. Controversy for us is not the opposite of reaching resolution but a *precondition* of doing so. (101, my italics)

But, again, when should this controversy be introduced? My own ten-year-long experience of disseminating the play has taught me that discussions about post-colonial political issues *before* the primary text has been read and properly digested—the very *pre*-condition in Graff and Phelan's imaginary case above—tend to be depressingly one-way traffic, hence rendering "passionate debate" a bit of a misnomer, given its inevitably monologic form. It also seems a relevant question to ask of a book that celebrates critical controversy as a pedagogical boon how much time one can reasonably spend on this play and its enormous debate in *any* classroom (in my own case maximum two weeks, plus one week for screening a film version)—especially in such cases when students' lack of contextual grounding and general preparedness render such debate unrealistic.

Furthermore, if students are challenged to take one of only two sides in this debate, one runs the overwhelming risk of simplifying first and foremost the play itself but also the complex nature of the critical controversy. My own challenge has often been to validate a neutral position or indeed a *non*-position that students can comfortably assume before or even after such extratextual issues have been properly researched or digested. Rather than the precondition of debate that Graff and Phelan's book calls for, which my own experience tells me is extremely difficult to elicit, it is perhaps a better and more realistic pedagogical goal to encourage fruitful exchange of ideas without expecting students to align their interpretation with one side of this important but by all means oversimplified schismatic divide.

Graff and Phelan in many ways anticipate such concerns, however, in their discussion over teachers' responses to the critical debate—some professors may feel that it is "counter-productive" and that it bars students' "direct and unmediated" responses (102). Graff and Phelan "respectfully disagree" with such claims, though, since a "distinction between a direct and mediated response does not hold up" (102). Furthermore, "[i]t is not possible for any class approaching *The Tempest* to escape the mediation established by the context of the whole course and by the instructor's particular approach to the material. The choice is not between direct and unmediated reading but between different *kinds* of mediation" (102–103, emphasis mine). While this seems like a solid point, my central disagreement with Graff and Phelan is that such facile rhetorical sweeps cloak a real pedagogical problem, for some responses are clearly *more* mediated than others, especially given the professor's training and level of specialization. To me, students' responses are extremely interesting precisely for their relative *innocence,* for their barometric indicator of a culture that, instead of an as-yet-to-be-acquired critical apparatus, students carry with them as their most important resource in the negotiation over meaning. Ironically, as we will soon see, it is such cultural and historical insights that enable my student Jessica White's term paper to anticipate much of the new historicist criticism of *The Tempest* before she herself has read it.

Students' cultural-political and therefore critical preferences are the focus of Christy Desmet and Roger Bailey's "The Shakespeare Dialogues: (Re)producing *The Tempest* in Secondary and University Education," which discusses frankly their own students' tendency to privilege traditional methods of textual analysis over textual-political post-colonial concerns:

> A similar nostalgia for tradition emerged briefly during the final interview.... Students expressed more skepticism about the utility of sociological approaches to art. During the debriefing, one student commented that he preferred to think of *The Tempest* as Shakespeare's farewell to the stage. Such a view, which goes back at least to Edward Dowden's nineteenth-century reading of Shakespeare's imaginary biography, is perfectly designed to drive a scholar wild. But if looked at in the context of the entire Shakespeare Dialogues, this comment shows that the students, instead of resting content on the Olympian heights of postcolonial theory, were still worrying the questions with which they had begun, *bringing back into court evidence that had been suppressed by the class anthology.* (130, my emphasis)

The great strength of Desmet and Bailey's work is its democratic acceptance of and respect for the students' sometimes reactionary modes of interpretation. As such, it is an enormously worthwhile study for displaying typical attitudes of students, especially as the authors themselves recognize that Graff and Phelan's selections tend to privilege the hegemonic readings of *The Tempest* as knee-deep in colonial discourse and post-colonial pathos. As ten years' experience (at a public state university as well as in a small, private liberal arts college) has bitterly taught me, though, the emotional rawness and sense of profound injustice that often underlie post-colonial criticism are extremely seldom entirely shared or fully understood by American undergraduate Shakespeare students in general—which makes intelligent student responses that appreciate and synthesize both so genuinely interesting and worthwhile cases, as will be shown below.

Part II

My own case study is Jessica L. White's senior-level Shakespeare term paper "*The Tempest*: A Warning against Colonization," which forms not only the basis for a pedagogical revaluation of my own practices as well as a barometric gauge that illustrates the pitfalls as well as the potentially rich readings *The Tempest* can produce in a senior-level Shakespeare class but also—fortunately, one must say—complicates my own hypothesis and prejudices, to say the least. Jessica's mature and (to me) surprisingly sophisticated grasp on both the co-texts of literary criticism and history problematizes my initial belief that few students manage to apprize the demanding New World-intertextual angle without having read Montaigne, Strachey, Robert Browning, W. H. Auden, George Lamming, Aimé Césaire, Ngugi wā Thiong'o, or Lemuel Johnson beforehand. This has certainly been the case in previous courses—not even my students from Francophone Louisiana, Haiti, or Kenya managed to make such a leap, despite the fact that their own post-colonial backgrounds would (or so I presumed at the time) have given them an upper hand on their fellow students with regard to empathizing with Caliban and understanding his plight as similar to dispossessed natives'.

But in her essay, Jessica points out that "[t]o a [post-1865] American, the images [of Caliban] invoked are reminiscent of slavery in the United States" (3). This is an extremely useful if, despite its careful wording, ultimately anachronistic parallel, yet Jessica's paper is here negotiating a presentist interpretation, namely that it is well nigh impossible for informed American students *not* to read it in exactly this way, the same way it is virtually impossible not to touch on the anti-Semitic voices so explicit, post 1945, in *The Merchant of Venice*. Hence, we can see here that a purely "Adamic" reading in this instance is almost impossible, as our history of slavery is a "co-text" we carry with us, a text we imprint upon the palimpsest that *The Tempest* necessarily becomes.

I have good reasons to believe that Jessica's reading is not influenced by my own. For, in a previous article written on Caliban's origins (which forms the basis for the third chapter of this book), I had argued a very different case, namely that there is a real danger that precisely this sense of flexibility and fluidity of meaning runs the risk of uprooting the character from the very text that brought him to life:

> [T]he final result of the emotion-centred fusion of the most subjective excesses of reader-response criticism and cultural studies is that *The Tempest* has undergone an interpretative odyssey... from text to self.... Many post-colonials now see themselves *in* Caliban or themselves *as* huddled masses of Calibans anonymous. But we get a profound sense of how ubiquitous—and, one feels tempted to add, subsequently meaningless in any Shakespearean sense—the adjectives [*sic*] "Calibanic," "Calibanismo," and "Calibanesque" have become, perhaps especially to the peoples of the New World they are often meant to address. (Brevik 197–198)

Bearing this fairly explicit conclusion in mind as a potential "noise" factor in the classroom (and the prejudice of privileging traditionally understood "text" whence it is admittedly derived), I take much satisfaction from the fact that Jessica has felt no compulsion while writing her paper to parrot my own article on the play but has instead taken her paper in the diametrically opposite direction from what I have argued on paper but, again, had tried, as an experiment, to keep silent about as best as I could during class discussions—even when such angles were brought up toward the end. It is nevertheless difficult to assess whether Jessica's paper neatly illustrates the point about the *relatively* Adamic readings for which I speak in favor, because, as her afterword implies, she may very well have been influenced by my own methods and bias. That is to say, the class discussions might have convinced her to eschew any moral condemnations or railings against imperialism, an attitude I have reason to hope was fostered by an organic and student-centered learning environment. Nevertheless, Jessica's paper achieves a sense of moral and textual balance that is her paper's strength, I think, in the face of any professor's caprice and unarticulated bias.

But her paper then shows the sort of sophisticated understanding of both text and co-texts that is indeed rare in these classes when she remarks that

> Shakespeare also brings into question the fruitfulness of such attempts of colonization by relating the island to the reader in a paradoxical form. At the time of his writing, much literature was propaganda in favor of the settlement and excursions to the New World, so it held an extremely biased view and often depicted an idyllic picture. Luckily, Shakespeare was subject to firsthand accounts that could negate these claims. (7)

Her paper bolsters its argument by carefully discussing "the [disputed] intended location of the island," which she deems "irrelevant in a colonial sense" because, "whether the play takes place in the Virginia colony, Patagonia, or Africa, the subject matter remains the same . . . [namely that] Caliban represents . . . 'otherness' and Prospero . . . sovereignty and power exercised by European colonizers" (7).

Jessica's paper further registers the linguistic and political struggles that Caliban has lost to Prospero and Miranda, that Caliban "can possibly be viewed as a victim," that he is "stripped of his land and his language, which are the same results that the Indians of the New World and other victims of colonization suffered," linking these parallels both to politics and ethics (8), *pace* George Lamming and others. Yet the equally fascinating and frustrating thing is that my students generally tend to be entirely unaware of the play's position as a site of such political and ideological conflict so enormously popular with post-colonial scholars. In fact, in a 1991 opinion article in *Newsweek* (of all places), George Will, very briefly, almost in passing, challenged the hegemonic interpretations of *The Tempest* that read the play politically "against the grain" as part of the Culture Wars. Stephen Greenblatt's passionate response a couple of months later touches on pedagogy in a way that is interesting to say the least, for, as Greenblatt proclaims, "[a]lso at stake is the *transmission* of that culture to *passive students*" (115, my italics). If one reads Greenblatt "correctly," one might say that he expresses a wish to challenge a "tame and orderly canon" or perhaps ask further questions of a "shared and stable culture" that such "passive students" have been discouraged from challenging in the past.

But it is also possible to read Greenblatt's response against the grain, as an expression of a wish to redefine the canon and our culture and historicity and modes of reading, surely a Herculean undertaking whose success might rely in some concerted measure upon the unfortunate possibility that even Socratically querulous students interpret like Milton's "new presbyters," too zealous to stomach thoughts of "liberation from liberation," as Harold Bloom puts it (*Canon* 16). In fairness, though, Greenblatt specifically urges students and professors alike "to ask the most difficult questions about the past" (115), about our Western culture and history, our colonialism and our cruelty, about the savageness on which much of our material comfort rests. Yet there is perhaps also a sense in which new historicists find themselves uncomfortable being in a position of Prosperian power, the ones subject to questions, the ones whose hegemony is challenged—for such a critical hegemony Greenblatt and other new historicists and post-colonial scholars at all interested in *The Tempest* must acknowledge theirs in 2011.

Jessica's paper instead focuses its attention on a markedly text-centered interpretation when it drily points out that the island setting itself is presented in a manner that is anything but hard and fast:

> The differing views are first encountered when Adrian claims "The air breathes upon us here most/sweetly" (2.1.49–50), to which Sebastian replies, "As if it had lungs, and rotten ones" (2.1.51). Antonio then adds, "Or as 'twere perfumed by a fen" (2.1.52). Later, Gonzalo makes a statement on the vegetation of the island, saying "How lush and lusty the grass looks!/How green!" (2.1.56–57). Antonio replies with "The ground is indeed tawny" (2.1.59). Though these men are on the same island, their interpretations of the land are extremely different. (White 8)

Rather than placing full faith in an "often . . . idyllic picture" painted by intertextually relevant New World propaganda literature, "these contrasting statements can be a comment on the differing views that surrounded the ideas of expansion" (White 8). In other words, Jessica's paper warns that the play registers an ambiguous attitude to colonialism—and surprises in its conclusion, where it reminds us that

> [o]ne must also remember that Prospero eventually leaves the island. If the land had proven to be fruitful and worth cultivating, then he may have stayed and continued to rule over it in preparation for new settlers and additional profit. The fact that he leaves the island causes one to question if he does not see potential for the land or if it is worth the hard work of cultivating. (9)

Thus, the paper seemingly eschews the (for many) tempting conclusion that the play is a snapshot of incipient Anglo-American colonialism for a more nuanced position: "We are left with the idea that Shakespeare may have been against the expansion of European settlements and the effects on the natives who inhabit[ed] the lands before" (White 9). Jessica's interpretation is thus anomalously mature at this level insofar as it goes a long way in both acknowledging as well as challenging the predominant critical orthodoxy.

One of the most annoying/fascinating/pleasing experiences I have gained as a European professor in America is to observe how college students over here arrive at extremely different, sometimes outright eccentric or even exotic interpretations that from the outside seem to be peculiarly culturally governed. Too many of my late evenings have been ruined by freshman student papers that seem hell-bent on testing my patience with their ill-founded claims that America is the *only* democracy in the world. Other student papers, I darkly suspect, are trying to drive me mad with their bold-faced assertions that people living in Western Europe or Canada or Australia have no right to choose their own religion, that Africa has no middle class, that India has no rich people, that British people do not include the Welsh and the Scots but are nevertheless much smarter and more educated than Americans... and, perhaps most gallingly of all, that Christianity began in America, brought over here [sic] by the brave men and women on the *Mayflower*. To put it charitably, it is at times like these that my faith in the eventual success of the American educational system quickly dwindles to the level of the estimation in which I hold the media culture that does its very utmost to retard our best efforts. Under such challenging circumstances, then, it hardly seems reasonable to expect students to know the rich intertextual woof or tapestry against which Shakespeare wrote *The Tempest* or the historico-contextual matrix against which we read the play today. Yet the other side of the double-edged sword that forms the sad reality of students' ill-informed assumptions paradoxically constitutes a specific cultural *competency* that (often equally challenged)

European students naturally lack. Hence my own prejudice of the relative "Adamicness" of my American students, it happily turns out, is at the same time quite accurate but also far too pessimistic.

For the following example exhibits precisely the sort of American-specific knowledge that informs and governs Jessica's paper's particularly insightful angle:

> If we continue to view the relationship between Prospero and Caliban as similar to that of the Colonizer and the native, then it is possible to make likely connections to historical events. Wylie points out that "Initially the relationship between Prospero and Caliban was amicable" (47). Caliban assisted Prospero in learning about the island and its resources. He reminds Prospero that he "showed thee all the qualities o'th' isle,/The fresh springs, brine-pits, barren place and fertile" (1.2.339–340). One cannot help but note the likeness of the aforementioned situation to that of the English settlers who were shown by the Native Americans how to grow crops such as maize and were also given useful information to aid them in their survival in the New World. (White 9)

Even though she draws on John Wylie's recent work, and even though her argument illustrates knowledge and competency that, unlike what George Lamming's prefers, is learned and instructed rather than lived, it still serves well to illustrate a distinctly American cultural insight that my European students, understandably, would have a hard time generating. Hence, the above wisdom serves as an apt example of the sort of interweaving of previously acquired culturally contingent competency that American students carry and apply to the text as a *side* text without the professor's interference.

Teachers of Shakespeare's *The Tempest* have long been challenged by myriad historical readings since Octave Mannoni's seminal 1950 work *La psychologie de la colonisation*. Post-colonial and new historicist scholars have since managed firmly to historicize Caliban (and Prospero, Miranda, and other characters) in a way that has broadened our understanding of the cultural and political impact that texts can wield even (or perhaps *especially*) centuries after their composition. In the case of *The Tempest*, however, historical and political readings have been done with considerable violence to the genre of the text as a play and to the metaphorical and dizzying un-literalness of Shakespeare's language. Whereas New Critical obsessions with an artificially simplistic view of "the text itself" might have privileged certain forms of texts or knowledge at the cost of other equally valid texts, it is my experience that an equally ill-defined set of hierarchies of form popular with many new historicist scholars is even more difficult to transmit to undergraduate students. Significant problems of privileging one form of textuality over others nonetheless arise at the stage when, because of time constraints, one simply must decide, for the limited moment, which semiotic force field best addresses the textual problem at hand, perhaps in this process needlessly annihilating the other interesting angles of approach entirely.

Mea culpa. I admit that I tend to privilege the traditionally understood "text itself," the purported object of study, after all is said and done taking precedence over (yet hopefully also *beside*) other relevant information. Thus, *The Tempest, the* text that John Hemmings and Henry Condell "handed down to us" in their First Folio version of 1623—open-ended and imperfect as it is in its elliptical, indeed nearly apocryphal, nature—is nevertheless a perfectly fine place to start. For *The Tempest* is often read as politically engaging *despite* the confines of its own formalistic boundaries as a purportedly dramatic text. This political reading itself—and certainly our own recent tendency to privilege it over other interesting angles—could well be said to be a highly subjective lens or attendant "text" particular to readers after 1950, but to study the interaction between the primary text that is *The Tempest* and its myriad contexts, intertexts, sources, co-texts, subtexts, paratexts—and ultimately ourselves—is to *distinguish* between the nature of these different "texts" and to understand better both *The Tempest,* ourselves, and the critical controversy in the process.

I have hoped to argue briefly here that a sense of syntax is central to appreciate with regard to teaching the various stages of "literary and historical matters" imbricated in the play (Brown 48–71), in the order of their descending levels of priority, an order that hinges on acknowledgment of text, form, and genre as its first and most important premise. There are significant benefits to this approach: Firstly, students' own mastery and independence is paramount. Secondly, students' responses can be said to be the cultural canary in the coal mine, a set of articulated and unarticulated opinions about text and discourse that, thirdly and finally, becomes a meta-pedagogical point of introspective interest that raises the question of how our culture's understanding *The Tempest*'s multicultural appeal is a space continually negotiated in the interacting spheres of semiotic contact that happens between text, student, professor, and culture. It is perhaps as healthy as it is humbling that many of my own brave impressions of such a tidy syntax are challenged and contradicted in Jessica White's afterword that follows.

Afterword/Assessment/Metareflection, by Jessica White

I was first introduced to Shakespeare's *The Tempest* in the fall of 2009 in a senior-level course that was dedicated to the author. Prior to this introduction, I had only read the plays that are included within the normal high school curriculum: *Romeo and Juliet, Hamlet, Macbeth,* and a handful of sonnets. We spent time in those classes breaking down iambic pentameter and trying to decipher metaphors and heightened language that was unfamiliar to us. We would either listen to the play being read aloud by the teacher or have to suffer while listening to the drone of a monotone fifteen-year-old classmate who had been asked to read a part. The process was at times somewhat tedious for a teenager in high school who was more concerned with volleyball and maintaining a social life, but I found Shakespeare's work enjoyable, and I looked forward to reading more in the future. Honestly, I'm not even that sure that I enjoyed Shakespeare at that time. I just remember always hearing that the man was a genius, which caused me to believe that I should like him.

When I was offered the Shakespeare course at LaGrange College, I was excited and hoped to read some of the classics that I had not had a chance to study, such as *Julius Caesar* and *Anthony and Cleopatra.* Much to my surprise, the syllabus contained many titles that I had never even heard of, such as *Two Gentlemen of Verona, The Merry Wives of Windsor,* and *The Winter's Tale.* Among these titles was *The Tempest,* also a work that I was unfamiliar with. It was evident to me that this was a favorite of my professor's and turned out to be a play on which he had written scholarly articles and his dissertation. Knowing that this had been a play that he had researched very thoroughly allowed me to put full faith in whatever he said about the work. Oddly enough, my professor did not push any one interpretation of the play on us. Instead we were asked to interpret the work for ourselves. This was interesting to me because I never really saw any of the previous Shakespeare plays as ones that required as much interpreting. It was evident to me that *Romeo and Juliet* was about young lovers who were kept apart and tragically died in an attempt to be together. *Othello* was a story about jealousy and sprinkled with questionable racial comments and animalistic descriptions. *Macbeth* was about greed and the supernatural, but *The Tempest* was not quite as clear to me. I found myself with more questions when reading this play than with the others. Where is this island? Who or what is Caliban? Why is Miranda the only female? What is Shakespeare really saying? It has been my impression that Shakespeare tends to comment on the human condition in most of his more serious plays, so what was he saying here? The answers to these questions are still unclear to me, and the more research that I do, the more differing views I find. To be honest, some of these questions never even crossed my mind until my professor addressed them to me. I only assumed such things as the location of Prospero's island. It made sense, for me, to believe that the island was somewhere in the Mediterranean Sea since Prospero's home was originally Milan and the tempest that carries Alonso and his crew to the island as they are returning to Naples from Tunisia. Until I was asked to examine the text further and take into account the magical elements associated with the play, I would not have second-guessed such assumptions as this.

In my opinion, the most helpful aids in deciphering *The Tempest* are additional texts that the author would have been subjected to at the time of composing the play. Some teachers disagree with this method, such as one who states that "[a]t the undergraduate level, I insist on two or three *full* careful readings of the play rather than secondary critical sources. Don't let people find substitutes for their responses and values" (Hunt 8). I understand what this teacher is saying in regard to critical sources shaping students' views rather than forming an opinion for themselves, but I think historical sources are different. These types of sources can only inspire additional ideas in the student instead of forcing a specific idea about what the author's intentions are.

In my Shakespeare course, we were assigned an excerpt from Michel de Montaigne's "Of the Cannibals." We read the essay in conjunction with the last act of *The Tempest,* so the idea of the "noble savage" resonated with me during my interpretations, and I attempted to view Caliban with this idea in mind, as he is referred to as "savage" and is the only native of the island. The concept of "the noble savage" returned to me as I examined the text further and found areas that echoed the ideas that are expressed in Montaigne's essay—more specifically the idea that though the natives are savages and cannibals, they are more humane than the common more "civilized" man when it comes to the treatment of others. I was reminded of this idea during the banquet scene in the play when Gonzalo sees the spirits that he assumes are native islanders. He says, "[T]hough they are of monstrous shape, yet note/Their manners are more gentle-kind than of/Our human generation you shall find/Many, nay, almost any" (3.3.31–34). Gonzalo, much like Montaigne, could see that the natives possess something that, as civilized people, we lack. Had I not been introduced to "Of the Cannibals," I never would have made such a connection.

Montaigne's essay also caused me to view Caliban differently. I'm not sure if this was partially due to the fact that my instructor asked me to think about the character in terms of "the noble savage" or if it came naturally.

I think I automatically sympathized with the character as he is abused both verbally and physically throughout the play, and his place as ruler of the island is taken unfairly by Prospero, who acts as a tyrannical power, but the word "noble" never really crossed my mind. My instructor did in fact ask us if Caliban may be smarter than the average reader gives him credit for. Since this question was even posed to me, I assumed the answer was yes. I just had to figure out how Caliban could exemplify a noble creature. During my research I came upon a few potential answers. More recent interpretations of Caliban stress his "implicit virtues—his innate sensitivity, rough dignity, articulateness, and his intelligence" (Vaughan and Vaughan 145). Not only is he capable of learning a new language and servitude, but he also displays a love for beauty.

Another instance that causes us to question Caliban's intelligence is during the scenes where he is supposedly drunk. It is now my understanding that Caliban is not really drunk but is attempting to manipulate Stephano and Trinculo. This was definitely not my initial understanding of the situation, but my professor impressed upon me the idea that Caliban could actually be in control and simply using Stephano and Trinculo as a means of getting what he wants.

Another source that I found to be helpful, and that I would use in a classroom setting if I taught *The Tempest* myself, is William Strachey's "True Repertory of the Wrack." Although this letter was not published until 1625, it is an account of a shipwreck that occurred in 1609—a couple of years before *The Tempest* was written. Many people believe that this letter was an inspiration to Shakespeare for his play as it is the account of a ship called the *Sea Venture* that was wrecked in the Bermudas.

By reading additional sources, such as the Montaigne's "Of the Cannibals" and Strachey's "True Reportory," I think students are able to formulate ideas about the text that may not have been as easily formulated without the supplemental help. If I were teaching this play, I would definitely share these things with my students to see if they would develop a similar understanding to what I have or if they would come to a new and completely different conclusion. Although I tend to believe that Shakespeare is making reference to the New World—maybe more specifically the Virginia Colonies—I do not think it is possible to say that my interpretation triumphs over another. I think it's important for a teacher to be open and receptive to his or her students' opinions when it comes to interpreting literature; however, it is still important for an instructor to keep students on track when they may veer off into an interpretation that has no clout and nothing to back it. That is one thing that I greatly appreciated during my Shakespeare course. I felt that I was able to express my own ideas without fear of being shut down immediately after with a harsh reply. I've been in classes in the past where this was the common situation. Most students eventually became either too scared to speak in class or just didn't want to because they knew that whatever they had to say would be severely judged by the instructor or shrugged off as insignificant.

I have always found that an open classroom that allows discussion is the most helpful for my learning. In this type of setting, I am forced to process information and think about it more critically than had I been given a load of facts that I would only memorize. It also allows a student to hear questions and opinions from other students that may or may not be in line with what he or she is thinking but still prove to be helpful in his or her understanding of the text.

In addition to secondary sources and open group discussions, I believe that additional media such as film adaptations and artist renderings of the play are helpful to the student in understanding *The Tempest*. In my most recent course that taught this play, we watched Derek Jarman's film adaptation of the work. The film was not something I would be particularly interested in watching during my free time, but I must admit that it caused me to think about the actual text of the play even more. I asked myself if the characters were being portrayed as I saw them and, if not, how Jarman differed from my own interpretation. (The same applies for the many versions of Caliban that can be found in drawings, paintings, and other stage adaptations.) I also found myself trying to determine how closely the director followed the play in dialogue and action. By comparing the two works, I believe my understanding and knowledge of the text was increased as I was forced to think about it. I think this is an effective tool in the classroom while teaching a play like *The Tempest*. Films can especially be helpful to students in a high school course, as they show the action and give better understanding of dialogue.

If teaching this play to a group of students, I would also try to stress the important themes that are found throughout *The Tempest* such as magic, the quest for power, leadership and service, the illusion of justice, and also symbols found within the play such as water and Prospero's books. I would first allow my students to identify these themes and motifs and ask them to explain how they came to their conclusion by way of specific examples from the text. If they were to find it difficult to answer this question, then I think it would be helpful to give my own example from the text and ask them if they could interpret it in order to develop their own idea about the themes.

If, in the future, I were given the opportunity to teach this play to a group of students, I believe I would do it similarly to how it was taught to me, as it proved to be effective to my own understanding. I would introduce additional sources that may be helpful in understanding what the author may have encountered as he was writing the play and may help in the student's understanding of the play. I would encourage group work and class discussions and try to incorporate some form of media adaptations. I think it is also a good idea to assign individual research assignments such as papers and presentations as they encourage the student to dig deeper and find new and interesting views regarding the play that may not have crossed their mind in their own reading of the play. They would also be forced to identify some of the themes within the play to write a well-developed essay. I find writing papers a very tedious process for myself, but I also find that I have to do more critical thinking and deeper research in order to support a thesis rather than sitting in a classroom and having everything pointed out for me. I look forward to one day maybe having the opportunity to teach this play, and I would do so in the manner outlined above.

Part II

"Text" versus "Context" in Post-Second World War Criticism

Such Maps as Dreams Are Made On: Discourse, Utopian Geography, and *The Tempest*'s Island

It is hardly controversial to claim that Shakespeare often broke the Aristotelian unities. The late play *The Winter's Tale,* for instance, is set in both Sicily and Bohemia, yet the *theatrical* element of setting (although certainly not time) is tackled fairly easily—though one would be tempted to say geographically awkwardly, since Shakespeare would have his audience believe that Bohemia is by the open sea. Also in *Antony and Cleopatra,* which switches effortlessly between three continents, setting does not pose any significant theatrical problem. Even *Pericles,* which oscillates between Tyre, Antioch, Mytilene, Ephesus, and Tharsus, produces no insurmountable geographical confusion, since it is fairly clear from the text that the action takes place in many different yet interrelated locations in the Aegean Sea and larger Eastern Mediterranean basin. In contrast, *The Tempest* seems on the surface like a very tight play in terms of the Aristotelian unities (Quiller-Couch 16), spanning a mere three hours, and while there is little reason to discredit the assumption that *The Tempest* follows the classical rules in a theatrical sense, it ironically fails to indicate a guiding sense of *geographical* setting, and as a result, most recent scholars have resorted to metaphorically or discursively suggestive passages in order to "place" the play. This chapter, however, seeks to illustrate that a close textual reading of *The Tempest* reveals a complex setting that exists in a geographical limbo, on the knife edge of a liminal space that relies on both a direct, textually specific *locus* and a more indirect discursive *topos,* in sum producing an *idea of a space* drifting across many countries and continents. I argue that *The Tempest* is in fact willfully ambiguous about its geographical setting and that any attempt to understand the play's cultural and discursive themes ought to take this dense textual ambiguity into account. For *The Tempest* provides a setting that is at the same time both an anti-setting and a non-setting, a place that is no place yet every place: European, Asian, African, (non-)Bermudan, South American, ancient, and early modern— some, indeed, would say "prophetic" and futuristic (Marx 72). Also, as we shall see, the fact that the setting-related obfuscation is established so early on in the play as part of the exposition and then left off entirely would seem to indicate that the geographical references are indeed part of a ludic discourse, a game, a riddle that it is designed to obfuscate the geographical setting.

The paradoxical situation arises where the more closely and holistically one studies the text's setting, the more aporic its geography proves. It draws first on the Mediterranean (where the exiled characters, oddly, are astonished to witness that Italian is spoken and understood), then Bermuda (where, despite William Strachey's otherwise highly relevant intertext, the play does demonstrably *not* take place, since Ariel was once sent *away from* the play's island to "fetch dew" there), England (Trinculo's "were I in England now" throws the temptingly crowd-pleasing location away by its mischievous subjunctive), and North Africa (Sycorax, after all, was exiled *from* "Argier"). The dizzyingly ambivalent setting that results—unprecedented in all of Shakespeare—perplexes the audience to such an extent that it brings attention to the problem of setting itself. Setting, by both its bewildering presence and conspicuous absence, thus becomes a self-reflexive geographical lens of exposition.

My concerns thus depart from many New Historicist, Cultural Materialist, and post-colonial critics' tendencies to "land" the play discursively in a fixed New World setting that the text goes to almost indiscreet lengths to destabilize. My own method, which draws on both "old" and "new" formalisms,[1] is one that I hope and also believe is sensitive to historically grounded understandings of "text" as more fluid than the sometimes transcendental signified status accorded to it. For this particular "close reading" of *The Tempest*'s setting, as I hope to demonstrate, is one that takes both "textual" and "contextual" detail into account and reveals that the play's self-referentially theatrical meta-setting contains many inchoate discourses.

The Tempest's exiled and marooned characters envision an island that is geographically utopian in that it is irreconcilable with *any* cartographically acceptable location. Rather, the setting's Laputa-like trajectory gestures toward a hovering and exilic sense of place that is important to acknowledge when pursuing topical (frequently political) angles often limited in geographically discursive scope. For the play's sense of place comments profoundly on its own setting's epistemological status and ultimately gestures toward a theatrical *topos*. In the process, the play interrogates its audience, the theatrical tradition, and early modern scientific achievements—in a manner that is occasionally teasing, playful, nearly impertinent—about cartographic imperatives, in its own ironic case about an ideal, utopian Platonic geography versus reality-grounded Aristotelian maps that seek to reflect it, thus slyly commenting on the (lack of) significance and validity of the purportedly scientific exercise of early modern mapmaking.

One of the most challenging and, necessarily, highly subjectively defined problems vis-à-vis determining the play's setting is to tease out the slight differences in meaning between direct, island-specific geographical commentary found in the play and more indirect, discursive, connotative, and associative geographically relevant references that exist below the radar, as it were. For the words on the page in a play like *The Tempest* very often conflict with resonant words (or discourse) outside of the page, which makes it nearly impossible to establish objective criteria for what, in terms of the play's setting, we are to make of textual hints to, for example, "the still-vexed Bermoothes" as well as of William Strachey's commonly accepted source or intertext of 1609—"A True Reportery"—that describes a shipwreck off the coast of Bermuda in an eerily similar fashion to what happens in *The Tempest*.

Few scholars have so far addressed this problem very lucidly or even forthrightly. One notable exception, though, is Eric Cheyfitz, who tackles the play's setting as both physical and figurative:

> The figure of topos, or place, drives *The Tempest*.... Indeed, considering first two aspects of this figure, before turning to its linguistic dimension... we might characterize *The Tempest* precisely as a play obsessed with putting people in what the ruling class understands as their proper places, both geographical and social.... The island is *the* place in the play; and the criticism of the play has addressed the problem of place as that of the island's location. Kermode's gesture of placing the island beyond the territory of the "merely topical" by locating it in the New World is a sign of this problem, even as it tries to solve it with such an unequivocal placement. As Leslie Fiedler, Jan Kott, and most recently Hulme... have argued, the location of the island is equivocal, lying somewhere between the New World and the Old. (86–87)

Cheyfitz effectively problematizes the acute difficulties we encounter when we seek to separate (seemingly straightforward and naked) geography from the far richer rhetorical-geographical dimensions of the play:

> Because while Shakespeare has literally (in the letters of the play) placed the island in the Mediterranean, somewhere between Tunis and Naples, the literal and the proper here are not identical. That is, the literal cannot escape its entanglement with the figurative in this case. In *The Tempest*, the island has no proper place.... The island's "somewhere" is perpetually ideological, or rhetorical, as, for example, the exchange between Gonzalo/Adrian and Antonio/Sebastian about its topographical features attests. (87)

Again, we return to the meaning of words themselves, to their nominal denotations as well as contextual connotations, but whereas Cheyfitz frames the liminal space that exists between these two different forms of discourse as "rhetorical" or even "ideological," I maintain that we *can* plausibly speak of geographically explicit commentary as distinct from indirect signifiers, if for nothing else then as a place to start, insofar as phrases like "this island" or "the ground" comment directly on the island, on the setting, or on geography as pertains to distance and space.

Yet even with this admittedly unstable proviso in mind, definitions of geography are not hard and fast: if one can accept, for argument's sake, that the island does indeed lie in the Mediterranean, is it on the African side? Or closer to Europe? And is it an island that "belongs" to Italy, Greece, Tunis, or some other Mediterranean country? Governmental structures, well evidenced by Prospero's erstwhile Milan, experience sudden shifts in power, and *political* geography changes accordingly. Definitions of political and cultural territory are, in other words, as susceptible to change as the political power structures that lay claim to the same territories or are, perhaps just as aptly, as fleeting as the stormy sea surrounding the island. Hence, one operates with a profound sense of fluidity when discussing phenomena like cultural, political, and discursive settings in a play that is already unclear on the much simpler literal level.

Thus, recent scholarship has quite understandably resorted to more limited, far less absolute understandings of "discourse" and "discursive settings" that have nevertheless conspicuously often been New World or (post-)colonial in nature and that have drawn on indirect, topical, and thematic references to slavery, linguistic dominance, education, and power. Insofar as discursive setting has to do with resonances that happen on a level that is not explicitly literal or openly, logically attributable to one location, however—Montaigne's essay "On the Cannibals" or the play's discussion of Dido/Aeneas, for instance—this discursive setting is often connotative rather than denotative in nature yet at the same time remarkably closely intertwined with the physical, geographical setting in *The Tempest*.

New Historicists have been extraordinarily successful in establishing the play in terms of limited discourses and have all but (re-)located the play to the New World. The physical, geographical setting, however, has usually not been very important a factor in this maneuver, as Jonathan Hart has recently remarked:

> This play, set in the Mediterranean and torn between Italy and Tunisia in a storm, also has, through echoes of William Strachey and scarce allusions to the New World, American dimensions. *Regardless of the empirical evidence*, this play has become as much a controversy in colonialism and postcolonialism as it had been an aesthetic icon in the revolutionary age of the Romantics. (*Columbus* 143, my emphasis)

While I take courage from Hart's pat assessment that many previous readings have been lacking in empirical or textual evidence, my conclusions tend to differ as to whether this play has a setting at all in the conventional geographical sense. Discussions on exilic setting and unstable cartographic imperatives find more usable inspiration in Jean MacIntyre's recent work on *The Tempest*'s setting as analogous to movable stage machines often used by theater companies for masques and dances, which idea illustrates well part of the larger point that this chapter argues about geography, maps, and setting. As MacIntyre argues, "These floating islands (visibly mobile or not) exploit the commonplace that insular Britain was a world apart, mythologized as a 'demi-paradise' and protected by the sea from 'the envy of less happier lands'" (84). MacIntyre describes the island's geographical location itself as

> initially placed in the Mediterranean between Tunis and Italy. Dialogue names cities—Milan, Naples, Tunis, and Argier—well known to England's trade and diplomacy. Maps, sea charts, and the experience of diplomats, travelers, merchants, and ship-masters, would have meant that many in the audience would have an idea of their relative locations and distance from each other. Yet the marriage of Claribell [*sic*], "she that is Queen of Tunis," has removed her "ten leagues beyond man's life" (II.i241–42), unabridgeably far from Naples. Words link the island to "the still-vex'd Bermoothes" in the Atlantic and may suggest other "islands far away." Real geography thus becomes fictional . . . so translating the island from the world of its named places into a floating island like those in masques, findable only by the witch

Sycorax on the Argier ship, or by the white magician Prospero in the Milan "hulk." (87)

And it is perhaps exactly this *sense* of an indeterminable, uncertain setting that has led scores of *Tempest* commentators in the last fifty years to see it as a metaphorical or discourse-determined *topos* rather than as the island's precise geographical *locus* itself.

Baker, who draws on Derrida's idea of hypertopicality, points out that "[t]his is not a 'geographical problem' that can be solved by abstracting geography from the play, or the play from geography" (68). And, as de Sousa has remarked, "Prospero's island is a curious place. It seems to be a 'real' place and an imaginary one, where natural and supernatural phenomena often cannot be separated" (447). Further, "[c]ulturally and psychologically, the island . . . disorients the mind" and "the island refuses to become anything but an alien habitat, terra incognita, an uncharted territory" (448). According to de Sousa, "[n]either island nor the forest offers fixity," and hence "[e]mpirical observation proves impossible because human senses cannot discern illusion from reality, magic from nature" (451). For his part, Kristiaan P. Aercke stresses the sheer uncertainty that is associated with the setting (150), the lack of knowledge and lack of correct interpretation the characters suffer from, their tendency toward sudden sleep, the unreliability of sensory perception, and thus, "[w]e quickly dismiss geography as futile" (146). The strength of Aercke's reading points to the epistemological status of the setting as tenuous. But it is also true that the many geographical references add to this confusion for the audience and readers of the play and also true that, while they draw importance to themselves, they manage to tear any meaningful sense of geography down. In other words, a geography "on steroids" is tantamount to no geography at all in the end.

In such a vacuum, then, one could perhaps make the case for any geographical setting, also one in the New World. And in its spatial quality and cartographical emptiness, the island seems to remind curiously many of the (relatively) empty, metaphorically uninscribed New World loci or bodies. Perhaps the most oft-cited *evocative* New World textual reference to the island in recent criticism involves Caliban's dispute with Prospero over ownership to it:

This island's mine by Sycorax my mother,
Which thou tak'st from me. When thou cam'st first,
Thou strok'st me and made much of me, would'st give me
Water with berries in't, and teach me how

To name the bigger light, and how the less,
That burn by day and night; and then I loved thee
And show'd thee all the qualities o' th' isle,
The fresh springs, brine-pits, barren place and fertile.
Curs'd be I that did so! All the charms
Of Sycorax, toads, beetles, bats, light on you!
For I am all the subjects that you have,
Which first was mine own king; and here you sty me
In this hard rock, whiles you do keep from me
The rest o' th' island.

                                        (I.ii.331–344)

Caliban's in many ways profoundly touching claim to the island as well as his complaints about Prospero's harsh treatment have proved nearly irresistible as a *pathetic* link to New World peoples who would later be internally exiled and dispossessed, in a similar way, of their land by the colonizers. Some critics, indeed, see the above passage as anecdotal evidence that the play deals with the issue of colonialism and hence see the play's location, *a posteriori,* as New World, since it seems to "fit" better with our recent history. For example, George Lamming claimed already in 1960 that "[i]t will not help to say that I am wrong in the parallels which I have set out to interpret; for I shall reply that my mistake, *lived* and *deeply felt* by millions of men like me—proves the *positive value of error.* It is a *value* which you must learn" (95, emphasis mine).

One would nevertheless be amiss to assert that radical historical and political readings with regard to setting are a trend that begin with New Historicism, Cultural Materialism, post-colonialism, or the cultural studies. Traditional critics like Hallett Smith, for example, rather tentatively suggest that the play is set in a kind of geographical limbo between the Old and New Worlds for reasons he seemingly cannot quite put his finger on:

> The "uninhabited island," as the Folio calls it, which is the scene of *The Tempest,* is apparently somewhere in the Mediterranean, since the shipwrecked characters in the play were en route from Tunis to Italy. Yet the imagery of the play and some of the descriptive detail concerning the island setting strongly suggest the New World across the Atlantic. (6)

Smith here draws a connection between the unexpounded-upon "descriptive detail[s]" and the Bermuda islands described in Strachey's *True Reportory* of 1609 and tries to qualify the claim that the play's setting is in the New World on the basis of this source and other "imagery."

Pier Paolo Frassinelli nevertheless credits Edward Said for this and related tendencies of reading texts against the grain:

> Indeed, one is here reminded of Edward Said's suggestion, in *Culture and Imperialism*, that we reread the Western cultural archive "not univocally but *contrapuntally*," so as to articulate on the one hand the interconnectedness between metropolitan history and "those other histories against which (and together with which) the dominant discourse acts" . . . and on the other "how writers and scholars from the formerly colonized world have imposed their diverse histories on, *have mapped their geographies in*, the great canonical texts of the European centre." (174, emphasis mine)

These myriad claims to Americanness, New World relevance, and post-colonial-specific problems are usually attached to the thematic and topical links that the play poses to early modern colonialism, incipient trans-Atlantic slavery, and linguistic imperialism. Caliban poses a pathetically highly effective symbol of most any indigenous or previously oppressed people—despite the text's remarkable resistance to divulge *whose* island Caliban was born on or its geographical whereabouts.

These discourses, always relevant vis-à-vis setting in a play like *The Tempest,* have proved a valuable contribution to *Tempest* scholarship, but few critics have engaged openly with how the play's island's textual setting changes dramatically the topical or thematic (read: political) angle one wishes to pursue. Howard Felperin has also warned against the tendency among many recent scholars to over-invest the play with a supposedly "dominant" colonial relevance:

> My point is not that recent colonial critique of *The Tempest* has misread its slight and fleeting, indeed almost subliminal, colonial evocations, but rather that it has overread them, and in so doing, has mistaken the part for the whole, has ignored or overlooked the much larger vision of history within which they are encapsulated. For within this play, the colonialism of the New World is merely an episode within a projection of nothing less than a historical totality that puts that episode into a much larger critical perspective. (50–51)

Such over-invested "Americanist" readings, I contend, also remain to be proven in any meaningful cartographical sense and furthermore pay scant attention to the text itself, which seems to suggest that the island, wherever it might be, has no definable American qualities (Skura 49) beyond vague discursive and intertextual parallels.

For example, as to the explicit topography and climate of the island as well as its flora and fauna, we do know that it furnishes grapes or "berries" for Prospero to make wine or fruit juice and also that the island has both "barren" and "fertile" spots as well as "brine-pits," most likely for fishing and "fresh springs" for drinking water (I.ii.334, 338). However, the fact that the island is reported to have both "fertile," "green," and "tawny" spots (Gonzalo, Sebastian, and Antonio are actually bickering over the exact same spot) would seem to indicate a deeply problematic mistrust in language as far as placing the play's island is concerned. For if we can accept that rain-drenched tropical locales like Bermuda or equally saturated subtropical places like Virginia are more likely to be "green" and "fertile" than the much drier and "tawnier" Mediterranean islands of, for example, Sicily, Malta, Lampedusa, and so on, then it is anyone's guess as to what the island actually looks like—especially since Shakespeare's "theater of poverty" relied on language and words rather than on expensive and elaborate scenery that could illustrate the flora and climate with more visual assurance (Burke 11). Relevant to this duplicitous rhetoric, Hart has commented that the "contemporary shipwreck in Bermuda (and the slight allusion to that island) gives the play an American dimension that it inscribes and effaces" (*Columbus* 162). Yet the textual island does not appear to be a place that has any geographical signifier that suggests *one particular* location for the play, since fish, brine pits, and berries are found virtually everywhere.

Part II

A return to the text gives us a sober sense of ground zero in relation to the erstwhile controversy (until very recently nearly a deafening orthodoxy) over *The Tempest*'s standing as a New World allegory. For the new textual (anti-)setting first of all undoes the flimsy *grounds* upon which dubious New World claims have been formed, thus a geographically close reading seriously questions the political criticism that has been leveled against both the play and its playwright predicated on a New World setting that the play brings up only sporadically, liminally, in passing, suddenly and unexpectedly, far-fetchedly and surprisingly, always as a sub-discourse that forms by all means an important but after all only *one* leg of a textual "chair" as far as geographical (anti-)setting is concerned (Felperin 50). For the text (or "chair"), I maintain, presents a geographical setting that is complete and in balance, self-sufficiently ubiquitous and non-existent for its specifically and ultimately meta-theatrical and meta-geographical purposes, and *not* to consider the holistic totality of its strategy—for instance by staring myopically at its scattered New World dimensions alone—is to miss the larger point, the play's central ethical project. Thus, in this second part that follows, I attempt to analyze the text's most relevant instances of direct, island-specific references as well as discursively important passages that bear upon the play's physical or metaphorical setting.

Our first knowledge of the island is that Prospero and Miranda were sent away from Italy, thrown out to sea to disappear or even die, but they have survived in exile on this island, where three other exiles used to reside: Sycorax, Caliban, and the spirit Ariel (I.ii.140–151). Prospero then informs us that Caliban's mother, the Algerian witch Sycorax, was sent into banishment or exile to the island and gave birth to Caliban. The first direct geographical indicator in the text occurs when Prospero tells Miranda that he once used to be "the Duke of Milan" (I.ii.54), a fact that, rather unusually for a girl almost fifteen, she does not yet know. Geographically speaking, though, Prospero's history lesson is important since we feel as ignorant about the location as does Miranda—like the audience, she does not know where she is, where she has been, or where she is going. She is an unknowingly exiled young woman who seems to live in a wonderful cocoon, totally isolated from and protected against the outside world. She speaks Italian[2] but does not seem to have even the slightest *cultural* notion of Italy or Milan and even less so with regard to a fully formed national or regional identity. Hence her reaction to Prospero's information that "thy father was Duke of Milan" (I.ii.54) is important in that she seems to infer for a moment that Prospero is *not* her father, presumably because she may never have associated him with that place at all.

The information of Prospero's past in Milan is then repeated in I.ii.58, before the Italian-specific reference to the city states, or "signories," reoccurs in I.ii.71. As Prospero continues, he claims that his brother wanted his position as "Absolute Milan" (I.ii.109) and that Antonio "confederate[d] . . . wi' th' King of Naples" (I.ii.111–112), an act Prospero considers "most ignoble stooping" (I.ii.116) for his "poor Milan" (I.ii.115). Though metonymy is commonplace in Shakespeare and Renaissance drama, the frequent harping on geography as forming identities here nevertheless seems too remarkable to miss in a play that is so stingy with geography to account for the play's location.

Prospero proceeds to tell his story with exclusively Italian references to his past and the men who preyed on his weaknesses as a ruler, all within a European and Mediterranean matrix of geographical and cultural references—until Ariel, in a way that might seem rather labored, tells Prospero that "[s]afely in harbor / Is the King's ship, in the deep nook, where once / Thou call'dst me up at midnight to fetch dew / From the still-vex'd Bermoothes" (I.ii.226–229). This key word might lead the audience to go along with the working assumption that the island is in close proximity to the Bermudas and perhaps also to the Virginia colony (Baldo 138–139). This is the first direct mention of the New World in *The Tempest,* and, unfortunately, it tends to obfuscate more issues than it clarifies. The audience may indeed wonder why Ariel was sent out to the Bermuda islands to fetch dew or how great a distance there is between the two islands—and whether Ariel, who is a spirit beyond the constraints of gravity and distance between different physical places and geographies, can roam freely all over the world. The express mention of the Bermuda islands, at the very least, is a loud alarm bell in the early stages of the play and, if the audience had *not* appreciated the clear similarities that the play and its island setting pose to recent travel narratives, is one that makes everyone understand it here. In a play that appears so careful not to divulge its geographical setting, "the still-vex'd Bermoothes" poses a textual indiscretion that seems to serve no distinguishable purpose beyond a sense of playful displacement and bewilderment. The reference gives us serious pause, but if the audience has been paying strict attention—the genre of past-paced theater happening in Aristotelian "real time" (both a first and a last for Shakespeare) is admittedly a very different experience from a studious close reading in our own good time—they would perhaps recognize that since Ariel goes *away from* the island *to* the Bermudas, those two locations are geographically antithetical. The play's Bermudan non-sojourn is at any rate brief—only five lines later, Ariel, like some kind of teasing and playful Peter Pan, takes his audience along on his swift wings back to Europe again: "The mariners... are upon the *Mediterranean* float / Bound sadly home for *Naples*" (I.ii.230–235, italics mine). Thus, in a matter of not fully two scenes, the play manages to teeter between three continents and makes trans-Atlantic setting switches with stupendous *sprezzatura*.

Another such mercurial change in discursive and topical "setting" is made just twenty-three lines later, where, in I.ii.258, Prospero refers to "the foul witch Sycorax," whose name seems Latin or Greek in origin[3] but whose background is emphatically *not* European, as the seemingly self-conscious exile Prospero takes conspicuous pains to extract directly from Ariel: "Where was she born?/Speak. Tell me" (I.ii.259–260). And only five lines later, Prospero impatiently answers his own rhetorical question by confirming explicitly that Sycorax is African:

> I must
> Once in a month recount what thou hast been,
> Which thou forget'st. This damn'd witch Sycorax,
> For mischiefs manifold, and sorceries terrible

To enter human hearing, from Argier
Thou know'st was banish'd.
(I.ii.263–266)

In this jarringly indiscreet passage, Prospero appears anxious to convey across the fourth wall an important point, that Sycorax not only lived, once upon a time, in Algiers, North Africa, but that she was in fact also a *native* of that place.

We may infer that the island is close enough to Algiers for its inhabitants to send a convict into exile there (and, one would perhaps think, far enough away for her to be of no further trouble). Perhaps this act of exiling Sycorax was more geographically deliberate on the part of the Algerians as opposed to the Milanese and Neapolitans, who, like thieves in the night, whisked Prospero and Miranda away (I.ii.144–151) and sent them off to the open sea with no safe harbor at all in mind. Partly because Shakespeare has made the old magician our definitive source of knowledge, very little else is known about the history of the island—the Neapolitans, Milanese, Tunisians, or Algerians seem to make no political or territorial claims to it. But what we are able to extrapolate from Sycorax's exile is that the island is first of all close enough to Algiers to serve as a fit place for banishment, a real place that is at the same time far enough removed from the mainland to protect the inhabitants of Algiers from her dark magic. In other words, the island is familiarly alien, in perfect balance between the political, real, physical core and the thematic, topical periphery, occupying a liminal space that seems to exist in between reality and fiction, geographically and physically real as a plausible plot premise first of all but more importantly as an increasingly thematic space that interrogates the boundaries of the physical, the geographical, and the strictly literal, toward a place "rich and strange," toward what Cheyfitz holds is an ideological *topos* (87) rather than a physically real *locus* but which I maintain is actually *both,* a euphony of cacophonic discourses.

One such example of euphuistic dissonance has to do with Caliban, his name, his status as slave, and his clear parallels to colonial subjects later in history. His name is an oft-cited point of interest as an anagrammatization of "cannibal" or "Caribbean," as Fleissner has noted (297), yet Caliban is, with the notable exception of his name, probably a staunchly European mythological creature, as I have argued previously (Brevik 190–197)—in many ways far more European than Othello is African, for instance. And if Caliban's claim to the island does strike a poignant resonance that places him (and therefore, as in some Trojan horse, the play and its setting along with him) metaphorically in a (much later, anachronistic) South or Central American historical and cultural context, he remains there for a brief thirty-three lines, when the deformed slave himself reminds us that he speaks a European "language" Prospero and Miranda have done their worst to teach him (I.ii.354).

But the geographically relevant reference to "your [Italian/European] language" is followed by an oblique New World reference from Caliban himself when he admits in an aside that Prospero's magic "is of such pow'r,/It would control my dam's god, Setebos" (I.ii.372–373). As Langbaum's Signet edition of the play glosses, "the name 'Setebos' derives from Robert Eden's *History of Travaile* (1577), which mentions 'the great devil Setebos' worshipped by the Patagonians" and can therefore be seen as an indirect American pointer (126).[4] Whether Shakespeare himself intended to draw upon Eden's accounts or whether he expected his audience to "catch" the almost subliminal drop of cultural-geographical information remains, of course, pure speculation.

But the name "Setebos" itself becomes part of a larger pattern when it is seen in relation to the play's other seemingly haphazard references to the New World, little geographical and cultural drops or hints of similar import. Caliban's mother, then, who *could* have worshiped Allah, Jahve, Odin, or any other well-known or even obscure Old World deity, clearly answered to a god whose name is New World in origin and who was also thought, according to Magellan and Eden, to be diabolical (Orgel 121) or even Satanic in nature. Thus, Setebos could be seen as a New World-specific cultural-geographical referent that "is clear evidence that the Americans were in Shakespeare's mind when he was inventing his islander," as Orgel has claimed (33).

The text stubbornly resists, however, any attempts at proscribing the play's setting or themes as *singularly* New World, even in the highly topical initial encounter between Ferdinand and Miranda. This romantic subplot may very well be taken from Captain John Smith's *A True Relation* of 1608, as the Vaughans have noted (*Caliban* 41). This is the narrative of the love relationship that forms the basis for the many subsequent romantic myths and stories about trans-Atlantic love struggles and is particularly interesting with regard to *The Tempest* since, as the Vaughans again point out, Smith "describes Pocahontas as Chief Powhatan's only 'Non-pariel' [*sic*]" (ibid. 43). The romance main plot (as we might choose to see it with the New World as setting in mind) is nevertheless muddled by the strange fact that Miranda speaks Ferdinand's "language! heavens!/I [Ferdinand] am the best of them that speak this speech,/Were I but where 'tis spoken"

(I.ii.429–431). In light of—and in addition to—the, in many ways, tempting parallels to Captain John Smith and Pocahontas, we may indeed wonder why Ferdinand is so astonished to hear his own, Italian language. For if the island is supposed to be in close proximity to Naples, then Italian might reasonably be expected to be spoken and understood even by people from the Levant and North Africa or larger Mediterranean fringe.

Hence the fact that Ferdinand, for reasons that *may* be geographic or cultural in nature, displays such a surprise—we note that Ferdinand actually swears at hearing his own *lingua franca*—could possibly be seen as too strong a reaction for the play to be credibly set in the Mediterranean, especially somewhere close to Italy, where hearing Italian spoken would rather be expected. And yet it is at critical moments such as this that our classifying even the Italian language as a European geographical hint becomes problematic vis-à-vis the "normal" or expected cultural and geographical setting that would usually accompany it—namely Italy. For the reference to the Italian language here—or indeed Ferdinand's expected *absence* of it—points in several directions, first toward Italy and the Mediterranean itself, but when mentally processed in logical relation to language and geography, the import of the reference would seem to dictate a spatial and linguistic motion *away from* the presumed European setting. In other words, the ostensibly Italian-specific reference becomes a seemingly intentional textual red herring, a distorting prism to the map or a magnet to the mental compass of the audience, who have thus far been taken aboard a tempestuously dizzying tour over several countries and continents as far as setting is concerned.

The same problem of opposing denotative and connotative terms is emphasized and elaborated on when Prospero immediately replies: "How? the best?/What wert thou, if the King of Naples heard thee?" (I.ii.431–432). Prospero's darkly stinging reminder about Ferdinand's supposedly dead father is answered in a solemn way by a dazed and stunned Ferdinand: "A single thing, as I am now, that wonders / To hear thee speak of Naples" (I.ii.433–434). The characters here seem self-consciously aware of their own proper Italian place, but these meta-Italian references, though they certainly confirm the characters' background, serve a multiple purpose in that they form a linguistic riddle, words manipulated in an almost euphuistic mode to express a paradoxical distance to their own, nominal meaning. The result is that the connotative and *logical* setting, in this passage's holistic sense, is ironically removed from the Italian setting that each individual term would strongly seem to denote.

As far as direct, textual references to setting, though, the old councilor Gonzalo transports the audience quickly back to the *terra firma* framing the Mediterranean Sea with his remark that his clothes "are now as fresh as / when we put them on first in *Afric,* at the marriage / of the King's fair daughter Claribel to the King of / *Tunis*" (II.i.69–72, italics mine). These direct geographical reminders are then followed by a frantic exchange over the precise location of Ancient Carthage and contemporary Tunis, touching upon geography, historical knowledge, Greek mythology, and Renaissance dramatic adaptations (like Christopher Marlowe's) of the love story between Dido and Aeneas. Antonio and Sebastian pointedly comment that Gonzalo has created a whole new city by his "miraculous harp" (II.i.87), a sarcastic reference to Gonzalo's garrulity and Greek mythology that is glossed in most editions as Amphion's harp raising the walls of Thebes.[5] And even though Gonzalo may be technically wrong about the location of Ancient Carthage as *precisely* identical to that of contemporary Tunis, he has managed to stress that the play owes a great deal to the Old World and the Mediterranean in its maritime topicality and setting (Brotton 33). The hefty exchange importantly shifts our attention away from contemporary Bermuda, Virginia, and the New World toward the ancient world of Europe and North Africa, seen through the prism of Greek mythology and Moorish conquests. But Antonio and Sebastian's mocking lines nevertheless pose an indirect New World relevance when they half-seriously suggest that Gonzalo has raised a new city on his own—again, what the whole play manages to do in its totality with regard to setting.

And in what we may well call a neo-Atlantistic fantasy, Gonzalo further elaborates on his dream of the perfect "plantation." In a way that Leslie Fiedler might term "prophetic" (Fiedler, qtd. in Frey 31), *The Tempest* alludes here to an ancient city raised from the "music" of Gonzalo's incessant chatter, but it is a city or plantation that is at the same time a (re)vision of the biblical city shining upon a hill or perhaps even a mockery of the as-yet-to-be-seen prototype of the Puritan version of it. The sheer cultural and religious density of this comment thus manages to question and scratch the surface of what appears to be a clear-cut Mediterranean passage. Thus, the potentially confusing banter forms the backbone of a meta-geographical discourse that reflects also the play's larger strategy, because what happens in the Tunis-versus-Carthage exchange manages to bring up the tip of the same iceberg of geographical confusion that the play itself does consistently with regard to a geographical setting that seems so self-consciously distracting that it calls attention to itself as a phenomenon that thus becomes an alarm bell, if not purposeful overkill.

Interestingly, though, the geographical uncertainty that surrounds Gonzalo's New World-relevant plantation reverie ends up in a *third,* classical location that is mostly rhetorical and linguistic in nature and one which importantly manages to contain both geographical claims, New World as well as Old. This rhetoric of containment is neo-Atlantistic, both in the geographical sense that the Atlantic Ocean is at the same time both a hindrance and a conveyor between Europe and America as well as in the concomitantly cultural sense that the ancient myths of Atlantis are able to express both the past and the future, the New and the Old Worlds, the hope and the memory.

In symbiotic ways this third sense feeds into a fourth, religious dimension, a Judaeo-Christian significance that in terms of philosophical setting importance ranks below only the Globe Theatre. For the theater, as Bartolovich (18) has recently claimed, could be seen as the ultimate setting for the play. It is difficult not to think that, after a long life dealing with sparse props in the theater, Shakespeare might have felt that the plays performed at the Globe could transport the audience in time and space and "create new islands" out of the sheer "baseless fabric of our vision," exotic and new places that are nevertheless permanently intertwined with a topos and ethos that is increasingly close: England, London, Southwark, the Globe.

And yet the English link is interestingly enough both tantalizingly raised and mercilessly shot down in Act II, scene ii, which opens with Caliban taking cover underneath his gaberdine. Trinculo discovers Caliban and deduces from Caliban's odor that he is "[a] strange fish":

Were I / in England now (as once I was) and had but this fish / painted, not a holiday fool there but would give a piece / of silver. There would this monster make a man;/any strange beast there makes a man. When they will / not give a doit to relieve a lame beggar, they will lay / out ten to see a dead Indian. (II.ii.27–33)

The overt mention of England here is significantly tempered by Trinculo's hypothetical "[w]ere I," a contingency that here leads us to understand that England is definitely *not* the intended setting for the play, but since the play was of course staged in London, the English reference nevertheless brings the audience's attention to a place they all know very intimately.

And the English angle is also a valuable one in that there is a sense in which the play's totality and hovering sense of setting are all reunited and encompassed by the burgeoning and increasingly cosmopolitan city that could contain in both fiction as well as in real life such strange sights as "dead Indian[s]" on display, as Vaughan has shown ("Trinculo's Indian"

49–50). The seemingly pandering reference to England bears symbiotically upon the issue of setting and location, since it is both self-referential and three-dimensional with regard to the *loci* of the country, the city, and the theater, which all in turn contain and playfully comment on their complex interaction. By understanding the play as set back home, as it were, in England and London, the audience may start to reflect on the conflux of the theater and the cosmopolitan city in which the Globe Theatre is located. The reference thus manages to draw attention to the omnipresence of the theater that is in a poetic sense not only an inferior Platonic reflection of the larger *theatrum mundi* but actually *greater* than the world itself, as Prospero more than hints at both during the masque-within-the-play and in the Epilogue.

This idea of the world as a stage and the stage as the whole world is equally relevant with regard to Platonic maps and Aristotelian geography (or vice versa). The play offers about 150 lines of relative quiet as far as setting is concerned, until direct, island-specific evidence of the setting's flora and fauna are brought up by Caliban, who offers his services to Stephano and Trinculo:

> I prithee let me bring thee where *crabs* grow;
> And I with my long nails will dig the *pig-nuts*,
> Show thee a *jay's* nest, and instruct thee how
> To snare the nimble *marmazet*. I'll bring thee
> To clustr'ing *filberts*, and sometimes I'll get thee
> Young *scamels* from the rock.
> (II.ii.167–172, my italics)

Of all these foods and animals, only the "marmazet" (a monkey) is particular to the New World—it lives only in South America.[6] "Pig-nuts" (or peanuts) now grow in both England and America but are native to South America, while crabs, jays (of Eurasia and North Africa), filberts (Eurasian shrubs, bearing nuts that are similar to but larger than hazelnuts), and the mysterious "scamels" (in some editions "sea-mews," a seabird) are found in both America and Europe.[7] In other words, the audience is presented with a range of animals and plants that are not native to any one place but which spans different continents.[8] But if the audience should be tempted to conclude, from the exotic signifier "marmazet," that a South American setting is intended, Ariel's problematic assertion that "this island" is one "where man doth not inhabit" (III.iii.56–57)[9] later seems to disqualify the geographical location as New World, except, indeed the Bermudas, where no people lived at all in 1609—yet Ariel has already worded himself so that the island *cannot* be Bermudan.

The play's increasingly obfuscated geography further *un-charts* the setting seventy-six lines later, when Antonio and Sebastian wonder who would be "the next heir of Naples" if Alonso were to die (II.i.245). The answer to the question is of course "Claribel," "[s]he that is Queen of Tunis; she that dwells / Ten leagues beyond man's life; she that from Naples / Can have no mote, unless the sun were post— / The Man i' th' Moon's too slow—till new-born chins / Be rough and razorable" (II.i.246–250). It seems that the crime Antonio and Sebastian are intent to commit would go largely undetected since Naples is simply too far away from Tunis for Claribel to learn about her father's death. William Boelhower argues that "[f]ortified by such geopolitical thoughts most likely blowing in from the newly discovered Bermudas, the two noblemen give the issue of filiation a decidedly cartographic inflection" (29). Yet we do well to note that it is not the island but the city of Naples that is described as being far away from Tunis. Hence, Antonio's information here does not provide us with any geographical coordinates as far as the island's location is concerned, but the passage is important in that it furnishes the play with an *exaggerated* sense of spatial distance between two locations that are actually very close indeed.

The Tempest hence operates with a *theatrical* setting that is entirely utopian, a setting that does not really exist in terms , first of all, with regard to geographical coordinates but also with regard to physicality and reality itself, as Prospero suggests with his relativization of the entire concept of reality: "We are such stuff as dreams are made on; and our little life / Is rounded with a sleep" (IV.i.156–157). If maps are a reflection of humanity and our world's myriad spaces, then the "theatrical" map—with its *illusions* of life, of people, of reality—could be said to be fittingly empty in this case insofar as putative geography is concerned. And yet the science and maps that reflect this unstable reality is central to understanding the setting of *The Tempest,* for, as Michèle Duplessis-Hay has argued, the play "conflate[s] Classical and Renaissance mappings of wonder" (8). Boelhower also stresses the importance of Renaissance ships and maps as "undoubtedly the two major emblems of the genesis and taking hold of the modern world system" (33). More to the purpose of this chapter, though,

they have also worked against each other in a competitive way that generates epistemological loopholes. While in the sixteenth and seventeenth centuries ships were invariably breaking out of their cartographic frame, maps in turn were equally busy converting this movement into a readable and salable image. Due to this breathless exchange, because the new Atlantic sensibility was quintessentially cartographic, both maps and ships can be labeled empirical universals. (35)

As Hamlet's play-within-the-play holds a mirror up to theater as much as to nature, *The Tempest* holds a mirror up to maps as much as to geography, to the fledgling *science* of geography, a mirror to all those credible and—importantly, I think—less credible accounts of phantom lands and islands (like Thomas More's island Utopia of 1516) that are yet to be found on any map except as "filling," as monsters, phantasmagoric creatures, strange animals, even stranger peoples, and other unbelievable phenomena.

John Wylie has argued that *The Tempest* "sits uneasily within . . . a retrospective 'colonial frame'" and that "critics seem to feel that they must *choose* between New World and Old World contexts" (48). Instead, he offers a compromise in which "the geographies of *The Tempest* involve an ambivalent mapping of both arenas. As Norbrook . . . suggests, 'there is a dual topography . . . in which American and Mediterranean features are kept in an unstable interaction, preventing . . . easy naturalisation'" (48). Wylie concludes confidently from this geographical ambivalence that "it no longer matters whether *The Tempest*'s island locale is situated in the Mediterranean or the west Atlantic, because from the poetic perspective of Elizabethan England *both* of these situations are 'exotically' distant" (50). Furthermore,

> one effect of this reading . . . is to loosen the play's historical and material moorings to the point where it becomes possible to read it purely as a reflection of European Renaissance visions of "the distant". In fact it may be from exactly such a position that Gillies is able to straightforwardly offer a quite strongly atlanticist reading, in which *The Tempest* is intertextually woven with a number of contemporaneous accounts of the English Virginia colony. (50–51)

Wylie's point about the island's ambiguity and resultant openness is well taken, but my own conclusion is that attempts at geographical grounding are *not* equally valid but rather equally *in*valid, for the text operates with a setting that in its inviting openness is actually the opposite, the *precise* "picture of nobody" (III.ii.127). It is a setting that is an *aporia*, a mystery, a textual and entirely theatrical topos that draws constant attention to what it *seemingly* is and what it pretends to be—and therefore also to what it is *not*, namely a conventional geographical locus. In its labyrinthine nature, the play's setting is a textual construct that resembles an unsolvable Rubik's cube where the play's competing geographical claims and discourses send us headlong into maps and atlases for some sense of topographically scientific reassurance. Our Odyssean efforts, though, are "all lost, quite lost," as the setting reveals itself as a self-referentially theatrical as well as rhetorical topos that emphasizes a Judaeo-Christian vision that makes use of both benign New World discourse and sinister phantasmagoric Old World characters like Caliban in order to fill the map that the textual setting has so successfully managed to erase and obliterate.

3

Calibans Anonymous: The Journey from Text to Self in Modern Criticism

Caliban is thought by many to be one of the most ambiguous and fascinating characters in the Shakespearean canon, a fascination mirrored in his remarkably wide array of critical and theatrical manifestations. Symbol of nearly everything and everybody, from beastliness and cannibalism to Rousseauvian Noble Savage, Caliban has undergone a dramatic and semiotic metamorphosis in especially the last fifty years. In theaters he has previously been cast as prehistoric monster, as tortoise, fish, Victorian-Darwinian missing link, Yorkshireman and Irishman, the Kaiser's Germany during the First World War, and more lately as rebellious African American militant or as punk rocker (Vaughan and Vaughan, *Caliban* 3). My own reaction to the, in many ways, confusing problem of Caliban's status and origin aims to be more textually faithful than most recent analyses. Thus, both in assessing predominant interpretations of Caliban and in dusting off the outer layers of several more likely origins of the character himself, I try to do so with the *whole* text of the play as touchstone. This chapter's greater emphasis on the primary text sketches a Caliban who takes on a decidedly different, more mythological hue than do many post-modern ideas of Caliban as *ourselves,* a pathos-predicated angle clearly evident in various readings that discuss Caliban as New World indigene, diasporic slave, or post-colonial native. While seeing Caliban thus is an understandable and perhaps also cathartic reading with regard to our own recent history and culture, I argue that it tends to neglect and obscure the textual details concerning Caliban's physical appearance, religious origin, and cultural interstices. Partly on the basis of the highly eccentric fact that *The Tempest* has an *inferred, dramatic* setting that, like Swift's Laputa, is not situated geographically, I contend that Caliban may better be understood within an Old World (inter)textual and mythological context rather than one that relies on the island's discursive (or fixed) location in the New World. This text-centered interpretation is also strengthened by Caliban's glaring *intertextual* dissimilarity with, for example, native Virginians, of whom we find many positive and optimistic views in Renaissance travel narratives. Thus, I find it plausible to claim that the textual Caliban can better be understood in terms of the European *mythical* savage rather than as a *historically* accurate symbol of New World men.

What is so peculiar—and, I think, highly problematic—with regard to *The Tempest* and Caliban in the last sixty years of interpretation is that the play's rich and highly complex *textual* setting is often neglected or even erased and actively re-inscribed along the lines of *Caliban*'s different historical, political, and cultural interpretations.[1] As a result, Caliban's oscillating metaphorical status has rendered the play so fluid and open to interpretation that *The Tempest* is frequently deconstructed and dismantled in favor of *"A Tempest of One's Own"* (e.g., Aimé Césaire's *Une Tempête*), ultimately an absolutely subjective revision of the text that can realistically hope to exist only as one voice clamoring to be heard in the wilderness among legions of equally valid and polyphonic *Tempests* or as increasingly faint interpretative echoes of the same. I have no desire here to challenge the fact that those myriad Calibans—and their often ancillary *Tempests*—are formed, interpreted, and discussed *mutatis mutandis* but rather to show that their private and often very narrow emphases extend little applicability and focus outside their own parochial agendas,[2] and thus I contend that they fail to illuminate the *Shakespearean* text in any holistic, accurate, and ultimately convincing fashion.

Admittedly, the text itself fails to give us a perfectly clear picture of what Caliban looks like, even though, of all the characters, his visual appearance is by far the most detailed in the play. What does seem clear from the start, though, is that neither his reported appearance nor his qualities draw on the New World in any explicit manner the way the play's pseudo-narrator Prospero (re-)relates them to Ariel: Caliban's mother, Sycorax, the banished Algerian witch, is claimed to have been a "blue-ey'd hag" (I.ii.269), whereas Caliban himself is described as "A freckled whelp, hag-born" (I.ii.283). Rather than resembling typical features of some New World native, Caliban's qualities take on a clearly Old World-religious dimension and lineage, a dubious and ambiguous heritage that—because of Prospero's incensed temper when he relates it to us—we must be careful how to construe: "Thou poisonous slave, got by the devil himself / Upon thy wicked dam, come forth!" (I.ii.319–320). This very early attempt by Prospero to make us, too, see Caliban as a demonic and devilishly unholy figure provides a wonderfully dramatic opening, and the slave's first lines spoken in full exposure are fittingly dark: "As wicked dew as e'er my mother brush'd / With raven's feather from unwholesome fen / Drop on you both! A south-west blow on ye, / And blister you all o'er!" (I.ii.321–324). At this crucial point, when Caliban enters the stage, the audience in 1611 would have been able see for themselves how much (or little) of a "m[a]n of Ind" or "deformed slave" Caliban cut,[3] but, as I think most critics would agree, it is difficult even to imagine a misshapen and freckled Indian demi-devil with a blue-eyed African witch for mother.[4]

Nevertheless, many critical interpretations in the last fifty years have ignored this veritable red flag and have instead focused on Caliban's thrall-dom and linguistic plight as similar to those of Native Americans or exploited colonial slaves. Post-colonial writers and literary critics alike have sought to suggest New World-specific discourse as relevant to the setting for *The Tempest*, emphasizing limited passages, phrases, or words in the text—for example, Miranda's gleeful outburst "Brave New World" (para-doxically when she is commenting on the play's Old World characters)—as "displaced from its own historical and tropological roots, from precisely what a contemporary audience must have recognized as its primary refer-ential horizon: the New World as historico-geographic trope" (Gillies 181). Furthermore, "[i]n addition to the words themselves, the very construc-tion of this moment (a species of 'first encounter' scenario) inscribes it within New World discourse" (Gillies 181).[5] Thus the back door is open for Caliban to be re-introduced, this time as an "aboriginal" Native American (Lee 257), an exploited black African (Mannoni 107–108), a Caribbean indigene by virtue of his name (Cheyfitz 87), or any other emotionally poignant representative for the previously colonized lands once under par-ticularly English[6] or French rule. In other words, *The Tempest*'s meaning, like the meaning of so many great works of art, is read in textually prob-lematic ways, supported by scant fragments, that reflect the feelings and agendas of its interpreters—an increasingly common tendency in modern interpretations of Shakespeare (Taylor 6)—which means that Caliban has lately undergone a facelift both physically and morally in terms of race and cultural origin.[7]

Poignant thematic and discursive parallels notwithstanding, one would perhaps expect that drastic ethnic character changes must rely to a great extent upon setting, so that in order for us to see Caliban as a Native American (or Asian, Arab, African, or virtually any post-colonial Other) the play's setting ought to reflect such mirages in a plausible and consistent cultural-geographical fashion as a first premise. Problematically, though, the admittedly fascinating prospect that *The Tempest*, and Caliban of course with it, is geographically, textually, *properly* taking place in and actively, politically engaging with "Enter Your Country of Choice Here" often seems to be taken for granted, seemingly under the assumption that it does not matter that the text stubbornly resists the notion of a fixed place or discourse: again, its setting-discursive conundrum early on results in a non-setting that veers *between but never properly in* geographical places like "Milan" (I.ii.54), the Italian "signories" (I.ii.71), "Naples" (I.ii.112), "the still vex'd Bermoothes" (I.ii.229), "Argier" (I.ii.265), and "Afric" (II.i.70). Ignoring this airy, trans-geographical (non-)setting, some recent critics instead comment on the play as though—often *because* of Caliban—it were set in a *discursive* New World locale, thus relocating from the traditionally preferred Mediterranean "letters of the play" (for our purposes, its material *locus*) to an "ideological" or "rhetorical" American "topos" (Cheyfitz 87, 88).

And this journey from textual *locus* (which suggests a geographical non-setting) to such *topoi*—which can be virtually everything but especially "other colonial documents" (Cheyfitz 87)—in turn invites fierce political castigation, particularly from adherents to a New World-metaphorical Caliban, whose discursive prowess strong-armed such an odyssey in the first place. Hence this recent critical tendency has managed to carve a political, geographically real *locus* out of a *pathetic topos*, resulting in an *emotional* "somewhere" (Cheyfitz 87). Like some Trojan horse, this "somewhere" harbors condemnation of colonial and/or contemporary Western politics,[8] moral as well as political accusations expressed in ways that often obviate important textual detail, such as the play's self-referentially ambiguous setting mentioned above.

One pointed instance of *The Tempest*'s pathetic[9] and extratextual New World landing appeared in 1971, when Cuban writer Roberto Fernàndez Retamar's essay "Caliban" declared kinship on behalf of his nation with Caliban: "What is our history," Retamar asks, "what is our culture, if not the history and culture of Caliban?" (14). Retamar further asserts that "[t]here is no doubt *at this point* that *The Tempest* alludes to America, that its island is the mythification of one of our islands" (8), before confidently concluding that "Caliban is *our* Carib" (9, italics mine). Later, the Barbadian poet Edward Brathwaite, Kenyan author Ngugi wā Thiong'o, and Lemuel Johnson of Sierra Leone made similar claims to "Calibanness" on behalf of their countries' experiences as well (Vaughan and Vaughan, *Caliban* 168), gesturing toward Caliban's linguistic plight, forced as he is to use Prospero's language in order to express himself, a familiar post-colonial paradox that has led Johnson to write in a fierce local dialect and wā Thiong'o to write in (the local Kenyan language) Gikuyu, all "to distance themselves still further from Prospero's colonialist clutches," as the Vaughans puts it (168).

This view of Caliban as colonial or post-colonial victim is relatively new, however, for Caliban was at one stage synonymous with the opposite. For example, in the aftermath of the Spanish-American War of 1898, South American poets, philosophers, and intellectuals resented the United States and the North Americans for their "Calibanesque"[10] imperialistic tendencies, materialistic greed, lust for power, and spiritual torpor. The Vaughans observe that as late as 1918, Venezuelan journalist Jesús Semprúm expressed a fairly common attitude in South American intellectual circles when he ranted that their non-Iberian neighbors to the north were "rough and obtuse Calibans, swollen by brutal appetites, the enemies of all idealisms, furiously enamored of the dollar, insatiable gulpers of whiskey and sausages—swift, overwhelming, fierce, clownish" (*Caliban* 152). Intriguingly, ninety years ago, South American intellectuals *expected* their readership to share this vision of Caliban as a fitting symbol of all that is ugly, brutal, violent, vicious, and greedy—and asked their readers to apply this set negative image to the North Americans.

It is interesting to ponder why it was not until the 1950s that Caliban was considered a suffering Promethean New World hero semi-prophetically gesturing towards (post-)colonial independence but perhaps especially so for our purposes to analyze *how* these interpretations were made. The idea of a New World *Tempest* setting that would later provide the very grounds for such liberationist views was briefly introduced by Edmund Malone as early as in 1808, and then picked up in 1896 by Sidney Lee, who believed that "Caliban is an imaginary portrait ... of the aboriginal savage of the New World" (257). The champions of the *négritude* movement would later amplify this claim to hold Caliban as one of their own, but it seems fair to say that the zenith of liberationist *Calibanismo* was reached by Robert Márquez, who in 1974 saw in Caliban a noble resistance to European domination, a character in many ways similar to South America's own political heroes and martyrs:

> The stories, poems, play, essays and art work collected in this issue are ... a contemporary echo of the rebellious Antillean slave in Shakespeare's final play. [Caliban is a symbol of] a struggle for liberation and cultural authenticity whose roots must be traced back, from Salvador Allende, Che Guevara, and Toussaint L'Ouverture, to the original revolts of indigenous Indians and Black slaves .... Against the hegemonic, europocentric, vision of the universe, the identity of Caliban is a direct function of his refusal to accept—on

any level—that hegemony . . . . This, then . . . a fragment of the world-view of the victim, is the world of Caliban. (6)

The key misreading in Márquez's passage is of course the "*Antillean* slave" who is somehow located "*in* Shakespeare's final play" (my italics), seemingly a slight prepositional glitch—or semi-intentional overstretch. But that little word "in" (rather than the more cautious and precise phrases "symbolically in the background of" or "discursively similar to") carries with it enormous ramifications with regard to setting and Caliban's origin. For the text has, as the *dramatis personae* informs us, of course no Antilleans "in" it at all but rather a more generic "savage and deformed slave" living on its "desert island," a purely theatrical setting that, the text goes to exceptional lengths to stress, has an *unstable* geographical location, as we saw in the previous chapter. But since Márquez's literal (*not* discursive or symbolic) reading stipulates that Shakespeare's Caliban really *is* "an Antillean slave," the play must perforce be set on an island in (or close to) the Caribbean Sea. As we can see, one's interpretative strategy and the openness and honesty in which it is declared are crucial components toward understanding such subtle sleights of hand vis-à-vis the play's text, since they ultimately change how we (re-)interpret the play's (new, modified) themes.[11]

In a critical climate grown increasingly relativistic to text, Peter Hulme can now safely defend George Lamming's attempts to see the play as speaking about Caribbean-specific issues such as torture of Haitian slaves, questions of race and color, nationality, and personal experience—though Lamming himself clearly expected criticism of his extratextual reading in 1960. He protests already at the outset that "[i]t will not help to say that I am wrong in the parallels which I have set out to interpret; for I shall reply that my mistake, *lived* and *deeply felt* by millions of men like me—proves the *positive value of error*. It is a *value* which you must learn" (Lamming 95, emphasis mine). Forty years later, Hulme proclaims that Lamming "was not wrong" in discussing the play and its setting as Caribbean and suggests that Lamming be moved to the canonical center of *Tempest* scholarship (232–233). Hulme's position is important as a critical as well as moral judgment, for it hinges entirely on a radical demotion of text and its preeminence in professedly literary analyses. In both Hulme and Lamming, clearly, personal reception and raw pathos are privileged at *The Tempest*'s expense, pushing into the background the primary textual passages that (supposedly) produced such recognition and resultant emotion in the first place. Perhaps the most evocative and certainly most frequently cited example of this nature is spoken in dignified verse by Caliban early on:

This island's mine by Sycorax my mother,
Which thou tak'st from me. When thou cam'st first,
Thou strok'st me and made much of me, wouldst give me
Water with berries in't, and teach me how
To name the bigger light, and how the less,
That burn by day and night; and then I lov'd thee,
And show'd thee all the qualities o' th' isle,
The fresh springs, brine-pits, barren place and fertile.
Cursed be I that did so! All the charms
Of Sycorax, toads, beetles, bats light on you!
For I am all the subjects that you have,
Which first was mine own king; and here you do sty me
In this hard rock, whiles you do keep from me
The rest o' the island.
                                    (I.ii.331–344)

Caliban, the son of an exiled Algerian, accuses Prospero of having stolen his birthright to the island, in a similar way to how Native Americans and African slaves were robbed of land and freedom. But as is eminently clear from the play's main plot and ending, Prospero's concerns are not colonial or imperialistic but rather apolitical and essentially morally and spiritually regenerative,[12] proof of which we find in the passage when he drowns his book, the source of power and magic, wishing instead to "return to Milan, where / Every third thought shall be upon [his] grave" (V.i.311–312).

Lamming's reading instead claims the text as a *pathetic* space, an emotional Room Nineteen where his "parallels" enjoy a morally superior position, which, problematically, therefore places them above dialectical scrutiny and discussion. This tactic is as old as the ancient Greeks: Lamming's position reminds us, perhaps, of how Antigone's impulse-turned-convenient-principle is sanctified by her emotions of family love and sisterly loyalty. Her sacred emotion, however, quickly turns out to be an anti-intellectual and anti-rational conversation stopper, one that in its own morally superior universe puts all discourse and argument to rest, to thin, suffocating air, as we see in her early dismissal of her sister Ismene. Antigone channels her sorrow for her brothers to make a religious claim from which, in turn, she demands a right and a space within (or indeed *outside of*) the law, a claim that is first of all extremely personal but that seemingly only Creon keenly senses has enormous *political* consequences for Thebes as well. In the meantime, Antigone, the bully of familial loyalty and love, makes a claim to a *moral* authority, a redefinition whose success is contingent upon *our* willingness to accept that it is pathos—not Creon or his law—who is king. As we see with Lamming, a not dissimilar specter of moral *kingship* lies readily available to us in *The Tempest* through the discovery of emotional *kinship*. In spite of the text's geographical non-setting, critics have discursively and emotionally relocated the play to the Caribbean (like Lamming and Césaire), to Africa (like Mannoni and Cartelli), to Ireland (Paul Brown, David Baker), or to any conceivable place from whence Caliban might speak pathetically to us—or indeed for us. *The Tempest* has thus, *via* Caliban, lately begun to deal primarily with ourselves. Critics no longer see the need to demonstrate—and quite understandably very rarely do—that the island is *textually* set in the New World before discussing New World-specific problems and (post-)colonial themes.

There are three major problems with viewing Caliban as our New World indigenous and oppressed selves. First of all, such interpretations frequently rely on anachronistic discursive references. One problem with interpreting Caliban as a specifically African American slave, despite the widely reported British pirate slave trade, is clear from the historical fact that the English themselves had not yet employed the practices of trans-Atlantic slavery in the 1611 Virginia colonies. As Vaughan observes, the first black African slaves "came to Virginia in 1619" (Vaughan, *American Genesis* 143). Indeed, "Englishmen might have avoided all association with Africans, and to a large extent they did. Contacts between England and Africa were few and far between; even the slave trade of the seventeenth and eighteenth centuries involved only a few hundred English sailors and a handful of resident agents... England did not need black labor" (ibid. 145–146).

Secondly, the Calibanic anthropological criteria (to coin a rather awkward phrase) seem far too uniformly negative to apply to the Algonquian New World population with much accuracy, for if Caliban is indeed to be associated with native Virginians, he is a pessimistic departure from the predominantly optimistic views of Indians found in Renaissance travel narratives. Contrary to what appears to be unanimous popular belief, from Columbus through Montaigne and William Strachey, few travel accounts of the New World present the natives in such harsh terms as befall Caliban in the play, as colonial historians are also quick to point out (Vaughan and Vaughan, *Caliban* 275). Furthermore, Caliban's association with animal qualities in the text tends to place him outside of the ethnographic perimeters of the historical New World natives: in light of the tradition of nearly panegyric praise of native life so successfully established by Christopher Columbus, terms like "cat" (II.ii.83), "debosh'd fish" (III.ii.26), "half a fish and half a monster" (III.ii.29), and "beast" (IV.i.140) seem like far too negative a set of characteristics to match American aborigines. In contrast, to

Columbus, the Indians were *not* "monstro[us]" but "amiable and kind" (Columbus 48). Montaigne believed that the Indians were men of "valour" and "glamour," proud and decent men who spoke in a sophisticated language strangely akin to the "Greek tongue" and "Anacreonti[c]" poetry (Montaigne 98). Sir Francis Drake's descriptions come perhaps the closest to resembling those of the textual Caliban's proneness to idolatry and sacrilege[13] when he notes that the Indians living in what is now Brazil used to "sacrifice to the devils" (Drake 156) and that the natives in California mistook the Europeans in the expedition for gods (165). Drake takes pains to stress, though, that the native people in present-day Argentina were "cleane, comely, and strong" and that the inhabitants of the Island of Barateve were "civil, just, and courteous" (157). The contrast to Caliban's dirtiness and monstrosity is obvious: "A fish, he smells like a fish!" (II.ii.25–26). George Percy's account of 1607 Virginia does describe the natives by the common epithet "savages" (like Caliban in this one respect) but admits that "[they] beare their yeeres well" (Percy 18). Captain John Smith intermingled with and learned much from the natives and recorded many of their words, which fact alone suggests that he was highly unlikely to have conceived of them as people who "gabble like [things] most brutish," the way Miranda[14] accuses Caliban of having done in *The Tempest* (I.ii.356–357).

Thirdly, as Meredith Anne Skura notes, the text of the play does *not* echo or harmonize with historical descriptions of Native Americans as far as Caliban is concerned, for Caliban, she points out,

> lacks almost all the defining external traits in the many reports from the New World—no superhuman physique, no nakedness or animal skin (indeed, an English[15] "gaberdine" instead), no decorative feathers, no arrows, no pipe, no tobacco, no body paint, and—as Shakespeare takes pains to emphasize—no love of trinkets and trash.... Caliban is in fact more like the devils Strachey expected to find on the Bermuda islands (but didn't) than like the Indians whom the adventurers did find in Virginia. (49)

And this last sobering point should have great ramifications, foremost of which is that the play ought to be significantly *limited* as a target for various political condemnations: Caliban's "freckled" skin (I.ii.283) and "blue-ey'd" mother (I.ii.269) provide clear key words in a textual snippet that stridently "refuses to mean" (as Stephen Greenblatt might have phrased it) that charges of European racism and imperialism against New World natives by Prospero (or even Shakespeare) are in any way textually justified.

For if we can momentarily suspend the belief that the setting is *symbolically* Bermuda, Virginia, the Caribbean, or the larger (post-)colonial New World, Caliban again changes along with it, casts off his New World-metaphorical coil and reveals his complex, textual hue—the (Old World) "monster" he is so often accused of being in the text: "This is some monster of the isle with four legs" (II.ii.65); "This is a devil" (II.ii.98); "this moon-calf" (II.ii.106); "this puppy-headed monster. A most scurvy monster" (II.ii.154–155). Caliban's physical as well as cultural attributes here suggest that he is to be seen in an Old World light, a monstrous, (familiarly) foreign, and thoroughly exaggerated and sensationalistic character whose ancestry is at least in some (nominal and unexpounded-upon) measure North African and whose cultural oddity, human beastliness, and European-defined Otherness is of a different complexion altogether than the *unheimlich* differences posed by New World natives.[16] For we can see from the isolated lines "the son that she did litter here,/A freckled whelp, hag-born" that Caliban has freckled or spotted skin, that he is born of a hag or witch, and that Prospero sees him as a "whelp" or a puppy dog or wolf rather than as a fully grown man.[17] It is true that Caliban's status as a human being is somewhat acknowledged, but the parentheses in which he is rather reluctantly classified as a man—which would no doubt have to be spoken in a lower tone or cadence to contrast it wearily to the more heated rant Prospero is delivering—quite literally make him an afterthought as regards humanity, a freak anomaly never to be considered an equal:

> Then was this island
> (Save for the son that she did litter here,
> *A freckled whelp, hag-born*) *not honor'd with*
> *A human shape.*
> (I.ii.281–284, my italics)

This monstrous impression is reinforced by the proximity in the text and line to the very opposite notion that these lines were meant to contradict, namely that Caliban is "not honor'd with/[a] human shape." In his rage, Prospero touches grumblingly yet nonchalantly on Caliban as being some kind of man, but the lines that immediately follow are orally difficult, to say the least, to rejoin with the general purport of the angry passage above, so that the way these lines are delivered orally—as well as the way in which they appear in print—will tend to accompany and modify Caliban's nature against their own *ostensible* rhetorical purpose. And this doubt is then further stressed two lines on, when Prospero continues to call him a "[d]ull thing" (I.ii.285). In short, Caliban, whose nature *is* acknowledged human, appears ambiguously nonhuman because of the passage's jumbled syntax and consequently misleading emphasis.[18]

And in contrast to the many positive European travel accounts of American natives we saw above, Caliban is certainly no gloriously noble or even handsome savage, nor does Prospero treat him as such: "What ho! slave! Caliban!/Thou earth, thou! speak!" (I.ii.313–314). These harsh invectives subtly hint at slightly different geographical and cultural-semiotic settings, for even if we accept the premise that the early modern English understanding of "slave" were equal to our own, chiefly as a refer-ence to a trans-Atlantic African/indigenous slave in the New World rather than to an Old World "thrall" or "serf" of European origin, then the rather odd identification with Caliban as "earth" is (paradoxically) not easily placed in terms of geography anywhere. The most tempting parallels slav-ery poses to the play tend to accentuate the abuse and hardship that befall Caliban under Prospero's rule and tutelage, but slavery was far from a new, or indeed New World, phenomenon. Europeans had been familiar with *internal* slavery—that is to say, the practice of enslaving one's own coun-trymen and citizens—since the days of ancient Greece and Rome up to the Vikings in the Middle Ages, and the practice of enslaving, for a limited time, fornicators and adulterers was given very significant attention and narrative (if not authorial) approval in Sir Thomas More's 1516 *Utopia*.

Caliban's conspicuous lack of central textual links with the American New World natives, then, suggests that his origins lie elsewhere. As John Hollander and Frank Kermode have noted, Caliban, and perhaps also the element "earth" with which he is here associated, is representative of nature as it is understood in a hierarchically inferior sense—stones, dirt, plants, and animals are below humans, and thus Caliban is similarly "based on the wild man or *Wodewose* of European tradition—treacherous, lecherous, without language . . . in an intermediate position between man and beast, natural in a bad sense" (Hollander and Kermode 446). Back to the textual scene, Caliban, who thinks his master wants more wood for the fire, replies rather curtly from behind the scene that "there's wood enough within" (I.ii.313). Earthy Caliban, then, who is frequently associated with the ele-ment of water via reference to his fishiness, is here called upon to make the fire, thus encompassing three of the four natural elements—air is of course Ariel's domain. And it is within this familiarly Old World frame of the natural kingdom, I choose to see Prospero, subsequently (in line 316) referring to him as a "tortoise," a naturally slow animal whose characteris-tics Caliban is claimed to share in his perceived laziness and a very familiar anthropomorphized creature (albeit portrayed with far more sympathy) in Aesop's *Fables* and European folklore.

Plausible Calibanic avatars and intertextual parallels may be found in the general fascination with monsters and freaks in much of English and European literature. We know that Shakespeare's contemporaries drew heavily on the tradition of the savage[19] in literature, as we can see in Spenser's *The Faerie Queene* (Bullogh 253–255). The similarly uncouth character Bremo of the anonymous play *Mucederos* has raised interest by scholars like Frank Kermode and William Hamlin (28). Furthermore, Günter Walch provides a German dramatic parallel vis-à-vis the conspicuously similar plot of Jakob Ayrer's play *Die Schönen Sidea* (236–237),[20] and Bernard Knox has noted the often ignored classical dimension that Caliban, Ferdinand, and Ariel's thralldom poses to the comic and "sullen slaves" in Roman plays by Plautus (177).

And if it is correct, as Hamlin has argued, that Caliban in no way relies exclusively on stage monsters and wild men of English mediaeval tradition (19, 22–23), then it certainly behooves us to consider that his physical monstrosity finds a fascinating set of parallels in Greek mythological creatures like the misshapen and ugly blacksmith Hephaestus, also mentioned in Homer's *Odyssey,* on which *The Tempest,* in turn, draws in central parts. According to Betty Radice, Hephaestus was "[t]he god of fire and a metalsmith, son of Zeus and Hera, said to have been flung from heaven in one of their quarrels and lamed by falling on to the volcanic island of Lemnos" (127). Thus, the paraplegic Hephaestus "is also a comic figure limping among the gods" (128). With regard to Caliban's otherwise textually unspecified misshapenness, the Greek mythological references find some support in the fact that, like Caliban, Hephaestus is ugly, deformed, and quite literally an outcast. Note, too, that Caliban carries firewood for Prospero. Additionally, in his most grotesque and misshapen *reported* form, Caliban finds useful general avatars in the minotaurs, satyrs, and shape shifters of Greek and Minoan literature and mythology, as Hulme has already suggested ("Hurricanes" 70).

Caliban's monstrosity, interestingly, can usefully be seen in *both* an Old World-religious as well as aggressive New World colonial-political light when he tacitly confirms Prospero's worst accusations of having attempted to rape Miranda: "O ho, O ho, would't had been done! Thou dids't prevent me; I had peopled else this isle with Calibans" (I.ii.349–351). Caliban is here rhetorically manipulated into a theatrical trial of sorts where he seems to take a destructive and stubborn sort of pride in his dark past: duped into making his devastating admissions in front of the audience by the orator and rhetorician Prospero, Caliban splutters curses of witchcraft and plagues (I.ii.363–365) and thus, perhaps, forever condemns himself to be seen by theatergoers as Prospero would have us see him, namely as a satanic worshiper of the dark forces of witchcraft.[21] And of course, the grotesqueness of Caliban's appearance, added to the hateful lines above, tend to give an indelible impression on any audience, a first encounter that spawns a mental picture of savagery and diabolism that Caliban can never seem to erase. If not so much for his (or the play's) direct reliance on biblical characters like Cain, Jezebel, Absalom, or Judas Iscariot, Caliban forms a conveniently satanic dialectical opposite to the airy and angelic Ariel in a Christian worldview of good versus evil.

And perhaps in this Judaeo-Christian context, we do best to see Prospero's accusation that Caliban is *a* "devil" whose father was allegedly "*the* devil."[22] In other words, what may seem like a rather desperately angry and insincere rhetorical exercise in identifying Caliban with a folkloric dimension of religious-mythological diabolism is here ultimately to be associated with the very roots of evil, the devil himself. Such characterizations would of course be familiar to a contemporary audience in 1611 from common morality play stock characters like Vice, Sin, Greed, Evil, and so forth.

And Caliban's towering Otherness, paradoxically, is exactly that which is (bordering on the) nonhuman and non-European in a distinctly classical European fashion. According to the hardly neutral Prospero, Caliban is the offspring of an Algerian witch and the Devil himself and thus fits snugly into a European, Old World, and Judaeo-Christian cultural and religious matrix. Applying the same tactic of *familiar* alienation or othering, the writer of *Beowulf* makes Grendel fit into *his* own, Christian culture by slipping in edgeways the information that Grendel's mother begot her (rather devilish) amphibious son by the banished Cain in what is universally understood by Christian readers to be hell. Caliban represents a similar pattern in *The Tempest:* his is precisely the sort of alterity the European tradition may contain without having to be stretched beyond its own cultural boundaries.[23] Paul Brown, for his part, refers to what he terms England's core and periphery and locates Ireland and the Irish as a semi-periphery that poses an island setting, a colonial situation, and masterless people as analogous to *The Tempest* in 1611. Such a reading, which deals with the alien that is closer to home or the core, tends to relocate or zone in on the more familiarly European and Old World.[24]

It also makes much sense to extend this further inward-gravitating attention toward Shakespeare's own, previous dramatic output. His plays present perhaps more convincing *thematic* parallels to Caliban than specific discursive references. Seen in relation to the gloomy and proto-Gothic furniture of *Macbeth*, for instance, the witches occupy a similarly demonic role to Caliban's role in *The Tempest*, where his status as the son of a witch—a "hag-seed"—only makes the link seem more plausible, seeing as how "hag" is an oft-recurring word in *Macbeth*, as well as in *The Tempest*. The Scottish features of the play, as Shakespeare presents and exaggerates them, generally seem to pose a highly fitting background to Caliban (more so than to Milan-bound Prospero) as a would-be black magician, witch, or wizard (Caliban, like Dr. Faustus, we do well to remember, wishes to gain insight into the arts of magic by stealing Prospero's books). Furthermore, Caliban's very real (lately downplayed and ignored) evilness could be said to draw on Iago or the bastard Edmund[25]; his admittedly brief thirst for alcohol might be set in pointed relief with Sir John Falstaff and his sometimes comical Otherness with that of the Jew Shylock. Caliban (unlike Edmund) is a *comical* bastard, a *real* orphan (different in this central point from Perdita or Marina), evil heathen, liar and coward (again, like Falstaff), forever a unique outsider but one whose separate features and qualities find myriad parallels in *1 Henry IV, Macbeth, Othello, The Merchant of Venice* and *King Lear,* to name but a select few.

New Historicists and Cultural Materialists have done exceptionally well to stress that by seeing the text as only one of many cultural utterances, we can better understand its significance as a product of a larger society, as only one voice within a broader culture and discourse, thus helping to redefine and problematize what a "text" really is. But the final result of the emotion-centered fusion of the most subjective excesses of reader response—inspired criticism and cultural studies is that Caliban has undergone an interpretative odyssey that has taken us from text to self. *Symbolically,* Caliban has long since departed from the text in Shakespeare cultural studies: many post-colonials now see themselves *in* Caliban or themselves *as* huddled masses of Calibans anonymous,[26] and hence we get a profound sense of how ubiquitous—and, one does feel tempted to add, subsequently *meaningless*—the terms "Calibanic,"[27] "Calibanismo," or "Calibanesque" have become, perhaps especially to the peoples of the New World they often are meant to address and (re-)identify. Caliban's *dis*entanglement from a limited discursive and emotionally symbolically predicated New World, therefore, is one suggestion toward an increased understanding of the character Caliban and the play—as iconoclastically liberating as it is faithful to the text, it also draws more fruitfully on several Old World traditions and intertexts, some of which are only beginning to be properly acknowledged in *Tempest* scholarship.

Part III

Subversive American Adams and Anarchic Utopists

4

The Tempest Beyond Post-Colonial Politics: Vargas Llosa's *The Storyteller* as Topical Retrotext

This chapter reads *The Tempest* with Mario Vargas Llosa's *The Storyteller* as a presentist intertext-after-the-fact—in other words, what I choose to call a retrotext—and as an eco-critical and post-colonial work of fiction that, partly because of the creative playfulness its genre permits, casts a new illuminating light on the play that produces some spiritual and ideological perspectives that politically centered post-colonial criticism of the play has heretofore entirely overseen. The methodology of this chapter is in large part modeled on Rebecca Ann Bach's "Mrs Caliban: A Feminist Postmodernist *Tempest*?" which (for obvious reasons) reads Rachel Ingalls' novel *Mrs. Caliban* as a feminist commentary on both contemporary society as well as the play. When I suggest here a similarly retrotextual post-colonial reading of Mario Vargas Llosa's novel *The Storyteller,* I do so in the knowledge that, whereas the novel does not employ overt *Tempest*-specific metaphors or references, its central themes revolve around primitivist utopias, language, alienation, religion, politics, and post-coloniality in a fashion that resonates closely with the play's own setting, plot, and dialogue. The convincingly eco-critical and post-colonial lens through which the novel's Western co-narrator interprets the novel's fascinating Others does not necessarily owe much to Shakespeare or to the play, nor is the novel in any explicit form to be taken as some sort of critique of *The Tempest*—dissimilar in this respect from the overt evocation of the play in the title of Ingalls' novel. I nevertheless suggest that Vargas

Llosa's novel addresses a wide range of the play's similar (post-)colonial themes in a manner that in its ironic and playful probing is infinitely closer to the rhetorical and aesthetic strategy of the play itself than is, for example, Aimé Césaire's *Une Tempête*—not to mention Rachel Ingalls' self-same *Mrs. Caliban*. While the post-colonial situation, as it is documented in history and in literature, clearly has also a political dimension that is always relevant to literature dealing with the same colonial or post-colonial plights, I suggest that this one aspect of power alone unsatisfactorily illuminates *The Tempest* as a text that is relevant to post-coloniality.

For the sake of clarity, I find it useful to specify already from the start what I mean by the term "political." Alexander Leggatt begins by defining politics by its opposite when he asserts that "if everything is political, then nothing is, for the world has lost its edge" (ix). My own working definition of politics in this chapter is similarly restricted to that which concerns the governing of the *polis* (or state), in contradistinction to the claim often espoused by Marxist critics that politics pervades everything and is therefore paramount in any given text since the textual product is itself (consciously or not) an utterance that ultimately stems from conditions that are political in nature. Hence, instead of seeing Prospero's power over Caliban, Ariel, Ferdinand, and Miranda as strictly and singularly in political terms, this chapter and this book seek to diversify this political discussion by exploring moments and situations in which the text actually does move "beyond politics," toward more utopian and spiritual aspects of ideology, identity, and culture.

Vargas Llosa's novel neatly dovetails with such an emphasis. Chronicling the development of Saúl Zuratas, a Jewish outsider who eventually leaves behind all urban pursuits to live among the Machiguenga in the Amazon forest, the novel resists facile political analysis. Its multiple voices and narrators create a dialectical rhetorical complexity that, when read in thematic conjunction with *The Tempest,* moves our reading of the play's relevance to post-colonialism forward. While I attempt in this chapter to acknowledge and recapture the political impulse of Aimé Césaire's *Discourse on Colonialism* and *Une Tempête* as well as George Lamming's *Pleasures of Exile,* I seek primarily to redefine and enrich their political angles in relation to similar and important *cultural* first-encounter issues discussed in *The Storyteller.* The cultural problems that Vargas Llosa's novel treats so carefully are at any rate also highly relevant to the extended political and ideological discussions of *The Tempest.* These issues typically include those of national identity and independence as well as cultural and linguistic confusion in the face of European or Western pressure seen from the viewpoint of smaller Amazonian tribes. The pressure the Machiguenga suffer is critically analyzed by the protagonist Saúl Zuratas, then ironically and retrospectively scrutinized by the co-narrator, in sum forming an impassioned as well as urbanely oblique set of observations on the more or less tangible lures of Western society. The novel usefully illustrates well for my purposes here how the play's much-touted political dimension might be seen as only part of a larger discourse wherein *The Tempest*'s text may be read in the more holistic light that Vargas Llosa's novel sheds on aspects like indigenous identity, culture, religion, and folklore. It thus serves as a useful modern background against which both the issues of *The Tempest* and the attitude of post-colonial *Tempest* critics may be apprehended.

Another dimension that the novel and the play raise in tandem is an eco-critical focus on the tensions that exist between nature and culture and how nature furnishes the material surroundings against which and within which this culture can come to exist and thrive. The purpose of this chapter is to explore ways in which *The Tempest*'s post-colonial relevance can be seen to resist simplistic political classification but rather move the discussion ahead of politics toward a richer and more holistic understanding of a larger cultural and linguistic discourse.

In order properly to justify the nature of such a reading, a brief critical contextualization is perhaps necessary. Overtly political criticism of *The Tempest* came about in the 1950s and 1960s and coincided with post-colonial independence. Fewer works spoke more clearly and politically from and to the initial post-colonial experience than Aimé Césaire's *Discours sur le colonialisme* (or *Discourse on Colonialism*) from 1955, a work that in its righteous rage identified the colonizer with the ultimate barbarity. Briefly, Césaire turns the tables and claims that colonialism makes a brute and a beast of the *colonizer*—he becomes primitive, frightened, animalistic. The colonizer has much in common with the behavior that he has previously accused his victims of displaying. The colonizer, claims Césaire only ten years after the end of the Second World War, is essentially a "Hitler" or a "nazi" in his inner self. Most ironically, though, colonization, the way Césaire sees it, is civilization's antithesis, an impulse that serves to degrade the colonizer and that makes him resort to violence and his baser instincts (*Discourse* 11). With specific regard to *The Tempest*, Césaire's fascinating and useful general analysis in some ways inverts the picture of the "colonized" Caliban as third world victim that was to gain great traction later and sees instead the European colonizer—often identified as Prospero in the play—as the victim of his own vices. Césaire's work reacts strongly against a perceived apologia for colonialism found in a more *Tempest*-specific analysis that was offered by Octave Mannoni's groundbreaking analysis *La psychologie de la colonisation* in 1950, where, like so many critics before him, Mannoni quickly identified the character Prospero with Shakespeare (Mannoni 107) but with the—for Césaire— tremendously troubling distinction that while Mannoni sees Prospero as a prosthetic figure, the latter's imperious treatment of Caliban is a natural reaction or even *state* brought about as a result of inherent psychological needs and urges to dominate and to obey. As such, Mannoni's seminal essay on the power relations between the two of the play's characters is to Césaire taken as a much broader blanket excuse for colonialism and imperialism cloaked as psychological pseudo-science.

Later political-psychological analyses interestingly often depend on New World-specific settings, a problem that is dealt with explicitly in Lamming's *Pleasures of Exile* of 1960. Speaking of the island setting as a perfect location for a colonialist power struggle, Lamming chooses to see the setting as an island in the Caribbean, "[f]or there is no landscape more suitable for considering the Question of the sea, no geography more appro- priate to the study of exile. And it is that ruthless, though necessary wreck, which warns us that we are all deeply involved in the politics of intrigue" (Lamming 96). To Lamming, too, Prospero is a dictator, a jealous old man who is cynical and evil, while Caliban is his underestimated slave. Lamming revisits Césaire's psychological study of the colonizer's depravity and seems to align his reading with Césaire rather than with Mannoni in that he lays no blame on Caliban for his physical urges but rather on Prospero. The New World (or third world) native that Caliban is by extension thought to represent, then, cannot be said to be responsible for his own "nature" since this nature has been corrupted by the white man's nurture—to Lamming, it would seem, Prospero has been only too successful in imparting his "print of goodness," a print that is here to be seen as corrupting and evil, of course, and which leads Caliban to lie, to lust, to want to dominate and kill.

In 1972, Leslie Fiedler focused on the political and ideological impact of the play as particularly relevant in a New World, American-specific, post- colonial context:

> [T]he whole history of imperialist America has been prophetically revealed to us in brief parable: from the initial act of expropriation through the Indian wars to the setting up of reservations, and from the beginnings of black slav- ery to the first revolts and evasion. With even more astounding prescience, *The Tempest* foreshadows as well the emergence of that democracy of fugi- tive white slaves, deprived and cultureless refugees from a Europe they never owned, which D.H. Lawrence was so bitterly to describe. (qtd. in Frey 31)

Obviously, Fiedler stresses instead the play's link with American history as experienced by refugees, black slaves, and the downtrodden. In doing so, Fiedler manages to raise attention to the history of the lower classes and the exploits of the rich—*The Tempest anno* 1972, then, serves a new and larger political purpose in that it reminds contemporaries not only of similar pastoral themes described in classical American literature but also of the histories of the underprivileged masses. Fiedler here discusses the play in a similar way to Lamming, Mannoni, and Fanon but significantly with a purpose to encourage an understanding of extratextual history that is essentially political in nature.

This increasingly political interpretation of both history and literature lends itself to a view of especially Prospero (and with him, Shakespeare) and *The Tempest* itself as complicit with colonialism and the rise of capitalism, and they are hence to be held accountable for the perceived injustices that later capitalist governments have bred. For example, in 1979 A. James Arnold wrote of Césaire's adaptation that "[o]ur latter-day Prospero is presented as the agent of European capitalism at its inception" (238). Arnold shifts attention from the *négritude* of Césaire's play and instead sees it in political-economic terms in a way that also comments on Shakespeare's play. Moreover, Arnold also casts in a new light Césaire's criticism of Gonzalo's dreamy passage:

> Utopian elements are submerged so as to render Gonzalo's position as a mere variation on colonialism. Gonzalo, too, intends to colonize the island but without corrupting the noble savage by importing European values. He would keep his Utopia as a place of rest and recreation for tired Europeans: in terms of contemporary Martinican reality a prototype for the Club Méditerranée (idyllic but rigidly set apart from "native" life). Césaire's derisive critical spirit thus spares not even the good Gonzalo, who emerges (in II.ii) as a Renaissance proponent of international tourism. (240)

Césaire's play, according to Arnold, takes issue with the notion that Gonzalo's reverie is noble and without negative consequences—it is in fact part and parcel of the same haughty, touristic, and perhaps slightly xenophobic impulses that have rendered an organic and "genuine" place like Martinique into a plastic garden for rich and jaded Europeans, a tropical dystopia devoid of its once-vibrant soul. What Arnold here adds to Césaire's play is a sense of continuity and developing political thought— after the initial fervor of decolonization had abated, Arnold finds new dimensions in the Western psyche to criticize. These dimensions includes a neo-colonial form of tourism, and Arnold does well to manage to stress that the cultural legacy of colonialism lives on in new and veiled forms and that *The Tempest* is relevant political and (post-)colonial reading also today precisely for its presentist relevance.

However, the play's thematic link to colonialism and racism, with all their attendant political aspects, would not be confined only to the American hemisphere or the third world. In an influential essay written in 1985, Paul Brown argues that *The Tempest* might be seen as operating along the geographical lines of "centre" or "core" (England), "semiperiphery" (Ireland), and "periphery" (the New World), represented, respectively, by the characters Prospero, Stephano and Trinculo, and Caliban (51–52). More to the point, Brown argues in favor of an extended understanding of colonialism and sees Ireland and Wales as English colonies in the "semiperiphery" and their often rebellious inhabitants as a threat to the English by virtue of their "masterlessness" (52–53). In *The Tempest*, likewise, Brown claims, what unites the aristocracy politically against the lower classes is the common fear of the masterless man (52–53). Such rebellious types as vagrants, gypsies, or blackamoors in England were seen as a potential threat from within as the rebels in Wales and Ireland were from without, and they were all regarded with great skepticism and suspicion. As several rebellions and subsequently failed settlements in the New World would also remind the English, the impulse toward masterlessness was indeed a threat also to the colonial enterprise in Virginia. In Brown's analysis, the play is

> not simply a reflection of colonialist practices but an intervention in an ambivalent and even contradictory discourse. This intervention takes the form of a powerful and pleasurable narrative which seeks at once to harmonise disjunction, to transcend irreconcilable contradictions and to mystify the political conditions which demand colonialist discourse.... The result is a radically ambivalent text which exemplifies ... a moment of *historical* crisis. This crisis is the struggle to produce a coherent discourse adequate to the complex requirements of British colonialism in its initial phase. (48)

Brown stresses that the text of *The Tempest* seeks to establish a fitting narrative to address early British colonialism and is therefore self-consciously involved in a political strategy to raise awareness about the colonial enterprise. And this enterprise and its attendant suppression rely on some negative stereotypes, according to Brown, as seen where the English would emphasize the beastliness of both the Irish and the New World population: "As with the Negro or the Amerindian, the Irish might be constituted as bestial or only marginally human and, as such, totally irreformable" (55). The suppression of the more mobile and "footloose" Irish people therefore "became a symbolic statement of British intent for the whole of uncivil Ireland" (56). Brown links such "masterless" types to especially Stephano and Trinculo, but he also finds a connection in Gonzalo's utopian passage:

More positive versions of Ireland were also produced, particularly in those texts which advocated plantation of the English beyond the Pale. Such versions produce Irish culture, generally, along the lines of a "negative formula" in which the alien is afforded no positive terms but merely displays the absence of those qualities that connote civility, for example, no law, no government, no marriage, no permanent settlement. Again, *The Tempest* is implicated in such a strategy. Gonzalo's description of imagined island kingdom in I.ii, culled from Montaigne, rehearses the standard formula by which the colonised is denigrated even as it appears to be simply the idle thoughts of a stranded courtier. (56)

Brown, like Arnold above, is highly skeptical of Gonzalo's plantation passage, but rather than seeing Gonzalo's ideal society as a touristified, whites-only island in the sun, Brown claims that Gonzalo's rhetoric is a recipe for an *incipient* colonialism in that the lines are seen as testifying to the lack of European civilization to be found on the island, which would produce a pretext for future colonization. But the island also serves another political function, as Brown points out: "At its most optimistic the negative formula represents the other as a natural simplicity against which a jaded civility might be criticised, yet even here the other is produced for civility, to gauge *its* present crisis" (56). And it is here I believe Brown makes his best point, in that the play could very well be seen as an indirect critique of English/European society and the corrupted ideals it upholds while an alternative form of society is discussed. (I shall return to the political and utopian relevance of this alternative society in Chapter 6.)

An interesting and in many ways similar political argument was made in an article of 1987 by Thomas Cartelli, who takes the discussion of the play's colonial involvements even further:

It is no doubt true that *The Tempest* has long functioned in the service of ideologies that repress what they cannot accommodate and exploit what they can. One consequence of this subordination of text to ideological transaction is that it is still a generally uneducable, bestial Caliban who survives the adjustments that have been made in western racial prejudices; mainly a blindly, self-righteous, authoritarian Prospero who presides in Third World inversions of the same. Yet the text of *The Tempest* continues to allow Prospero the privilege of the grand closing gesture; continues to privilege that gesture's ambiguity at the expense of Caliban's dispossession; continues, in short, to support and substantiate the very reading of itself transacted by the ideologies in question. It is in this respect, among others, that *The Tempest* is not only complicit in the history of its successive misreadings, but responsible in some measure for the development of the ways in which it is read. (112)

If I have understood Cartelli's lament right, it suggests that, because of the text's static nature, it "continues to" create a nearly *sui generic* and prescriptive, ritualized way in which it also interprets itself, a reading that in turn lends itself not only to the ideology that supported English colonialism in the early seventeenth century but continues to this day to promote exploitation in post-colonial countries. For "[i]n this respect," Cartelli claims, "Shakespeare's staged fantasy establishes the parameters of a colonialist procedure [white explorers] will rehearse with a rougher magic in Africa" (111). In Cartelli's analysis, the play seems partly responsible first of all, for how the play has been *allowed* to be performed and interpreted and secondly, more problematically, of course, for the disastrous historical consequences this "misreading" has had in places like Africa, Asia, and South America. Obviously, if we can accept for a moment that the the text itself (as opposed, for example, to far more dynamic oral stories) is a permanent and static artifact, *The Tempest* is a self-regenerative product. Hence, it seems accurate to say that Cartelli criticizes the text for having *created* the same ideology he also claims has "successive[ly] misread" it. In other words, unless it is actually the readers and interpreters of *The Tempest* who have got it wrong, *the text itself* must necessarily contain a set of self-conscious devices that lead to interpretative obfuscation. As such, the ambiguity and "misreadings" that logically follow are produced by the play itself for odious political purposes that lend themselves quite handily to colonialism and racism, and the text is therefore seen as "responsible in some measure" for reproducing such political ideologies. In other words, Cartelli seems to bemoan the fact that influential texts survive their historical moments and continue to imprint their by now old-fashioned and restricting mark on us 400 years later.[1]

In *The Poetics of Imperialism* (1997), Eric Cheyfitz deals along the familiar lines of colonialism and post-colonialism as they pertain to *The Tempest* and observes with regard to race and color that "there is evidence in the Jamestown documents that the early colonists saw skin color, which in any event was not the crucial 'racial' category to them...as a cultural rather than a natural acquisition" (85). "*The Tempest*," Cheyfitz claims, "records" what he terms a "violent history of translation" that ought to be read "along other colonial documents" (87). Speaking of Caliban's wish to kill Prospero, Cheyfitz urges us to understand this wish in terms of recent political and ideological rebellions, for

> it is the settler [i.e., Prospero] ... who institutes the violence that triggers this dream of counterviolence. Revolution, whether it is Tayo's return in *Ceremony* to the communal world of the pueblo, or the Sandinista's communism,

becomes the possibility of replacing this dream with a social reality that is independent of the settler's institutions. (162)

The (more or less) presentist political lens through which Cheyfitz here poses Caliban as the communist rebel to an imperialist Prospero along the conflict lines of political unrest in South America is of course familiar territory. Cheyfitz sees language as a central component in this "violence" and draws a parallel from Miranda's teaching Caliban her language to the attitudes to the natives' language among some of the European explorers:

> Caliban's relationship to his own language or his lack of language becomes a figure for the Europeans' need to feel that the Old World languages were superior to those of the New. Europeans needed to feel, that is, that New World languages were virtually a lack of language. How else justify the *mission civilatrice* that rationalized and still rationalizes Western imperialism? (164)

Cheyfitz's somewhat confounding rhetorical question at the end of this quotation seems to imply that the linguistic violence he perceives in Prospero and Miranda's educating Caliban is either still tacitly accepted in Western countries vis-à-vis the rapid worldwide spread of such *linguae francae* as English, Spanish, French, and Portuguese, or that reactionary critics of the play still condone the sixteenth- and seventeenth-century "imperialism" that he sees at work in *The Tempest*.

For all of Cheyfitz's genuine attempts to rekindle a political spark that might resituate the play to a presentist-topical space, it seems far more sobering to reflect on the fact that whatever apologist views of "Western imperialism" might somehow have survived at all in academia until the 1990s, they had gone overwhelmingly out of fashion with any serious scholar in the field. To wit, in an article written in the same year (1997), Jonathan Hart points to the great sense of irony that lies in the fact that academics in both North America and South America

> find themselves in a position of identifying with Amerindians as a means of vindicating the wrongs done to, and prejudices against, those peoples in the past and as a declaration of independence from their own European past. While this position is understandable and even laudable, it is difficult to avoid contradiction and to erase the European contact with the first Americans so readily and with an exercise of conscience. (24)

Hart does well here to stress the historical and cultural currents that have shaped criticism and also manages to raise the question whether Western academics' unreserved yet in many ways culturally contradictory solidarity with the downtrodden is able to serve scholarship neutrally and credibly in light of such contradiction.

One of the more peculiar things about modern criticism of the play is that it has sometimes been preoccupied as much with some post-colonial creative works that employ *Tempest* metaphors as with the Shakespearean play. These creative adaptations in themselves are also often read as criticism. Indeed, appropriations and adaptations like Aimé Césaire's play *Une Tempête* and Rachel Ingalls' novel *Mrs. Caliban,* poems by Edward Kamau Brathwaite and Lemuel Johnson, and autobiographical (mis)readings by George Lamming have become so established in the last forty or so years as the critical orthodoxy that many scholars read Shakespeare's *The Tempest* with these other creative works foremost in mind. In this spirit, I therefore find it fruitful at this stage to turn outside or above the strictly defined political sphere to discuss the play's post-colonial relevance in relation to Mario Vargas Llosa's post-colonial novel *The Storyteller.*

For the novel poses valuable parallels to *The Tempest* in its treatment of the cultural first-encounter experience in general and comments in a new post-colonial manner on the political and cultural criticism of the play besides. By reading these two works in close thematic tandem, I believe that we can find ways in which to diversify, as it were, the strictly political sphere discussed previously and rather see certain textual passages in the play in light of cultural, religious, linguistic, and folkloric post-colonial problems. As will be shown, the intricate relationship between such various themes may serve as a better gateway to understanding also *The Tempest* than is the oft-cited political dimension of the colonial situation.

In some important ways, for example, the play can be said to anticipate the struggle over language in post-colonial societies. Haughty and nationalistic attitudes to the native languages are not necessarily to be seen as political per se but ultimately also touch on far more complex patterns of dialects, sociolects, idiolects, class, and local and individual identity. We see an example of linguistic ignorance/arrogance when Miranda scolds Caliban for his general bestiality, but the moral and intellectual focus of this criticism is here directed at Caliban's lack of gratitude and linguistic and cultural receptivity as two sides of the same coin:

> Abhorred slave,
> Which *any print of goodness wilt not take,*
> Being capable of all ill! I *pitied* thee,
> Took pains to make thee speak, taught thee each hour
> One thing or other. *When thou didst not, savage,*

Know thine own meaning, but wouldst *gabble like*
A thing most brutish, I endowed thy purposes
With *words* that made them known.
(I.ii.351–358, italics mine)

The linguistic problem that Miranda brings up also evinces a familiar political judgment in the sense that there was a more or less conscious desire
among the early colonizers to further their own interests via their own
language, and vice versa. It could also be said that the attitudes above
anticipate the notion of the *noblesse oblige* or White Man's Burden—that
is to say, Miranda's passage may be read as a recipe or process of not only
teaching the natives but un-teaching them as well, of their own past, language, identity, and religion. Miranda's passage importantly also articulates
far more clearly than most early modern travel narratives do—more honestly than these carefully crafted rhetorical Eurocentric documents could
possible be expected to do—the caprice of language and the vagaries of
translation, especially a "violent" kind of translation that refuses to see in
the native's mother tongue a proper language but only gibberish and brute
sounds. We also note that the focus of Miranda's educational efforts is on
the *printed* word, while her diatribe against Caliban emphasizes his *oral*
"gibberish" and "lack of language," in Cheyfitz's words (164). This particular attitude could obviously be seen as analogous to the articulated
as well as unarticulated notions of Renaissance explorers trying to bring
the natives of the New World to understand the Bible and written culture in general, a practice that results in situations of absurdly unsuccessful
intercultural communication and translation that are blithely passed off
as successes. In the above passage, though, there is a dark tone of cultural arrogance and aggression that most Renaissance travel narratives, for
reasons to do with rhetorical agenda, manage to gloss over in their one-
sided nature, but from the point of view of a "Calibanic" culture that has
relied chiefly on oral accounts of history, culture, and artistic expressions,
encounters with an orthographic Prosperian culture that relies almost
solely on written accounts will often be seen as threatening and dangerous.[2]

As we will see, this threat is taken very seriously in Vargas Llosa's *The
Storyteller*. Vargas Llosa's novel is set in Peru in the 1960s and follows the
development of Saúl Zuratas, Jew, radical ethnology student, and eternal outsider, through his folkloric, linguistic, and cultural sojourn into
the Amazon forest, where he eventually settles with a Machiguenga tribe.
In a sense, Saúl experiences the Amazonian Other in a fashion that goes
one better than the manner in which Gonzalo merely fantasizes about
the phantom "islanders" in *The Tempest*. However, unlike Gonzalo, whose

approach is optimistic and curious, Saúl displays an almost desperate concern for the potentially ruinous effects that a rapid process of Westernization may cause for the indigenous population. Saúl is adamant "'[t]hat these cultures must be respected,' he said softly, as though finally beginning to calm down. 'And the only way to respect them is not to go near them. Not touch them. Our culture is too strong, too aggressive. It devours everything it touches. They must be left alone'" (Vargas Llosa 99). Saúl sees Western culture—in this case the academic disciplines of ethnology and anthropology—as a pollutant that is fatally toxic to a fragile little community like that of the Machiguenga tribes living in the Amazon forest. A student of ethnology himself, Saúl harbors great moral qualms about his field of academic study, since he sees it as too insensitive and curious in its nature. He fears that this insensitive curiosity will obliterate what it seeks to study; according to Saúl, as soon as the Machiguenga are infected with the culturally lethal virus that is Western popular culture, they will perish. Saúl Zuratas's attitude is thus almost exactly the opposite of that expressed in the Miranda passage, which is to say he fears that the Machiguenga will lose their unique culture as a result of sheer exposure to the lure and convenience of mainstream Western society. The protective and pastoral-paternalistic attitudes that Saúl displays toward the natives here are in some meaningful ways seen in relation to Gonzalo's utopian dream in *The Tempest,* where the old Neapolitan councilor dreams about abolishing letters entirely and law and all other urban-specific pursuits with it. The general pastoral inclination that forms the basis of Gonzalo's primitivism is hardly new, of course, as both the Greeks and Romans dreamt of getting away from the hectic and bustling cities of Athens and Rome, as if to acknowledge in so many actions and words that not only can the countryside be seen as a refuge but can serve a necessary regenerative function for the city, to which we will by necessity return.

Also, Saúl here expresses a dualistic commonplace in the pastoral genre, one that sees everything rural as positive and natural—and urban sophistication in exclusively negative terms. Relevant to the pastoral posture (which here takes a folkloric hue) that Saúl assumes, Roger D. Abrahams notes that such romantic pastoral ideas are "not the natural world view of the folk. It is the sophisticated person who has gained some psychic distance from country life who is capable of perceiving of the totality of the metaphor" (92). That is to say, Abrahams points out, like Frank Kermode, that the pastoral is fraught with several internal ironies and contradictions since it is a genre that is essentially urban in nature. But in Saúl's zealous opinion, of course, the *urban* (or Western) longing, curiosity, and "sophistication" have brought about enterprises like colonialism (which was, indeed, often highly pastoral in its impulse and rhetoric), imperialism, and their more distant cousins anthropology and ethnology. According to the increasingly radicalized Saúl, *all* these pursuits—whether imperialistic or academic in nature—contribute to a fast destruction of that which was their erstwhile object of fascination and attraction. Western urban civilization has not only an ironic and self-loathing longing to reside in harmony with nature but also an uncontrollably persistent curiosity and thirst for knowledge to learn about different cultures, to *read* Others in order better to understand ourselves and the world. This cultural *reading process* is, of course, a central theme in *The Tempest,* especially as pertains to Gonzalo and Miranda, a process of observation, recording, scrutiny, and research that *The Storyteller* problematizes with great acuity: "And yet he's taken it into his head, can you believe it, that the work [ethnologists are] doing is immoral' . . . He's convinced that we're attacking them, doing violence to their culture . . . [t]hat with our tape recorders and ball-point pens we're the worm that works its way into the fruit and rots it" (32). The flip side of this coin, still according to Saúl, is that we as Westerners also wish to put our "print" on everything, as Miranda also mentions in the above passage. We are a culture of "civilizing" others as well as ourselves, and this tendency, "imperialistic" though it may be to critics like Cheyfitz, is what sets Western civilization apart to Saúl as so uniquely "aggressive." Saúl Zuratas sees this civilizing tendency as a potentially disastrous threat to the Amazonian culture, but also his *own* view is colored by Western conceptions of the Other, no matter how hard he tries to persuade us otherwise. His attitude is representative of the longing toward nature and uncorrupted lands overseas latent in a crowded Europe, but in fairness to Saúl, he also moderates this view, and he never seeks to domesticate the natives as the colonists would—and did. He wishes above anything that the Amazon tribes *not* become Western but realizes, even as he sets out extremely cautiously and sensitively on a seemingly innocent mission—to gain academic knowledge of the Machiguenga tribes—that although he is very self-consciously not part of the process of imprinting, he is very much the part of the *reading* process that will form a narrative framework for the ultimate Westernization of the natives.

And yet one of the strengths of Vargas Llosa's novel lies in its double narration that creates a dialectic between the primitivist fantasies of the storyteller Saúl Zuratas and the jaded cynicism of the narrator:

> What was it that Mascarita was defending? Was it something as chimerical as the recognition of their inalienable right to their lands, whereupon the rest of Peru would agree to place the jungle under quarantine? Must

no one, ever, have the right to enter it, so as to keep those cultures from being contaminated by the miasmas of our own degenerated one? Had Saúl's purism concerning the Amazon reached such extremes? (33–34)

Problematically, though, Saúl—and, one feels tempted to add, scores of recent *Tempest* critics with him—seems to underestimate the resistance and flexibility of the native culture, a strength that is proven by the fact that they have officially and ceremonially adapted to Christianity (a written religion) but stubbornly evade the missionaries' questions regarding their most central cultural feature of yore, namely that of the *hablador*, or storyteller:

> "I mean, baptizing this place New Light and calling the village chief Martín. The New Testament in Machiguenga; sending the Indians to Bible school and making pastors out of them; the violent transition from a nomadic life to a sedentary one; accelerated Westernization and Christianization. So-called modernization. I've realized that it's just outward show. Even though they've started trading and using money, the weight of their own tradition exerts a much stronger pull on them than all that." . . . "I asked the school-mistress in New World, and Martín as well, about habladores. And they both reacted in exactly the same way: denying that they existed, pretending they didn't even know what I was taking about. It means that even in the most Westernized Machiguengas, such as the school-mistress and Martín, there's an inviolable inner loyalty to their own beliefs. There are certain taboos they're not prepared to give up." (172–173)

In relation to *The Tempest*, we could see this level of resistance fruitfully with regard to Caliban's most intimate yet almost demonstratively overt nostalgia about his mother's god Setebos: "I must obey. His art is of such power, / I would control my dam's god Setebos / And make a vassal out of him" (I.ii.371–373). While it is true that Caliban here acknowledges Prospero's power as greater not only than his own mother's but also her deity's and that this realization makes him feel that, for the moment, he "must obey," Caliban's invocation of an exotic New World god seems more than a nod in the direction of Magellan and Richard Eden. For the cultural and religious memory that Prospero and Miranda's language and culture lessons has not been erased but rather cemented and guarded (Caliban delivers these lines in an aside) as a treasured heritage from his mother, a legacy he must keep to himself as a taboo, ideally, perhaps in his "brutish" tongue that his tutors cannot understand. Of course, since Prospero, Miranda, and caricatured European explorers more generally insist that there simply never was any such thing as language or religion in native culture, the Machiguenga (but importantly—because of his rash temper—*not* Caliban) have taken a very similar stance to that of Saúl: what they wish to keep, they must hide from the white missionaries. It is this jealous stubbornness that keeps their ancient oral culture alive, as we soon learn when discovering that the role of the storyteller now holds an even stronger position than before and one that also reveals that the *official* acceptance of the written religion is ceremonial at best. The oral culture, religion, and practices are still held in sway when the white man is not watching.

In relation to the similar cultural and political assimilation that Prospero and Miranda force upon Caliban in *The Tempest* by teaching him their language, Saúl realizes that the only possible contribution on his part is not so much a student *reading* of the Machiguenga culture but rather a "suicidal" undoing of such passive pastimes toward active participation. Thus, he has to "go native." The novel's narrator—the older version of the persona who (like Antonio and Sebastian do with Gonzalo in *The Tempest*) has cynically challenged Saúl's visions of an undisturbed Amazonian *eutopia* in his past—grows increasingly philosophical about the important distinctions that differentiate Saúl's mania from the fleeting fancies of romantics:

> But Saúl had not gone off in the same way [adventure-seeking students in the 1960s and 1970s] had. He erased all trace of his departure and of his intentions, leading those who knew him to believe that he was emigrating to Israel. What else could the alibi of the Jew making the Return mean, except that, on leaving Lima, Saúl Zuratas had irrevocably decided that he was going to change his life, his name, his habits, his traditions, his god, everything he had been up until then? It is evident that he left Lima with the intention of never coming back, of being another person forever. (243)

In this way, of course, Saúl renders *himself* a *tabula rasa,* one who must first become *un*-civilized and then *re*-civilized on the terms of the natives. Saúl Zuratas dreams of a very similar place of activity rather than some pastoral-touristic *otium*—and in fact goes through with it—and lives with the Machiguenga in not so much a Golden Age or Edenic prelapsarian bliss but, to his mind, lives an active life as the most unlikely latter-day *hablador* just before the Western deluge. While it is true that Saúl's initial urges to do so might be criticized for being a romanticized, pastoral-paternalistic dream that could only have been dreamt by an intellectual urban dweller from a solidly Western background, those same contradictions resonate with *The Tempest*—and are in fact resolved to some satisfaction. For Saúl converts, like his biblical namesake, from a literate culture to an illiterate one, converts from a culture of convenience and advanced technology to one of basic necessity and discovers entirely without romanticized illusion that his life and the lives of the Machiguenga are active and meaningful rather than the sort of vacuum of identity and lifestyle that so besot the lives of the acculturated, Arielic "zombie" Indians for whom Saúl shows equal doses of pity and irritation early in the novel.

The right description for this impulse lies perhaps somewhere between self-fashioning and self-annihilation, if by such change one is required to give up part of oneself. Similar attitudes to such drastic self-fashioning are expressly articulated in *The Tempest* by Gonzalo, and by Trinculo and Stephano, too—but perhaps most convincingly displayed in terms of action by Ferdinand. And as Paul Brown has shown, there was a commonly held fear among colonizers in the Renaissance that the "blank spaces of Ireland [and of America, too] provided not only an opportunity for the expansion of civility; they were also sites for the possible undoing of civil man" (57). Such an anxiety might possibly be attributed to Prospero's unease about the *social* (and also possibly sexual) bond between his daughter and Caliban—he may fear that by speaking in his native tongue, the slightly older Caliban might "infect" Miranda in her cultural vacuum and sterile linguistic innocence.

And such a view of languages and cultures as miasmas and viruses is very much adopted by Saúl Zuratas, who, instead of writing an ethnographical dissertation in the form of an elegy of the (soon-to-be-)lost cultures of the Amazon jungle, decides to *reverse* what he sees as a lopsided and unilateral cultural development of assimilation:

> Do our cars, guns, planes, and Coca-Colas give us the right to exterminate them because they don't have such things? Or do you believe in 'civilizing the savages,' pal? How? By making soldiers of them? By putting them to work on the farms as slaves to Creoles like Fidel Pereira? By forcing them to change their language, their religion, and their customs, the way the missionaries are trying to do? What's to be gained by that? Being able to exploit them more easily, that's all. Making them *zombies and caricatures* of men, like those *semi-acculturated Indians* you see in Lima. (26, my italics)

In contrast, Saúl abolishes the nostalgic and romanticized lens through which the West sometimes views the natives and chooses instead to un-textualize and re-contextualize himself by "going native." As the co-narrator of the novel points out, Saúl held these views before they became faddish with the intelligentsia in the 1960s and 1970s, and Saúl is therefore not so vulnerable to critical remarks that he might be a simple romantic dreamer like the Gonzalo whom the play satirizes and praises in equal measure, but also Saúl is unable to rid himself completely of his identity as a Peruvian Westerner (26). For when we are given the natives' point of view, it is through the ambiguous and culturally hybridized—indeed almost schizophrenic—medium of Saúl. Hence, what we see through the "eyes" of the Machiguenga is somewhat tainted by Saúl's extremely rich and complex cultural background. We are presented with the plight of the natives through the cultural filter of a Jewish South American academic, and we are unsure of whether his portrayal of the Machiguenga is, or ever can be, the true representation of the aboriginal Amazon cultures.

This problem of interpreting and representing New World natives through culturally biased translators has often been stressed vis-à-vis *The Tempest* and colonialism (Greenblatt, *Learning to Curse* 26–27). Such problems of intrusive translation (in both reading and print) are also relevant when studying the impact that Western civilization has had on oral communities round the world. Nobody denies that this impact has been extremely powerful, perhaps nowhere more profoundly felt than in the realm of religion. One would perhaps think that since it is a written account, the Bible—and indeed holy scriptures of other religions as well—provides greater consistency in interpretation than an orally transmitted set of beliefs forever subject to dynamic change, simply due to its static literary vehicle. And in some useful ways a rural oral community can indeed be seen as the *tabula rasa* onto which, most literally, print may be put, and via this process of writing, the writer will redefine the recipient culture. And, of course, in an imperialistic sense, the central point is to imprint upon the Other one's own culture and tastes, language, and ways of life.

Shakespeare had of course written explicitly about such imperialism earlier, in *Antony and Cleopatra*, where Antony, sent out by Rome to demand both a military and a cultural act of submission on the part of the Egyptians, fails tragically in his imperialist designs. Antony fails, I believe, chiefly because he is fascinated and pacified by Cleopatra and the Egyptian culture in general, and undergoes an act of voluntary cultural assimilation that is similar to the openness (and what almost seems like streaks of cultural self-annihilation) found in both Gonzalo in *The Tempest* but particularly in Saúl Zuratas in *The Storyteller*. In *Antony and Cleopatra*, there is a marked reversal of fortunes and atmosphere when Octavius finally conquers Egypt for Rome, but by then both Antony and Cleopatra are dead from suicide. And it is this sense of cultural humiliation that Cleopatra avoids by taking her own life, avoid, that is, the embarrassment it is for her to be dominated by an outside culture and be paraded on the streets of Rome like some exotic bird in a cage. Although her country is eventually conquered to become part of the Roman Empire, Cleopatra personally suffers no cultural domestication. Antony can boast no such accomplishment, though, for he has instead voluntarily yielded both his militarily superior cultural background and his sense of manliness. Geraldo de Sousa has claimed in a recent work that Antony, through his Egyptian sojourn, has become "a self-indulgent guest of the Egyptians and a gypsy vagabond" (129, *Cross-Cultural*). Playing on the word "gypsy," which is of course a corruption of the word "Egyptian" (but which has since come to mean a person of the Romani people), de Sousa does well to distinguish between the more genuine culture of Cleopatra's Egypt and Antony's rather shallow sense of hybridity. In Antony's case, we are led to infer that Egyptian culture, militarily weak though it might be, is dangerously beguiling and intoxicating, and Antony is fatally smitten with its *virus,* that extremely attractive sense of Otherness which Gonzalo so cherishes in *The Tempest* and for which Saúl Zuratas so enthusiastically gives up his lifestyle, career, and indeed his entire previous identity. It is this wandering sense of masterlessness that Paul Brown sketches out as very dangerous for Renaissance Englishmen, the same fear of a multiculturalism where one dominant culture consumes another that Saúl Zuratas is clearly so skeptical about, "maintain[ing] that [ethnologists] have taken up where the missionaries left off. That we, in the name of science, like them in the name of evangelization, are the spearhead of the effort to wipe out the Indians" (33). From the adopted point of view of the Machiguenga, the sense of cultural annihilation—which Caliban has suffered to some extent in *The Tempest*—is very much Saúl's nightmare scenario for the indigenous population.

This is a view I personally find to be too pessimistic and simplistic. For with regard to religion in Vargas Llosa's novel, the missionaries misinterpret the natives' seemingly passive regurgitation of Christian doctrine. And as the Machiguenga's clever performativity of Christian rituals and sacraments demonstrates, the tribe fully masters, fully apprehends the *masque* of the ceremonial aspects of religion when they pay lip service to their "benefactors" of the Christian/Western persuasion while at the same time continuing their own religious and cultural practices. To regard people of mainly oral cultures, therefore, as simply passive recipients of the Christian gospel and to expect the natives to have no intellectual resistance and no cultural or religious substance in them at all is not only a fiercely arrogant view—it also views people as essentially static and collectivistic rather than as thinking individuals. It is precisely this condescending attitude the Machiguenga seem to have understood and consciously pander to when they robotically perform the rituals of the local church. They display what the white missionary wishes to see, but they understand, like Caliban, Stephano, and Trinculo do in *The Tempest,* that he cannot read their minds: "Thought is free," Stephano sings as the drunk rebels prepare to usurp Prospero (III.ii.123). Unlike the written word, this intimate thought and stuff of the soul, and the spoken word that is used to express it, can be hidden from sight, kept a secret. It can furthermore be orally rehearsed in a strange tongue as a tool of subversion in a moment of a crisis of cultural identity, as in the Machiguenga in Vargas Llosa's novel, or during a crisis of power, as with Caliban and his co-conspirators in *The Tempest.*

Thus, it becomes useful to see *The Storyteller* as a "shadow-Shakespearean" response to the many naïve and romanticized "Noble Savage" accounts of the Amazon tribes that started with Montaigne already in 1580. In some meaningfully similar ways to how Aimé Césaire's *Une Tempête* actively speaks back to Shakespeare's play, *The Storyteller* challenges and redefines the 500-year-old dialectic that poses Europe as the engraver of America, one that sets its mark upon it culturally, linguistically, and religiously. For Vargas Llosa's novel manages to dwell on cultural instances that resist such facile sweeps; instead of seeing the natives as bearing the mark of European civilization, these passages hint that the process by which cultural contact is taking place affects and impacts *all* sides. It seems a trite but useful reminder that Peruvians of Spanish descent, like Vargas Llosa, are, remain, and will develop into markedly different "Spaniards" after their encounter with the Amazon cultures, and this fusion of cultures is what sets Peru so clearly apart from Spain and Europe.

In *The Tempest,* colonial politics may be found within culture, culture within religion, personal spirituality within ideology and politics. Quarrels over attempts to sort and interpret these multiple aspects according to theories of either dominant or subservient material forces or spiritual longings are perhaps inevitable. For a long time, though, especially in *Tempest* scholarship, the generalized misconception has been allowed to take hold that such—in some ways organic, natural—change has been intentionally and unilaterally to the detriment of indigenous New World tribes, in keeping with a critical political analysis of exploitation, imperialism, and European/Western aggression. Historically correct though this analysis may be with regard to much military as well as economic and cultural conquest, it tends to neglect some pressingly important points, foremost of which is the fact that revolutionary change took place also in European culture and religion as a result of the impact or the initial encounters, as many historians have documented: "James Merrell reminds us that the Indians found themselves living in a world that from their perspective was just as 'new' as that which greeted the European invaders" (Breen, Divine, et al. 7). Importantly, too, and contrary to popular belief in political criticism of *The Tempest*, "Native Americans were not passive victims of geopolitical forces beyond their control" (ibid. 7). For example, the view of both geography and anthropology that most Europeans held before the encounters was forced to be seriously readjusted, if not discarded altogether—the "Indians," in a way, undid the very meaning of European and Western thought, simply by virtue of their existence, as Hawkes has argued ("Swisser-Swatter" 28). As such, the reciprocal process of influence and counter-influence seen especially clearly in *The Storyteller* but importantly also in the separate cases of Gonzalo and Caliban in *The Tempest* is not necessarily militaristic or political in nature but relies perhaps even more heavily on "softer" factors like religion, spirituality, folklore, theater, and culture. Hence, the colonialism and imperialism implicit in the early European military and political aggression develops into a more culture-specific realm, one that, in its intimate, profound, and sometimes clandestine nature, in many ways resists the reduction of textual meaning to politics or ideology as these terms are understood in this work. Historical examples of such cultural development "beyond politics" are actually abundant in North and South American history, as the intermingling of Spanish, French, Portuguese, African, and indigenous peoples proves with regard to the sense of *new*, creolized regional and national identities. This brave new sense of identity forms the most hopeful passages in the play, perhaps especially in Ferdinand's case, as we shall see in the next chapter.

"Any Strange Beast There Makes a Man": New World Manliness as Old World Kingliness in *The Tempest*

In the remarkably few gender analyses that have been written on *The Tempest* in the last forty or so years, feminists have focused almost exclusively on its one female character, Miranda, and have typically interpreted her position in the play as a romantic foil for Ferdinand or as a pawn in Prospero's political game. Masculinity has been almost totally ignored as a factor in these analyses, and this chapter seeks to redress this imbalance by linking the powerful sense of manhood that the play navigates to my book's critically revised and readjusted New World themes. I seek, in particular, to sketch out some previously uncommented-on New World qualities in especially Ferdinand that are paradoxically distinctly Old World in their *ideal*. This chapter, which tries to trace and at the same time attempts to *redefine* a sense of New World relevance for the play, hears in Ferdinand echoes of both early modern European travelers to the American continent as well as many of the qualities that those same chroniclers attributed to the natives. Ideas of masculinity are central to this undertaking, and my argument relies on an understanding of New World manhood as a particularly acute and anxious version that could in many ways be said to be different from Old World manliness. Of course, I rely here on what some may perceive as fairly conservative yet firmly established and remarkably stable Renaissance masculine ideals, on commonplace ideas about what men should and should not be, about how men ought or ought not to behave,[1] yet, with the advent of the New World, also how men could change—for the better—within accepted modes of male conduct. I argue that travel is part of this male formation, not only to "effete" European locales on the Grand Tour but increasingly to places unknown, uncharted, and dangerous, like Othello's Africa, like Marlowe's Asia (Hopkins 115), and to wild America, which Strachey's *Tempest* intertext certainly affirms. This New World-topical sense of manhood, as we shall see, is paradoxically yet inextricably linked with ideas of Old World kingship.

Men in English Renaissance literature express their athleticism, their prowess, in fact their *maleness* increasingly in terms of their movement. When middle-aged Othello, for instance, reflects on how he managed to woo young Desdemona with such surprising success, slavery, escape, exile, and the adversity of admittedly involuntary but nevertheless fascinating travel present to Desdemona an irresistible spectrum of distinctly *male* experience:

> Wherein I spoke of most disastrous chances
> Of moving accidents by flood and field,
> Of hair-breadth scapes i' th' imminent deadly breach,
> Of being taken by the insolent foe
> And sold to slavery, of my redemption thence
> And portance in my [travel's] history;
> ....
> And of the Cannibals that each [other] eat,
> The Anthropophagi, and men whose [heads]
> [Do grow] beneath their shoulders. These things to hear
> Would Desdemona seriously incline;
> ....
> My story being done,
> She gave me for my pains a world of [sighs];
> She swore, in faith 'twas strange, 'twas passing strange;
> 'Twas pitiful, 'twas wondrous pitiful.
> She wish'd she had not heard it, yet she wish'd
> That heaven had made her such a man.
>   (*Othello* I.iii.134–163)

The significant difference in age—not to mention race—between Othello and Desdemona is eclipsed by not only her pity but more to the point by the fact that younger, more appropriate suitors need the help of "heaven" to be able to measure up in terms of being equally fully "a man." The rhapsodic elegance and economy of Othello's relation aside, we know from the Venetians' initial suspicions that the Moor's narrative is responsible for the same psychic reactions that "witchcraft" and magic were believed to be able to stir in especially young women (I.iii.169). Thus, Shakespeare's habit of self-referential muscle-flexing again makes the common but useful point that words and the narratives and poetry they form (certainly as testified by Iago's) have enormous power.

William Strachey's universally accepted *Tempest* source and intertext, the "True Reportory" of 1609, echoes similar narrative and literary strategies, a storytelling technique that titillates the senses and moves the emotions of its expressly intended *female* audience and readership with tales of storms, danger, grief, and salvation. Strachey's story makes much of this latter angle, seen at the very outset of the storm when it describes not only the quiet before the storm but also St. Elmo's fire, a natural phenomenon that was often seen as a religious portent by sailors:

> Only upon the Thursday night Sir George Somers, being upon the watch, had an apparition of a little, round light, like a faint star, trembling and streaming along with a sparkling blaze, half the height upon the main mast and shooting sometimes from shroud to shroud, 'tempting to settle, as it were, upon any of the four shrouds. And for three or four hours together, or rather more, half the night, it kept with us, running sometimes along the main yard to the very end and then returning; at which Sir George Somers called divers about him, and showed the same, who observed it with much wonder and carefulness. (12–13)

Other, more fictional and sensationalistic literary strategies that deal with danger involves cannibalism, as we saw with Othello. Even though, by his own admission, Columbus, in his letter to Luis de Santángel of 1493, found no "monsters," he claimed that on "the second isle as one enters the Indies ... [there reside] a people considered in all the isles as most ferocious, who eat human flesh" (*Travel Narratives* 212). Amerigo Vespucci's *Mondus Novus* of 1504 revels in far more graphic detail in its descriptions of the ultimate taboos:

> The elders by means of certain harangues of theirs bend the youths to their will and inflame them to wars in which they cruelly kill one another, and those whom they bring home captives from the war, they preserve, not to spare their lives, but that they may be slain for food; for they eat one another, the victors the vanquished, and among other kinds of meat human flesh is a common article of diet with them. Nay be the more assured of this because the father has already been seen to eat children and wife, and I knew a man whom I also spoke to who was reputed to have eaten more than three hundred human bodies. And I likewise remained twenty-seven days in a certain city where I saw salted human flesh suspended from beams between the

houses, just as with us it is the custom to hang bacon and pork. (*Travel Narratives* 220)

Whereas such descriptions had cleverly contrived political purposes toward a sense of dutiful *mission civilisatrice* that is a favorite pretext for subsequent colonial plunder and exploitation, the passage itself has clear literary qualities in its ability to shock, to pique, to repulse, and the narrator seems to assume that the exoticness and sheer danger that such phenomena imply reflect positively on his own bravery and masculinity.

Such masculinity is also an almost universally praised quality in the New World populations Europeans encountered, as found in Sir Walter Ralegh's *Tempest*-intertextual "The Discovery of the Large, Rich, and Bewtiful Empyre of Guiana" of 1596:

> These Tivitivas are a very goodly people and very valiant, and have the most manly speech and most deliberate that ever I heard of what nations soever.... Of these people those that dwell upon the branches of Orenoque called Capuri and Macureo, are for the most part Carpenters of Canoas, for they make the most and fairest houses, and sell them into Guiana for gold, and into Trinedado for Tobacco, in the excessive taking whereof, they exceed in all nations, and not withstanding the moistness of the air in which they live, the hardness of their diet, and the great labors they suffer to hunt, fish and foul [*sic*] for their living, in all my life either in the Indies or in Europe did I ever behold a more goodly or better favoured people, or a more manly. (*Travel Narratives* 334)

The most interesting aspects of a very traditionally defined sense of manhood to note here, perhaps, are the natives' appetite for simple but nutritious food, their skill in hunting and building houses and canoes, and their still exotic habit of smoking, only later to become fashionable with Europeans. The natives as they are described by Ralegh are at any rate similar in their very maleness to Caliban in their ability to fish and hunt, like Ferdinand in their valiant conduct, and also find conspicuously precise echoes in Gonzalo's prelapsarian "plantation" in that "they never eat anything that is set or sown, and as at home they *use neither planting nor other manurance,* so when they come abroad they refuse to feed of ought, but of that which *nature without labor bringeth forth*" (334, italics mine).

Thus, New World and European men alike are measured *as* men in relation to how they travel, stray, survive in the wilderness, to how they are active and ingenious agents in their own narratives. In Renaissance travel literature, men very often make their own ways where none exist, forge their futures, and thus fashion themselves via hard labor and the fruit that it alone yields in the face of an oft-touted virginal and female nature (Hopkins 116) that nevertheless often turns out *initially* to be a masculine locus to be battled with, rather than seduced and cultivated. In Shakespeare's last unassisted play, Ferdinand subscribes to this particular formula for male conduct only in some part, and the focus I am concerned with in this chapter is how *travel* to faraway places like the Virginia colonies becomes not only a hallmark of such early modern daredevilish manliness but in fact also a *cure* or redemption, as it were, for characters like *The Tempest*'s Ferdinand, a representative of a class of pampered men desperately seeking what was in mediaeval times called a quest, a cause, a project tinged with significant overtones of manhood.

Understandably for a play that has one female character, *The Tempest* has drawn very little feminist critical attention. Ania Loomba's *Gender, Race, Renaissance Drama* from 1989 draws on Nixon to account for part of "the play's declining pertinence to contemporary third world politics" (Loomba, *Gender* 389) as "the difficulty of wresting from it any role for female defiance" (Nixon 577; qtd. in Loomba, *Gender* 390). Loomba's main concern is what she sees as the failure of post-colonial criticism to operate with a feminist prism when dealing with a text like *The Tempest*: "If varieties of feminism are guilty of racist practices, it needs hardly to be detailed here that sexist versions of anti-racism abound as well" (*Gender* 392). Loomba then proceeds to conduct a feminist reading of both Sycorax and Miranda[2] in light of the educational practices that the British colonists imposed on the Burmese people:

> Colonized women were also subjected to untold sexual harassment, rape, enforced marriage, and degradation, both under direct slavery and otherwise. Sycorax's illegitimate pregnancy contrasts with Miranda's chastity and virginity, reminding us that the construction of the promiscuity of non-European women served to legitimize their sexual abuse and to demarcate them from white women. Therefore Prospero as colonialist consolidates power which is specifically white and male, and constructs Sycorax as a black, wayward, and wicked witch in order to legitimize it. (*Gender* 394)

The tenuous Burmese parallels notwithstanding, the main problem with this reading is that Prospero hardly needs to "construct" Sycorax as anything at all other than what Ariel in shuddering gratitude has related to him—the narrative of her wickedness and implied grotesque sexuality are in other words not so much corroborated but in fact handed down to Prospero. Secondly, her racial aspect, though reportedly Algerian/North African, can hardly be said to be unproblematically "black"—no less of an authority than Prospero himself concedes that she was "blue-ey'd" and her son Caliban "freckled" (I.ii.269, 283).[3] Thus, the towering racial dimension with which *Othello* and *The Merchant of Venice* are invested with such great success is rather disappointingly downplayed in *The Tempest* and therefore seem to "legitimize" very little on the whole. By 2002, in *Shakespeare, Race, and Colonialism,* however, Loomba points to a general problem by admitting that few politically inclined *Tempest* critics, commentators, and "writers engaged at any length with Shakespeare's play" (*Shakespeare* 164). Also, while her position remains that "Sycorax returns us to the fears evoked for African and Moorish femininity" (*Shakespeare* 166), Loomba more recently admits that the North African references register as Old World rather than New World colonial (*Shakespeare* 167).

Fusing the feminist reading suggested by Ania Loomba and the intertextual methods offered by New Historicists, Melissa E. Sanchez's "Seduction and Service in *The Tempest*" claims that

> Shakespeare's late plays evoke . . . narrative structures to participate in an ongoing debate regarding the location and scope of sovereignty in early Stuart England. Read in such a discursive context, *The Tempest*'s attention to female desire and consent registers the participation of both populace and ruler, women and men, in sustaining structures of authority. Miranda's enactment of political subjection differs conspicuously from that of Ariel, Caliban, or any of the shipwrecked Italians, for her femininity accentuates an erotic dynamic that is less visible—but equally significant—in Prospero's relations with his male subjects and rivals. (50)

And like Stephen Orgel and Ann Thomson before her, Sanchez voices a by now common lament:

> Given the prominent conjunction of courtship and politics in early Stuart discourse, it is surprising that female figures have generated little interest in criticism of *The Tempest,* which has typically responded more to the masculine struggles emphasized in the play's comic sub-plot than to the male and female negotiations staged by its romantic main plot. (50–51)

This relative dearth of feminist scholarship on the play is perhaps "surprising" primarily in light of its hegemonic critical position since the 1970s rather than due to textual passages in the text that scream out for feminist analysis—the play lists, after all, one sole female character (barring the make-believe banquet goddesses) against at least fifteen male counterparts. The point of critical hegemony is well illustrated by the fact that, whereas it might be correct to claim that criticism up to Leo Marx's *Machine in the*

Garden of 1964 has dealt predominantly with "masculine struggles" rather than with feminine, it would be an enormous stretch to imply that *recent* scholarship has been anything but neglectful of the play as a *studium* of English Renaissance masculinity.

For her part, Ann Thomson admits that, in light of the play's scarcity of women, doing a feminist reading of *The Tempest* "may seem perverse, but my choice is a deliberate one and relates precisely to the *absence* of female characters. I want to ask what feminist criticism can do in the face of a male-authored canonical text which seems to exclude women to this extent" (404). Thomson, like Stephen Orgel's "Prospero's Wife" (of 1984) already had done in its focus on the absence of women in the play, protests that the play "den[ies] the importance—and in some cases the presence— of female characters" yet "simultaneously attributes enormous power to female chastity and fertility" (408). The main strength of Thomson's work is found in its honesty and ability to reflect over her own prejudices and the critical status quo while respecting the play's textual integrity in a fashion that few politicized *Tempest* readings these last four decades have felt compelled to do:

> Both psychoanalytic and political theoretical approaches nevertheless deny some of the pleasures experienced by earlier generations of audiences and readers who were apparently able to identify more readily with the viewpoint of Prospero as white male patriarch and colonizer. Today, white male critics in Britain and the United States understandably feel uncomfortable and guilty about participating in these attitudes. Reading the play as a woman and as a feminist, it is possible to feel good about delineating and rejecting its idealization of patriarchy.... [I]s it possible for a staging of *The Tempest* to convey anything approaching a feminist reading of the text (without rewriting it or adding something like Leininger's epilogue) ...? (412)

While it is never entirely clarified—except, possibly, of a sense of presentist pathetic catharsis—what "feel[ing] good" or "guilty" or "uncomfortable" might usefully do to *Tempest* scholarship, the fact that Thomson warns about "rewriting" the play for one's own political purposes is as refreshing as it is unusual in recent *Tempest* criticism, where the tendency has often been to comment on what one wishes the text *should rather have said* than to analyze what the text actually does communicate (Brevik 181–201).

Rebecca Ann Bach's "*Mrs. Caliban*: A Feminist Postmodernist *Tempest?*" is not necessarily a case in point, since her article clearly enough identifies a secondary spin-off product (Rachel Ingalls' novel *Mrs. Caliban*) as a *commentary* on the play itself rather than confuse the novel as the play.

Still, Bach follows familiar lines in feminist scholarship when she interprets Miranda as Prospero's political bait, and her attention to Caliban strikes a double chord in its fusion with post-colonial concerns: "Whereas Ariel is set free at the close of the action, the other two will be forever enslaved; Caliban will do Prospero's work, and Miranda will belong to Ferdinand by his contract with her father" (392). Yet the reading simply seems far too cynically "against the grain" that Miranda is somehow "shackled to Ferdinand, chosen *only* under her father's direction" (400, my emphasis).[4] However difficult it is to disagree with Bach's astute observation that Miranda is indeed a *loyal* marionette used for Prospero's immediate political gain, Bach pays little attention to the love that we are led—rather convincingly—to believe exists between Miranda and Ferdinand or to the fact that the political control that Prospero manages to regain from Antonio and Alonso will be to the benefit of the entire family, Miranda especially. Despite Bach's claim that "*The Tempest,* after all, mystifies a political and economic settlement between men as a marriage based on love at first sight" (398), it furthermore makes little textual sense to accept wholesale the axiomatic assertion that Ferdinand is a patriarchal suitor who, like Miranda, becomes a mere pawn in Prospero's game. Rather, Ferdinand, as we will discover later, displays first rebellion but then a sense of obstinate acceptance, provocative calm, and controlled masculinity that echoes Roman-Stoical ideas of manly composure and restraint as well as New World-native bravery.

Extremely little attention has been paid to Ferdinand in gender studies. A notable exception among Shakespeare scholars is Robin Headlam Wells' excellent *Shakespeare on Masculinity* from 2000, whose chapter on *The Tempest* is indispensable reading for those who seek a post-feminist understanding of New World manhood and gender relations that goes beyond the predictable formulas rehearsed by feminists and post-colonial critics since the 1970s (Headlam Wells 192). For Headlam Wells nuances and tempers the tried and tested protests that Prospero has stolen what Cartelli (not entirely unproblematically) calls "Caliban's island" (186) with the unusually radical assertion that "Prospero is also an unwilling exile" (188–189), that "[h]e too suffers a 'sea-sorrow'" (189), and that, crucially, in light of overwhelming textual evidence, "Prospero is not a colonizer" (190). Instead, Headlam Wells' book distances itself from Leslie Fiedler's politicized approaches (192) by calling attention to the fact that, in his "Rarer action" of forgiveness, "Prospero is in effect re-defining masculine *virtus*" (195). Most interesting about this insight is its implication of manhood and faith as converging rather than mutually excluding qualities that do not necessarily demand military valor as a saving grace. In light of this revised and more complex sense of masculinity, then, Prospero's self-control could very much be said to be inspired by Ferdinand's calm and collected manliness, one that Headlam Wells claims is *atypical* rather than foppish (200–202).

Ferdinand's sangfroid is a remarkable sign of a traditionally under-stood masculinity that is punctured with sorrow at few but dramatically poignant intervals in the play, thus allowing his character a sense of emo-tional depth, balance, and believability, seen most clearly when he laments what he is led to think is his father's demise. The most relevant work in this respect is Jennifer Vaught's *Masculinity and Emotion in Early Modern English Literature* from 2008, which studies masculinity in a wide range of English Renaissance texts as relevant to and convergent with "feminist project[s]" (6). Vaught argues that "[i]ncluding the study of men in the field of gender studies implicitly challenges the misleading association of men with the mind and women with the body and avoids perpetuating the illusion that men are the ungendered sex" (6). She further demonstrates how Renaissance men who align themselves with women and display emo-tion come out of their various ordeals "empowered" (15). In fact, rather than subscribing to "hegemonic categories" of gender, Vaught sees them as "cultural constructions that are performative and even masquerades" (7). And especially this (meta-)theatrical dimension is indeed a central one for a character like Ferdinand, who plays his "part" in Prospero's "play" with a peculiar mixture of genuine pathos, heroic bravado, and galling inso-lence in a way that almost seems studied, perhaps even hollow, and at times highly self-conscious of the rhetorical/dramatic situation Prospero has rigged up.

Still, while this chapter is much indebted to both Headlam Wells and Vaught in its understanding of the play's exposition of various and fluid masculinities, my own focus here is mainly on Ferdinand rather than on Prospero and most crucially how the former's extraordinary display of exemplary male conduct is significantly shaped and honed by the New World-topical experiences that the play's island setting furnishes. This point owes much to Leo Marx's *Machine in the Garden* from 1964, which, although it was patently in no position to speak at length about gender studies or redefined masculinity far ahead of its own zeitgeist, is a book that recognized several particularly American dimensions in the play:

> [W]hen ... we consider the action of *The Tempest,* a more illuminated con-nection with America comes into view. The play, after all, focuses upon a highly civilized European who finds himself living in a *prehistoric wilder-ness.* Prospero's situation is in many ways the typical situation of voyagers in

newly discovered lands. I am thinking of the remote setting, the strong sense
of place and its hold on the mind, *the hero's struggle with raw nature* on the
one hand and the corruption within his own civilization on the other, and,
finally, his impulse to effect a general reconciliation between the forces of
civilization and nature. Of course, this is by no means a uniquely American
situation. The conflict between art and nature is a universal theme . . . . Nevertheless, the theme is one of which American experience affords a singularly
vivid instance: an unspoiled landscape suddenly invaded by advance parties
of a dynamic, literate, and purposeful civilization. (Marx 35, my italics)

It is of course no coincidence that the play's romantic hero *Ferdinand*
so quickly masters what Marx identifies here as "Prospero's situation," a
highly physical struggle that the latter managed to transcend only via the
slave labor of Caliban, who "does make our fire, / Fetch in our wood, and
serves in offices / That profit us" (I.ii.311–313). Yet the erstwhile Milanese
Duke and the Neapolitan *dauphin* differ centrally in that Ferdinand
meets his hard, dangerous, and involuntary labor with stoical serenity,
even enthusiasm, in an attempt to redefine himself as a man. According
to Catherine Belsey, "self-fashioning is another name for the American
Dream, exemplified by any number of immigrants whose rags-to-riches
stories display the endless *adaptability* of human beings" (43, my italics). There is, likewise, certainly an "American" or New World-meritocratic
sense in which Ferdinand for the first time in his life does something
useful (read: masculine), even though his pioneer-like labor is humbling,
difficult, and entirely involuntary. In some respects, Ferdinand displays
a proto-American ethos of hard work that further refines, strengthens,
and *ennobles* him through semi-voluntary humiliation. This adversar-
ial but ultimately rewarding process for Ferdinand involves his highly
New World-topical combat with the elements themselves that calls for
an immediate sense of vigorous physical dexterity that is as poetically
recited and praised as any heroic act by Beowulf or Hercules. In the textual passage where the Neapolitan party debates whether Ferdinand is
dead or alive, Francisco recalls a glorious visual image of the missing
prince battling the (admittedly phantom) waves of Prospero's (hypnotic)
storm:

> I saw him beat the surges under him,
> And ride upon their backs. He trod the water,
> Whose enmity he flung aside, and breasted
> The surge most swoll'n that met him. His bold head
> 'Bove the contentious waves he kept, and oared
> Himself with his good arms in lusty stroke

To th' shore, that o'er his wave-worn basis bowed,
As stooping to relieve him.

(II.i.115–122)

Ferdinand's heroic struggle with (the Prosperian mirage of) nature here ostensibly shows that he is a strong, rugged, and capable swimmer. More to the point, though, Ferdinand's "lusty" and almost frolicsome command over the forces of nature finds a most distinct resonance in later American literature and culture: the passage invites modern readers to fill it into Ishmael's mysterious escape from the Pequod and beckons us to swim and fly with Walt Whitman, who like some Arielic spirit, "trod the water" over America.

Like Whitman's metaphorical flight, Ferdinand's walk on water—which of course not so much accentuates as *shouts* out his Christian faith as well and strength and nobility—remains an image of an image, a dream inside a play, a hypnotically induced vision within a performance that takes place inside of a dry theater but nevertheless manages to delineate Plato's favorite poetic example as the sort of *real* man that the Virginia Company initially sought to attract to the New World (but in reality never could, of course) in that he possesses a "bold head" and "good arms." Interestingly, too, as Joan Pong Linton has pointed out, is the fact that he also displays sexual restraint (156–157). It is true that Prospero's stern warning about the dangers of premarital love expects the right, *chaste* answer:

If thou dost break her virgin-knot before
All sanctimonious ceremonies may
With full and holy rite be minist'red,
No sweet aspersions shall the heavens let fall
To make this contract grow; but barren hate,
Sour-ey'd disdain, and discord shall bestrew
The union of your bed with weeds so loathly
That you shall hate it both.

(IV.i.15–22)

And Ferdinand's own colorful, nearly proto-Gothic response to Prospero's bucket of cold water is by now predictably measured:

As I hope
For quiet days, fair issue, and long life,
With such love as 'tis now, the murkiest den,
The most opportune place, the strong'st suggestion
Our worser genius can, shall never melt

Mine honor into lust, to take away
The edge of that day's celebration,
When I shall think or Phoebus' steeds are founder'd
Or Night kept chain'd below.

(IV.i.23–31)

In this almost too perfect vow of chastity, though, Ferdinand successfully mollifies Prospero with a level of political wisdom that dwarfs whatever physical restraint and patience the words themselves promise for what Ferdinand giddily understands is the last short stretch of chastity. In so doing, Ferdinand achieves a balance between what may be termed the virtuous vice of manly urges and the unmanly virtues of too much restraint. In *Masculinity and the Metropolis of Vice* (2010), Amanda Bailey and Roze Hentschell claim that urban "manhood was negotiated, made visible, and even engendered through the performance of misconduct.... Male misconduct thus not only calls into question masculine virtue, but also serves to define it" (3–4). Still, "[t]he yoking of moderation and proper masculinity meant that vicious behavior, associated with various forms of excess, was by definition a challenge to and potentially a departure from manhood" (4). Interestingly for my purposes, Bailey and Hentschell further argue that "geography matters to the construction of gender" (2) and "seek to complicate earlier studies that construe London as a feminine entity" (3). In some contrast, Joan Pong Linton fuses the New World-topical manly qualities illustrated above with fatherhood, kingship, and mature masculinity: "If Elizabeth was, in the historical hindsight of Samuel Purchas, 'our virgin mother' who initiated England's maritime enterprise, James was the paternal figure under whom colonists came into manhood" (158). In precisely this way the play carefully fleshes out Ferdinand not only as an admirable youth but in fact as a future ruler who is neither greedy, foppish, nor effeminate but a disciplined young man, the only one able to resist with some valor and honor Prospero's tempest in a teapot. For, again, Ferdinand *masters* the make-believe waves and is clearly on top, treading the water like some Christ-like Tarzan figure[5] in this one vital moment of survival, all according to Francisco, a character whose entire purpose in the play, tellingly enough, is to rehearse those sentiments only in the play. Geography, as Bailey and Hentschell also suggest, is central to this male-formative project but in Ferdinand's case with an essentially pastoral-pioneering modus operandi.

Importantly, though, Ferdinand conceives of his New World toils as a valuable apprenticeship whose success relies not only on his own resources. The fact that Ferdinand patiently enjoys his tenure under Prospero is most obviously explained in the text by his affection for Miranda but perhaps also by the oddly masochistic nature of these following euphuistic lines that mischievously comment on both the binariness and unity of the sexes with play on words that harp on grueling feminine "labor" as that most laddish domain "sport":

> There be some *sports* are painful, and their *labor*
> *Delight* in them sets off; some kinds of *baseness*
> Are *nobly* undergone; and most poor matters
> Point to rich ends. This my mean task
> Would be as *heavy* to me as odious, but
> The *mistress* which I serve *quickens* what's *dead*,
> And makes my *labors pleasures.*
> (III.i.1–7, emphasis mine)

Adonis-like boyish pursuits and amorous confusions notwithstanding, Ferdinand quickly proves himself the emblem of Roman *virtus:* he takes orders—but for a larger goal; he enjoys his labor in an atypical fashion (Headlam Wells 200–202) that would break the backs of other Falstaffian European noblemen unaccustomed to working out—but for a time he hopes will be short, and he thus triumphs over Prospero in this game of wills. For Ferdinand is reverent, polite, even when tastelessly and maliciously reminded about his father's presumed demise by Prospero, a tasteless stinger (I.ii.431–432) that brings a pang of grief that Miranda empathetically shares—"Alack, for mercy!" (I.ii.437)—and then seems willing to carry—"I'll bear your logs the while" (III.i.24)—sorrow quickly metamorphosing into an unselfish love that seems to nurture and support Ferdinand in a way that facilitates his own bravado throughout the ordeal.

Ferdinand's seemingly serenely composed and Roman nature hints at Castiglione's ideal courtier as a man perhaps more *innately* in tune with rather than intellectually steeped in Marcus Aurelius and other Stoic philosophers; his noble nature comes into fruition via struggle with the New World-topical nature (as we saw with Leo Marx) but also via the love of Miranda and his own faith. Ferdinand's own masculine composure is perhaps not explicitly philosophical and theological in nature but rather instinctive, more akin to Burke's wisdom without reflection; they constitute what a man is at seed, in his noble genes—more than, perhaps, any common man could socially become. This point is trite but central, because, with the would-be usurpers Trinculo and Stephano well in mind, it more than intimates that not everyone can *become* a manly (that is to say, ideal) ruler. And as countless cross- and re-crossdressing scenes in numerous plays remind us, Renaissance categories were stable, at least in the realm of ideas and ideals—princes, paupers, men, women, children, citizens, and outsiders were (eventually) to know their place. Yet the obvious paradox was clearly within Shakespeare's grasp that without these rigid social, sexual, and economic structures, there could be no mobility, and the (for Ferdinand) *negotiable* manliness that is measured by travel, discovery, and hard work in *The Tempest* is also one that human affection and the greater powers may effect and improve: in this play it is not so much the masculine weeping and wailing and tears that Jennifer Vaught's book defends (9) so much as his faith and humility that reinforce the prince's manliness. For Ferdinand certainly needs to *suspend* his grief in order to play a more important game while comforted by Miranda, who not coincidentally seems to do the most important part of the grieving for the both of them. Ferdinand manages to remain in balance because of her love and most importantly because of his quiet faith and humility.

Faith in God and proper observance of the societal order link Ferdinand and Gonzalo as two of the play's most likable characters. These two Neapolitan men—one old, the other young—display significantly different approaches to the "plantation" or New World aspects of the island. Even though Ferdinand's proto-American masculine agency is related to Gonzalo's view of the island as an Edenic colonial site, the old councilor's views are far more radical and utopian:

> Had I plantation of this isle, my lord—
> . . . . . .
> I' th' commonwealth I would, by contraries,
> Execute all things; for no kind of traffic
> Would I admit, no name of magistrate;
> Letters should not be known; riches, poverty,
> And use of service, none; contract, succession,
> Bourn, bound of land, tilth, vineyard, none;
> No use of metal, corn, or wine, or oil,
> No occupation, all men idle, all;
> And women too, but innocent and pure;
> No sovereignty—
> . . . . . .
> All things in common nature should produce
> Without sweat or endeavor: treason, felony,
> Sword, pike, knife, gun, or need of any engine,
> Would I not have; but nature should bring forth,
> Of its own kind, all foison, all abundance,
> To feed my innocent people.
> . . . . . .

I would with such perfection govern, sir,
T' excel the golden age.
                                            (II.i.144–169)

Gonzalo's vision is essentially a pre-Romantic idea of a utopian-anarchistic
society where man lives in ignorant bliss as a second Adam, a theme
American authors like James Fenimore Cooper would expound on more
than 200 years later. For instance, Deerslayer's (or Thoreau's, for that
matter) view of society and nature is that of Gonzalo rather than that
of Prospero—nature is preferred to societal company, for only in nature
can he maintain his noble savagery/savage nobility—or his integrity as a
man, in other words.[6] Ferdinand's accomplishment, similarly, rests in the
paradoxes that he experience savagery before assuming nobility, undergo
primitive labor in order to be sophisticated enough in his understanding of power, and subject himself at the mercy of an anarchic new
world so as to gain insight into Old World Machiavellian realpolitik. Yet
Ferdinand importantly approaches these inclemencies with a distinctly
New World frame of mind, his perhaps pampered past, a forgotten chapter.
The desire to cast off one's cumbersome past or identity finds echoes in
R. W. B. Lewis's idea of the American Adam, a "hero of the new adventure,"
who, like Gonzalo and Ferdinand alike, feels himself "emancipated from
history, happily bereft of ancestry, untouched and undefiled by the usual
inheritances of family and race; an individual standing alone, self-reliant
and self-propelling, ready to confront whatever awaited him with the aid
of his own unique and inherent resources" (Lewis 5). Lewis's American
Adam—like an exiled Prospero, too—fashions for himself a better future
through individual effort and genius and, like Gonzalo, is propelled by his
hope of a prelapsarian existence that will be untainted by the habits and
sins of the past, as evidenced by the sheer utopian optimism of the above
passage.

Crucially for my own purposes, though, the dystopian hard work that
Ferdinand is put through metamorphoses him from his old and perhaps
somewhat childish self into a new, more mature man. In a play so per-
vaded with binary contradictions, it is perhaps fittingly paradoxical that
such maturity be the psychological precondition for that radical *innocence*
that Ihab Hassan has located in the American Adam:

> His stance questions the "mystic centrality" of our day, which Richard Chase
> so ably condemned in *The Democratic Vista*, and his fate testifies to the con-
> tinuance of "the vivid contradictions and anomalies that in the past have
> engaged the American mind." His innocence, therefore, does not merely
> revert to those simplicities which, rightly or wrongly, have been identified

with vision in America. His innocence, rather, is the property of the mythic American Self, perhaps of every anarchic Self. (Hassan 6)

Ferdinand acquires these "vividly contradictory" "properties" of *mature* "innocence" via his hard work.[7] He does so in a way that posits a valuable parallel to the nature of the innocence of the American Adam, which is anything but a childish "simplicity" but instead related to growing young, growing into a man after years of feminization inculcated by a pampered upbringing. For, as Hamlet and Prospero both bitterly admit, an education in books can go only so far as "words, words, words."

The Tempest furnishes further parallels to America, the New World, and its auspicious effects on men. In many respects it is useful for our purposes here to look to the Jamestown colonizers as well as the Puritans in New England. Both set of experiences were in meaningful ways an "errand into the wilderness," as Perry Miller has argued so persuasively in his eponymous book: "Changes there had to be: adaptations to environment, expansion of the frontier, mansions constructed, commercial adventures undertaken. These activities were not specifically nominated in the bond Winthrop had framed. They were *thrust upon* the society by American experience" (Miller 9, emphasis mine). In America, especially the Puritans could come to form a new community of believers, a city on a hill that would shine as a beacon of light to the Old World. Tinged with this in many ways positive view, however, was the fear among the Puritans of the Native Americans, the dark woods, and the diabolism they believed existed in them.

Likewise in its religious aspect, the masculinity that *The Tempest* sketches out is one that takes into consideration the greater powers. For a telling contrast to Ferdinand's Christian New World masculinity is seen at the play's outset by the Boatswain, a character who, in some ways like Ferdinand, displays traditional masculinity in abundance, growls and roars, hoists and runs and pushes and shoves and tries desperately to steer the ship:

> Hence! What cares these
> roarers for the name of king? To cabin! silence!
> Trouble us not.
> ... .
> You are
> a councillor; if you can command these elements
> to silence, and work the peace of the present, we will
> not hand a rope more. Use your authority. If you can-

not, give thanks you have lived so long, and make
yourself ready in your cabin for the mischance of
the hour, if it so hap.—Cheerly, good hearts!—Out of
our way, I say.
. . . .
Down with the topmast! yare! lower, lower!
(I.i.16–34)

But the Boatswain's efforts are all in vain, since the storm is one of the
mind. When the Boatswain mockingly speaks about "command[ing] these
elements to silence," the Globe audience may well have recalled Matthew
8:23–27, where Christ, with Prosperian power, calms the ocean. Tom
MacAlindon, John Cox, and Robert Grams Hunter have recently done
convincing Christian readings of the play, but in relation to New World
masculinity and agency, not even recent eco-critical scholars have commented on the play's ironic view of a nature that is ruled by God, a nature
meek men can master only by respecting and *obeying* it, by playing along-
side it, whereas stubborn and haughty pioneers will be ruled by it—the
way Stephano, Trinculo, and Caliban experience as they are drenched in
"horse-piss" (IV.i.199).

It seems like an entirely appropriate and intended irony that the
Boatswain's sarcastic dismissal of Gonzalo's meddling by urging him
to "use [his] authority" is the only way out of the tempest, but our
Boatswain—like cursing and foul Sebastian and Antonio—is found spiritually wanting. And there is something allegorically familiar about the
Boatswain's situation, about his potent impotence, about his lack of faith in
faith itself, about his desperately exuberant (lack of) belief in skill and his
own agency, about his reliance on man's ability to save himself from perdi-
tion. The Boatswain interestingly also fails to appreciate Gonzalo's remark
"remember whom thou hast aboard" (I.i.19), which may not refer to the
king or his noble entourage but actually to God himself. This is an assumption on my part that I nevertheless think is corroborated when the mariners
and the nobles all go "to prayers" and in fact echo the word "prayers" with
desperate repetition (I.i.51, 53).[8] Thus, the misguided Boatswain has too
much faith in his own power, and his transgressions in decorum, I think
it could be argued, are not so much to do with civil authority but rather
indicative of a lack of faith in God, who is supposedly with all European
ships, if Strachey, Jourdain, Smith, Columbus, and countless other travelers
have taught us anything.

Ferdinand's otherwise silent faith and respect for nature are confirmed
not only in the fact that he is witnessed to have survived the storm in such

spectacular fashion but also by his optimism in the face of a seemingly tragic loss. His grief for his father and his entourage could be deemed oddly casual but is best explained by his piety the way that his father Alonso's grief, conversely, is a testament to his own guilt and lack of faith: "O thou / Mine heir of Naples and of Milan, what strange fish / Hath made his meal on thee?" (II.i.112–114). To Alonso, as we can see, life is defined as physical and temporal, its happiness accounted for in terms of political alliances and the power they yield as well as by material manifestations such as family relationships that are inevitably bound to cease. Hence, to a nominal but spiritually empty Christian, the shipwreck is a titanic tragedy, but to firm believers like Ferdinand—whose humble masculine faith triumphs over Prospero's initial misanthropy—life is full of limitless possibilities, full of joy to come *while* waiting for death. Flip sides of this coin can clearly be seen in the introductory tempest scene that gives the play its name, experientially speaking the characters' last hour on earth, designed by Prospero to instil a sense of fear (of God). For none of the other crew and passengers could this moment be said to be their finest hour: woefully few of them tackle the situation like Roman exemplars of *virtus;* they revert instead to regular frail humanity insofar as they panic, and except Gonzalo few seem to *believe* that they are cared for by a greater force, an important factor to Romans and other pagans alike as well as to Christian soldiers.

Other characters, too, display the "wrong" kind of male agency, one consistently associated with the worst aspects of the Old World. Antonio and Sebastian cowardly scheme to kill sleeping Alonso, for instance; Caliban, threateningly male to most concerned, likewise plots to "batter [Prospero's] skull or paunch him with a stake, / Or cut his wezand with thy knife" (III.ii.89–91) as his master is napping and also fantasizes about having children with an unwilling and defenseless Miranda: "O ho, o ho, would't had been done! / Thou dids't prevent me; I had peopled else / This isle with Calibans" (I.ii.349–351). Gentler representatives of Old World masculinity can be found in Gonzalo, who, although naïve and often comical, displays a patient and flexible mind, an ability to translate things old from the new. Importantly, Gonzalo shares some of Ferdinand's hopefulness and suffers much ridicule at the hands of Sebastian and Antonio for trying to lift Alonso's spirits, and his meekness, compassion, and learned sophistication are evidence of the sort of religious education and courage that the noblemen lack.

Instead, such spiritual fortitude finds its best intertextual parallels in New World natives, who were often enough thought of as similar to the Old World Spartans in their bravery, laughing at their captors and never willing to yield to an intellect outside of their own, similar in this central respect to Ferdinand's attitude to his *physical* enslavement (Montaigne 96). Furthermore, according to Montaigne, in the New World, "the reputation and worth of a man consisteth in his heart and will: therein consists true honour: Constancie is valour" (97). "Of the Cannibals," nearly verbatim recited by Gonzalo, thus becomes here an instance of playful intra-intertextuality via-á-vis both the New World and topical ideas of masculine conduct: "The very words that import lying, falshood, treason, dissimulations, covetousnes, envie, detraction, and pardon, were never heard of amongst them. How dissonant would [Plato] finde his imaginarie common-wealth from this perfection?" (94). While it is true that Gonzalo's attitudes are in many ways typical of those explorers who in ruthless fashion came, saw, and conquered in the New World, he explicitly also wishes to do away with part of his own past, or with part of his culture's past. It is in this sense that Gonzalo dreams not so much of a New Naples or New Europe in miniature that belongs entirely to himself but of a *locus alter,* of a refined sense of pastoral wilderness, of a redeemed urban sophistication that draws on all places, all cultures, in order to achieve perfection—but especially on the New World in terms of masculine valor and simplicity. We see that Plato's "Republic" to Montaigne is far inferior to the simple lives of the cannibals; in Gonzalo's reverie, we find a similar desire to do away with all the external accoutrements of civilized life, such as laws, letters, property, and so forth, but the important distinction here is that Gonzalo is a fit *king* of the island because he has both virtue and sophistication, New World and Old World qualities (as they were often thought to be, respectively) that come together in an admittedly (for Gonzalo) unintended and comically oxymoronic fashion. Montaigne admittedly deals explicitly within the New World sphere, as he is commenting on his friend's travels, but also he yokes together the wonder of the new with the glory of the ancient when commenting that the natives' language "is a kind of pleasant speech, and hath a pleasing sound, and some affinitie with the Greek terminations" (98). Thus, the physically and geographically real place that inspired Montaigne to write "Of the Cannibals" has become an ethnographic documentary text on which Gonzalo's hypothetical paradise is based in much the same fashion as the New World and the Old World worked in linguistic and cultural symbiosis, and in few ways is this ideal sense of cultural osmosis more important than in sketching out the qualities of men and kings.

It seems not entirely accidental, for instance, that the word "master," with all its distinctly masculine connotations, appears with such frequency in the play. To Ariel, Prospero is the savior, the master, and a physical man, while to Caliban, Prospero's sense of manhood and power takes on different, more intellectual dimensions that make Caliban's drunken gibes to "find a new man" as futile as to get "a new master" (II.ii.185). To Ferdinand, though, Prospero will be "master" and *pater familias* for a short time only, until Ferdinand can marry Miranda and thus become his own man, as it were, no longer filially bound by the older generation. Yet his understanding of his laborious tenure as a masculine rite of passage is quite possibly his saving grace—and his patience and good cheer are thus seen as valuable assets in this quest for manhood as well as kingship. Ferdinand's education as a man is at an end when sitting at chess at the end of the play, Ferdinand, now far from a pawn, symbolically enough winning (against) Miranda after having beaten her father in a far greater and more important battle of wills, confirming his power thus in a manner symmetrical to how Prospero relinquishes his own, leaving the island knowing that the future of his by now expanded realm and family are safe with Ferdinand.

Ferdinand is interesting as a study in masculinity because he is an exemplar of a nascent *virtus,* a sense of a king-to-be. More than the ferocious Hotspur or dillydallying Hal, the contemplative Hamlet, or even the highly self-conscious two noble kinsmen, Ferdinand is a man in perfect *balance.* Like Othello, like Aaron the Moor, like William Strachey, or like Montaigne's glorious cannibals—indeed, like most travelers coming from or sojourning to strange lands—Ferdinand relies upon traditional masculinity, seen in his physical combat with the waves, in his battle of wills with Prospero, and in his elegant courtship of Miranda, simply because the setting and his survival demand it of him. As such, not only does he display traditional manly bravado but also a sense of flexibility, pliability, agility, amphibiousness, and cultural and spiritual sensitivity that are also to be understood as masculine traits in Marcus Aurelius's version of Roman *virtus.* Ideal and successful travelers like Ferdinand, especially those who travel to the New World, then, must be more attuned to their surroundings than the drunkards Trinculo and Stephano (who wish to take the natives captive, to lure them with alcohol, and to ravish the women), more appreciative of their surroundings than the cynical Antonio and Sebastian, more hopeful and optimistic than the despondent Alonso, yet perhaps also more skeptical and less naïve than Gonzalo, whose own optimism is proven unrealistic rather than rugged when he dreams of his "plantation" where all work has been suspended (II.i.144–169).

Masculinity and composure, then, are more than vain butch agency: they hinge, first of all, on an unshakable belief in one's own vulnerability in the face of an angry God and secondly on the solace and comfort and forward-looking rugged optimism and agency that this belief alone provides. Similarly, to men staring death in the face in wars or in places strange, a religious belief was central to survival, and there is perhaps a similar sense in which the play's New World-topical experiences bring each character closer to his own soul. What he learns from this *internal* "first encounter" is an existential revelation about his own limits, worth, and potential as a man. The travels undertaken in *The Tempest* are rites of royal masculine passage that Ferdinand alone passes with flying colors.

"Thought Is Free": *The Tempest,* Freedom of Expression, and the New World

In this chapter I shift the focus from practical politics onto a more utopian understanding of ideology that is also predicated in some measure on the play's physical setting. I borrow Alexander Leggatt's working definition of politics as a practical concern over power: "if everything is political then nothing is, for the world has lost its edge. I want to concentrate on what is political in a more narrow, traditional sense: the ordering and enforcing, the gaining and losing, of power in the public state" (ix). In contrast, *ideology* is best understood in this chapter as (new) ideas, (old) culture, (free) thought, (an essentially Christian) spirituality, and (both ancient and Renaissance) philosophical longings for freedom and self-realization. In terms of utopian dreams, *The Tempest* sketches out the difference between those of an egotistical and an altruistic nature, but freedom of speech and expression is necessary to both. For instance, Caliban is hindered from fully expressing the idea that he reproduce so as once again to be master of the island, this time by sheer number; to the extent that Trinculo and Stephano express a clear utopian wish, they simply want to enjoy a lordly life of leisure and debauchery, for which ambition alone they are punished; Sebastian and Antonio wish to depose and kill the King of Naples, who himself, in turn, has wanted to expand his influence across the Mediterranean by marrying his daughter Claribel to the King of Tunis in Africa. Common to all of these dreams is their genuinely *political* practicality, but the play's most important impulse comes from the more religious, social, cultural, and *ideological* longings of Alonso, Gonzalo, Miranda, Ferdinand, and Prospero.

I interpret the totality of these latter urges as an optimistic general ideology that is heavily influenced by pastoral conventions clearly also present in *The Tempest*. This pastoral-ideological fusion, in turn, inclines toward a Judaeo-Christian religious worldview. The sum of these part-ideologies also bears heavily upon the play's empty and geographically ever-ambiguous setting—in fact, so much so that the utopian themes revisit and impregnate the possible New World setting discussed in Chapter 2. In other words, the play's many New World-relevant themes are created partly as a *result* of a vast and relatively empty setting that is otherwise simply too ambiguous to be seen as fully New World Atlantic or Old World Mediterranean. Hence, the themes of the play, in regard to the possible New World setting, tend to revisit and comment back on the same setting that shaped them, such as Gonzalo's dream of a utopian plantation. This is of course a vision that is partly dependent on the physical reality of the setting and partly dependent on ancient European cultural *topoi* like Atlantis and Eden. Thus, a proto-American relevance presents itself by setting-derived pastoral-utopian themes that impregnate, re-inform, and feed on the setting in a symbiotic and circular fashion. The central concern of this chapter is to demonstrate how this pastoral geography and utopian worldviews carve out a space that allows for and encourages an ethos of freedom of speech and freedom of expression that owes much to the materialism and geography of the New World.

One of the main Old World influences on the play is the genre of pastoral. *The Tempest* is widely thought to lean on previous pastoral English works like Spenser's otherworldly *Faerie Queene* (of 1596) and Thomas More's *Utopia* (of 1516), works, in turn, that both draw upon centuries of European yearning for a simpler, freer, better, more just existence. Whereas this tradition sought its pastoral utopias in a virtuous countryside unsullied by the vices of the city, an increasingly predominant tendency in Renaissance travel literature was to locate this pastoral-utopian dimension in the New World, and these travel narratives, in turn, are a palpable influence on works like *Utopia* and *The Tempest*. However, the pastoral and New World influences with which the play is vested forms a problematic and contradictory whole that draws on Old World ideas of Greco-Roman and Judaeo-Christian origin as well as a rhetorical and philosophical reaction to European civilization, as can be seen particularly clearly in Montaigne's essay "Of the Cannibals," a work that deals rhetorically much more centrally with European corruption than with the New World tribes themselves. This necessary balance between apparently irreconcilable binary opposites like New and Old Worlds finds much support in Frank Kermode's observations about the pastoral as an essentially *urban* phenomenon and artistic vehicle that makes use of the romanticized rural and bucolic life primarily for the redemption rather than the total transformation of civilization, as the mission that reconciles its seemingly contradictory impulses (Berger 781). The pastoral impulse, then, is a mode of expressing the longings and needs for a redeeming distance *from,* and *for,* the morally corrupted urban readership. The urban-based and *urbane* pastoral is hence an artistic (and artificial) vehicle for escape and release, but its courtly and urban origin and *raison d'être* go counter to the message it portends to uphold. In one sense, the pastoralism of the play might be seen not as the morally cleansing journey into a wild and uncontrollable nature that furnishes unfettered expression and free speech but rather as an idea of beauty and virtue that is cultured and contained, but the tensions within this containment are simply too fierce to be properly contained in any successful manner, as we shall see.

If we can accept that a narrative in which wishes for love, social companionship, peace, and quiet may be termed a utopian discourse—and especially where this discourse of "deeper meaning" conquers the hard-nosed scheming of Caliban, Antonio, and Sebastian—then such a utopian ethos exists in *The Tempest.* Such an ethos or discourse is also closely intertwined with both the pastoral form and especially the genre of the romance, as Jonathan Hart has recently argued:

> Another case of dramatic irony shows the limitations of those who oppose Prospero: the conventions of romance check political rebellion. Alonzo [*sic*] thinks the events "monstrous," that the wind seemed to call out the name of Prospero and make him so aware of his guilt that he will seek his son in the deep. Sebastian and Antonio think that they are fighting fiends. Realizing that Alonzo, Antonio and Sebastian are desperate and that "their great guilt,/Like poison given to work a great time after,/Now 'gins to bite the spirits," Gonzalo sends Adrian to restrain the three. (*Romance and Politics* 32)

In other words, Hart sees the elements of romance so dominant in the play that the political struggles Prospero has to contend with are resolved in a "naturally" magical and mystical fashion that is true to the genre of romance.

In a fashion befitting a romance, then, the harshness of the political reality is here seemingly gently brushed over with the benevolent magus's almost omnipotent powers, but the ideological impulse of course remains.

Hart mentions (as McAlindon did before him) the stress on forgiveness and blessings in the dénouement of the play, where "Alonso and Gonzalo bless the much-blessed couple as if to amplify the blessings of Prospero and Juno and Ceres in the masque" (34). The observation of religious rituals made by McAlindon and Hart here is very important for anyone wishing to discuss the play in terms of utopian or spiritual discourse, and McAlindon's stress in particular on the motif of blessings and curses found in *The Tempest* moves the often politically tinged discourse emphasized by most recent criticism into a more traditional Christian-allegorical realm that is essentially religious and spiritual in nature. Nevertheless, already in 1969 John Dover Wilson commented that *The Tempest* is not a Christian play per se—God, claims Dover Wilson, is not even mentioned in the play.[1] Dover Wilson feels instead that the play moves forward by a *poetic* rather than divine force (41–42).

The pastoral preference for nature over the court is very palpable in Gonzalo's reverie, but is perhaps even more clearly expressed in Shakespeare's *As You Like It,* where Duke Senior expresses the same sentiments when he presents the forest, Arden, not only as a pastoral demi-paradise or replica of the Golden Age of which Renaissance writers thought so much, but also as one that is *truly* Christian in nature:

> Now, my co-mates and brothers in exile,
> Hath not old custom made this life more sweet
> Than that of painted pomp? Are not these woods
> More free from peril than the envious court?
> *Here feel we not the penalty of Adam,*
> The seasons' difference, as the icy fang
> And the churlish chiding of the winter's wind,
> Which when it bites and blows upon my body
> Even till I shrink with cold, I smile and say
> "This is no flattery: these are counsellors
> That feelingly persuade me what I am."
> Sweet are the uses of adversity
> Which, like a toad, ugly and venomous,
> Wears yet a precious jewel in his head;
> *And this our life, exempt from public haunt,*
> *Finds tongues in trees, books in the running brooks,*
> *Sermons in stones, and good in every thing.*
> (*As You Like It* II.i.1–17, italics mine)

This fusion of religion with the pastoral is something we do not find as explicitly articulated in *The Tempest,* but Gonzalo's utopian passage nevertheless represents an important discourse that is part of a larger utopian impetus whose *general* tendency, in its benignity, is convergent with this same Christian-pastoral ethos. And if we can accept for a moment that there is such a thing as a Christian utopia, then we note with interest that Gonzalo's utopian passage in the play claims to outdo the Golden Age of Greek mythology, while at the same time being employed in a larger religious and equally utopian discourse.

Furthermore, seen in terms of power and politics, Gonzalo's *political* utopia here takes the form of anarchic lawlessness. (With the term "anarchic" here, I mean that which is etymologically derived from the Greek *anarchos*, literally "without ruler.") For, as we note, Gonzalo's ideal world, his "plantation," seems very much to imply such absence of rulers: "no name of magistrate" should exist in his commonwealth (II.i.150). The religious and secular freedom Gonzalo here envisions, although elaborated in earlier Renaissance works like Thomas More's *Utopia*, has its political roots in Christian pacifism. For in a setting where Christian believers quite literally turn the other cheek and reject the use of any form of violence or coercion, no one is in a position to *enforce* any laws. And laws that are not enforced are moot theories only, empty words that are "as sounding brass, or a tinkling cymbal," in the words of Paul the Apostle (1 Cor. 13:2).

Central to the tenets of anarchistic and utopian philosophy, though, is a *voluntary* peaceful order, clearly expressed in Gonzalo's idea of "innocent and pure" prelapsarian men and women living in peaceful, voluntary coexistence rather than in a Hobbesian chaos (II.i.156). "No sovereignty" is to exist in this island utopia, yet the plantation is as contradictory in this respect as the Renaissance poet Robert Herrick's paradoxical sense of "order in disorder," since it is clear that Gonzalo himself would "govern" it (II.168). In this sense, of course, Gonzalo's anarchical and freedom-seeking, Christian-utopian discourse and vision of an ideal society are undercut by his own totalitarian desire to impose his rule on the island commonwealth. Still, Gonzalo's "contrary" sense of a "govern[ed]" anarchy of "innocent people" still represents a potent, if highly ambiguous, utopian force, able to "excel the golden age" (II.i.169). For Gonzalo's daydream explores the very politically subversive ideas of literal lawlessness as superior to statism, safely couched within officially sanctioned discourse and courtly decorum, since he airs his ideas under the guise of trying to cheer the weary and depressed Alonso. I see his utopian dream in a *wider* political context as a statement that has a clearly defined pastoral dimension in both its sympathies and antipathies—the colony (the countryside) is a means by which power (the city-states of Italy) can be critiqued. *The Tempest*, and Gonzalo's impressionistic utopian passage in particular, thus seems to be involved in a similar strategy to the "typical" pastoral in that it follows the exact same ritual of praising the country life while critiquing the politics of town life. It is of course this strategy that allows Gonzalo to speak relatively freely—so freely and so garrulously, in fact, that his superiors Antonio and Sebastian struggle to interrupt him and his own king Alonso to silence him.

The parallel longings and desires seen above, then, include a pastoral vision that later develops into a conflict with (and eventual mastery over) raw nature, a sense of anarchic freedom, the stress on hard work and self-made men, and that very European-American yearning to find a utopia of one's own. The play's utopian moments are often invested with American qualities of free space and unfettered motion. The free motion and speech that results from this space are revisited to such an extent as reminds the historically retrospective reader of subversive mobility and masterlessness. Vagrancy and independence were often identified with both New World natives and early settlers described in Strachey and Jourdain but also with rebels and frontier types like Thomas Morton among the Puritans. Such subversiveness and lack of control, of course, give urgency to the debate over the need for a Hobbesian government, also found in the play. All these ideas—these very *American* ideas and dreams—are expressed in *The Tempest,* importantly not without an overriding sense of mission in all its somewhat hedonistic pursuit of freedom and happiness. The same desires and dreams would later figure large in the cultural and psychological fabric of classic American literature, as Leo Marx has shown (35). Yet their literary manifestation in America was in many ways foretold by historical experiences remarkably similar to those related in Shakespeare's last unassisted play.

Its relevance to America is found on multiple levels, and it is for reasons to do with this highly complex relationship between Renaissance travel literature, pastoralism, drama, and our presentist interpretation of past events that it seems like no exaggeration to claim that *The Tempest* encapsulates an American literary and historical ethos. More subtly so than Thomas More's *Utopia,* for instance, Shakespeare's last unassisted play, in its plot and ideas, not so much reflects as *foreshadows,* well before its time, that complex set of contradictory impulses later found in both early American history and literature, and free speech and expression certainly form important parts of this experience. Some scholars might very well question my admittedly light-handed treatment of the very meaning of the phrase "freedom of expression" itself. While I will welcome such corrections, I will for the time let the concepts and phrases "America," "freedom of expression," and "freedom of speech" stand naked, unadorned,

and unproblematized as hopefully still meaningful entities—especially
when considered together against a play so geographically ambiguous and
thematically topical as *The Tempest.*

For *The Tempest* is constantly discussed with regard to the New World
and America. As early as in 1960, Leo Marx claimed that *The Tempest* is
an "American fable" and prophecy because a similarly pastoral dimension
later develops in American literature and experience. Leo Marx considers
the particular nexus between the pastoral ideas and the historic moment of
colonialism relevant to *The Tempest* as far more than a coincidence:

> When . . . we consider the action of *The Tempest*, a more illuminated con-
> nection with America comes into view. The play, after all, focuses upon a
> highly civilized European who finds himself living in a prehistoric wilder-
> ness. Prospero's situation is in many ways the typical situation of voyagers in
> newly discovered lands. I am thinking of the remote setting, the strong sense
> of place and its hold on the mind, the hero's struggle with raw nature on the
> one hand and the corruption within his own civilization on the other, and,
> finally, his impulse to effect a general reconciliation between the forces of
> civilization and nature. Of course, this is by no means a uniquely American
> situation. The conflict between art and nature is a universal theme . . . . Nev-
> ertheless, the theme is one of which American experience affords a singularly
> vivid instance: an unspoiled landscape suddenly invaded by advance parties
> of a dynamic, literate, and purposeful civilization. (35)

To Marx, not only is there a "genetic connection between *The Tempest* and
America" but one "that can only be called prophetic. By this I mean that
the play, in its overall design, prefigures the design of the classic American
fables" (68). The play, according to Marx, seems to share so much with
later American experiences and literature that Leo Marx confidently terms
the play "prophetic" in this pastoral and historical sense. This sense of
Americanness could therefore be used as a pretext for the play's setting to
be seen as American or New World, a setting that is conducive to a political
and post-colonial analysis.

Marx did well to claim that the play deals with recognizably American
themes, but one of the most characteristically American of these themes
has gone entirely uncommented upon in *Tempest* scholarship, namely the
freedom of speech that is explored and tested as a direct consequence of the
empty space and unfettered movement the pastoral island setting provides.
For the vacuum of power that exists in pastoral locales like the Virginia
colonies clearly brings with it an anarchic sense of freedom that in *The
Tempest* feeds on the symbiotic relationship between Old World pastoral
ideas and American tracts of empty land. And on a deserted island where

the limited enforcing authorities are often out of sight or reach, both the pastoral's radical *topos* and geographical *locus* logically dictate a (temporary) political vacuum. In its deserted insularity, the island setting of *The Tempest* thus presents us with a near-perfect locale for free speech.

Concurrently with Leo Marx, as we have seen, the post-colonial authors George Lamming and Aimé Césaire saw the play in terms of English and European colonialism, and critics like Peter Hulme and Eric Cheyfitz have later defended the readings that see Caliban as a Native American or as a sub-Saharan African slave. Thus, even though one can say that the play has by now become heavily "Americanized," it was the post-colonialist views that gained momentum, so much so that many critics now read *The Tempest* with Césaire, Lamming, or Fanon in mind. For all their poignancy and success, however, such by now thoroughly orthodox and hegemonic interpretations have entirely neglected the play's New World and American dimensions of utopian free expression. These dimensions are also quite easily demonstrated in both dramatic and historical texts and thus form a sense of geographical and historical specificity and textual empiricism that criticism that sees a New World native or an African American slave in Caliban plainly cannot hope to do. I suggest instead we shift the attention away from the textually speaking extremely problematic idea of a fixed sense of a New World setting for the play and its resultant characters of flimsy "Indian" or black origin on to the play's more utopian-topical realm that more accurately explores the ideas and ideals of American-pastoral free speech.

For *The Tempest* is a play that for good but seldom clearly articulated reasons *feels* relevant to America like no other Shakespearean play. The play comprises several interrelated ideologies that are unified in their generally benevolent and humanistic attitudes: it displays utopian longings, anarchistic urges, and Christian-pastoral impulses, and importantly, these optimistic and life-affirming discourses seem to take precedence over the play's sterner practical-political concerns and come together to form the play's "American" vision. Holistically speaking, the play could be said to frame a certain free discourse by muted speech, even though the play would be seen to silence the perceived sauciness of the boatswain, ignore the appeals for justice made by Caliban, and punish the "unnatural" ambition of Stephano and Trinculo that Caliban exploits. Of course, to oppressed and destitute people in Europe, what made the idea of America such an attractive prospect was in many cases the absence of restraining laws that would otherwise curb one's freedoms, including the freedom to speak freely. In suggesting an original interpretation of the play and its sense of freedom that stresses the rise of capitalism as a backdrop against which the textual events and relationships may be explained, Paul A. Cefalu notes English fears of masterless men and laws against vagrancy and goes on to claim that these anxieties were transported to the colonies in Virginia. He suggests this nervousness as explanation for why the colonists failed so many times in their capitalist enterprise—because they strictly limited the freedom of movement, without which capitalism can never thrive. Further, Cefalu sees Caliban negotiating a similar, relative freedom when he moves away from the feudal lord Prospero and instead follows Trinculo, mostly out of a desire for profit and personal latitude. Importantly, Prospero also needs to confront this new development and skillfully negotiate his power in commercial terms by the asset that is his daughter Miranda (Cefalu 85–119).

Jane Kingsley-Smith has shown how emigrants from Europe and travelers to America were regarded with suspicion in Europe precisely because of this subversive desire to distance oneself from a repressive power:

> The association between colonialism and exile can be traced back to the anti-travel polemic of the sixteenth century, which deplored the metamorphosis and self-loss entailed by the voluntary renunciation of one's family, property, language and nation. It is also related to the various connotations of the term "wandering." A system of licenses or passports had been applied within English boundaries to try to control the movement of displaced peoples such as gypsies, beggars, various kinds of entertainer, soldiers, sailors and agrarian workers. Such "wandering" placed one outside the restrictions of law and of society, and therefore marked one as capable of all kinds of crime. (229)

This same variant of "wandering" and errant masterlessness that we see in Trinculo and Stephano is very dangerous to a society that relies on a static and transparent social structure rather than the potentially debilitating "metamorphosis" and change that faraway travel may cause. Hence, the island itself, in its emptiness and lack of a central or government control, furnishes a space where such anarchic "wandering" and masterlessness is facilitated.

And it is true that this anarchic freedom is particularly felt *if* we were to see *The Tempest* as set in the Virginia colonies or America, since both Gonzalo and Caliban seem to suggest that freedom and free speech may be found in the *absence* of kings. John Hollander and Frank Kermode have noted that Amerigo Vespucci, when he first encountered the American "Indians," found that what made their state such a carefree and harmonious one was the absence of restraining laws and rulers (*Literature of Renaissance England* 444).[2]

This political understanding is well illustrated in the text when Caliban drunkenly envisions a bright new future for himself with Prospero gone: " 'Ban,' Ban, Ca-Caliban / Has a new master, get a new man. / Freedom, high-day! high-day, freedom! freedom, high- / day, freedom!" (II.ii.184–187). The for-the-moment absent Prospero can thus be "ban[ned]" (perhaps further exiled?) or cursed by Caliban, if only in the metaphorical sense that a tree that falls in the forest actually does make a noise. Stephano and Trinculo both explore and use this sense of newfound freedom—that is, freedom *from* such enforcers—when they eye a chance to become masters of the island, as do of course Caliban and Gonzalo.

Common to these four characters is the fact that they normally do *not* have it in their right or power to speak freely, and the island hence presents more than a materialist fleck of land but in fact a more fundamental ideological opportunity to them in that they feel they may start the world all over again and reclaim their once-lost liberties. They are, in a proto-Rousseauian more than a proto-Burkean sense, free to *re*negotiate a *new* social contract. Even Gonzalo gradually comes to realize the radically regenerative potential the island's topically "American" space holds:

> Had I plantation of this isle, my lord—
> […]
> I' th' commonwealth I would, by contraries,
> Execute all things; for no kind of traffic
> Would I admit; no name of magistrate;
> Letters should not be known; riches, poverty,
> And use of service, none; contract, succession,
> Bourn, bound of land, tilth, vineyard, none;
> No use of metal, corn, or wine, or oil;
> No occupation, all men idle, all;
> And women too, but innocent and pure;
> No sovereignty—
> […]
> All things in common nature should produce
> Without sweat or endeavor: treason, felony
> Sword, pike, knife, gun, or need of any engine,
> Would I not have; but nature should bring forth,
> Of its own kind, all foison, all abundance,
> To feed my innocent people.
> […]
> I would with such perfection govern, sir,
> T' excel the golden age.
>   (II.i.144, 148–157, 160–165, 168–169)

In the euphuistically meaningful space between such obvious contradictions as Gonzalo expresses (and which I have discussed above), *The Tempest* struggles ideologically to reconcile terrible power with utter powerlessness. Paul Brown has argued that it is Caliban's goal to yield power—ultimately, Brown contends, "Caliban's dream is not the *antithesis* but the *apotheosis* of colonialist discourse," but

> [i]f this discourse seeks to efface its own power, then here at last is an eloquent spokesman who is powerless; here such eloquence represents not a desire to control and rule but a fervent wish for release, a desire to escape reality and return to dream.... This is to say, the colonial project's investment in the processes of euphemisation of what are really powerful relations here has produced a utopian moment where powerlessness represents *a desire for powerlessness*. This is the danger that any metaphorical system faces, that vehicle may be taken for tenor and used against the ostensible meanings intended. (66)

Brown locates this desire for universal powerlessness in Caliban since his own discourse sorts under "Prospero's narrative . . . reality principle, ordering and correcting the inhabitants of the island" (66) and points out that a similar contradiction is found when Prospero finds ultimate edification in giving up his powers (67), wherein lies the greater power of spiritual self-control. Hence, it is Gonzalo rather than Caliban who *articulates* or euphemizes this anarchic impulse toward powerlessness best, yet Prospero who does so *indeed*.

But in whomever it is found, this wish for powerlessness is closely related to the island's emptiness, a vacuum which represents, almost quite literally, a political no-man's-land, that does make the historical "Virginian" parallel to the play topically keener. This political non-entity is at the same time a conducive factor in producing as well as absorbing a utopian radicalism as regards freedom in general and freedom of speech in particular. As such, the emptiness of the island serves a dual political purpose in that it presents a political *tabula rasa* whereto radical, previously muted European political discourses may be relocated. The end product of this movement away from power is a combination of apolitical *and* subversive impulses that in the final analysis produce a highly radical longing toward something *new*, "something rich and strange" (I.ii.402)—for lack of a better word, America, or utopia.

Yet it is true that the play also seems disconcertingly at ease with *muted* speech, with proactive censorship, with constant surveillance, for via his secret police Ariel, Prospero hears and sees nearly all. As Caliban laments, "his spirits hear me, and yet I needs must curse. But they'll nor pinch, fright me with urchin-shows, pitch me i' th' mire, nor lead me like a fire-brand, in the dark, out of my way, *unless he bid* them" (II.i.3–7, my italics). Whereas a modern democratically inclined audience could interpret this sort of surveillance as a threat to free speech, the play's rhetorical structure and plot seem to present the situation blithely in terms of realpolitik as a way to protect the good Prosperian state against scheming Machiavels like Sebastian and Antonio or against blunt Calibanic threats of violence. Prospero wins in the end, Antonio and Sebastian are chastised, Caliban and his two co-conspirators are ridiculed, and even the Boatswain is put in his place by Gonzalo.

But as we find in several textual examples, a sense of free American speech is facilitated by natural forces. Firstly, the Boatswain in the very beginning scene of the play upbraids and rails at his betters, but with very good reason: "What cares these roarers for the name of king? / To cabin! silence! trouble us not!" (I.i.16–17). This tempest scene can of course easily be seen as a metaphor for an order that is about to disintegrate and collapse, as representative of the idea, so commonly seen in Shakespeare, that nature is the great equalizer and that when God's nature (or Prospero's mirage of nature, as in this case) works against men, there is an implicit understanding that the class structures and social distinctions they put in place are feeble, arbitrary, unnatural, and anything but favored by a God who controls the whole "chain of being" and "cosmic setting," as E. M. W. Tillyard argued in the very different critical climate of 1943 (42). More pressingly, though, the state of emergency that this (un)natural phenomenon causes makes the Boatswain and the sailors masters for the moment, even though the Boatswain wisely recognizes that the real "Master" is neither himself, Alonso, Antonio, nor Gonzalo but rather nature's awesome forces or the divine power behind them, and thus the loud-mouthed Boatswain speaks a prophetic truth to power in this moment of crisis. It is ironic that the passion and freedom with which he does so should so annoy Gonzalo that the kind, old councilor is moved to speak of "hanging," "gallows," and public execution on no less than four successive occasions (I.i.30, 32, 57) as fit punishment for the Boatswain's breach of what counts as decorum on land only.

The second instance of such lack of tactful conduct is found when Miranda interrupts Prospero, who, much like a child himself, is eager and impatient to be heard. In many ways, Miranda's relative freedom of speech and general expression rests in her privileged position, in her being Prospero's only daughter and only real social companion; unlike European daughters like Cordelia, Miranda is not bound up in quite the same way;

she doesn't know her power but keenly expresses it in front of a knowing father when she defends Ferdinand, technically treason in the way Prospero stages the rhetorical situation: "Silence! One word more / Shall make me chide thee, if not hate thee! What, / An advocate for an impostor? Hush!" (I.ii.476–478). It is worth keeping in mind, though, that whereas Prospero is provoked by his daughter's interruption and seeming lack of family loyalty, there is perhaps also a sense in which Ferdinand's silence and subservience can be even more provocative: he bears his yoke with galling dignity and patience, and he toils under Prospero's tenure with an annoying veneer of serene servitude, as we saw in the previous chapter. In other words, where free speech cannot not exist, other, more theatrical forms of expression speak in speech's place, often more effectively. The play's treatment of silence *within* the perimeters of freedom of expression could also fit into a larger example of how Prospero sanctions and forbids certain types of utterance. For the Milanese magus wishes to hear only certain things on his way to his own foggy and very absolutist utopia: his own "grave," in fact (V.i.311). We witness with stunned surprise his apoplectic outbursts against the ever-so-meek interjections of his own daughter, against Ferdinand's own right to object to his enslavement, against Ariel's yearning for his freedom, not to mention against Caliban and his own usurping brother, all of whom are either silent or silenced.

This stark but also meaningful silence stands in glaring contrast to the garrulity of Gonzalo, whose constant stream of words has the power to annoy Sebastian, Antonio, and Alonso but also to convey exciting and/or outlandish ideas, best seen in his "commonwealth" speech above. Derek Traversi claims that Prospero's keen understanding of human (and therefore political) nature is at the center of his sometimes illiberal conduct, in contradistinction to

> Gonzalo's commonwealth [which] is founded on an amorality which leaves place for "nettle-seed", "docks", and "mallows" to take possession of the ground. The fact that men like Antonio and Sebastian exist proves that some kind of cultivation of the human terrain is necessary. The state of nature is one which man must in the course of things outgrow; the crucial problem is whether this development will be towards good ... or towards the anarchy of unlimited personal desires. (311)

Traversi points out, quite rightly, that this "commonwealth" is one that does away with the political state, but, as usual, the "anarchy" that will logically ensue is inflected with a pejorative connotation that is imprecise, to say the least. The "anarchy" that Gonzalo envisions is in danger of "unlimited personal desires" because of an *absolutist* predisposition that is first of all alien to anarchistic thought and secondly the very essence of the weakness and logical absurdity of Gonzalo's vision. Yet his main idea of a perfect society is rather a state of anarchic *inexperience,* evocative of a prelapsarian place untainted by the Adamic vices that made the state necessary, in the Judaeo-Christian political mythology. The island presents a chance to start civilization afresh, and in order to achieve this utopia, Gonzalo envisions an illiterate yet *enlightened* populace where free speech seems a natural right.

One might very well interject, as Antonio and Sebastian certainly do with great panache, that the ironies implicit in Gonzalo's seemingly benevolent and illuminated wish to govern the ungovernable renders the proposed larger argument for freedom self-annihilating by its obvious self-contradiction. In the same spirit, similar objections could be made about the somewhat paradoxical sense of brute sophistication and illiterate education and polish seen at work in *The Tempest.* Yet the inhabitants Gonzalo envisions would seem to be avid readers of the "books in the running brooks" found in the forest of Arden in the play *As You Like It*—his commonwealth would perhaps be unlettered but wise people more than reminiscent of the transcendentalists Thoreau and Emerson.

As David Norbrook has argued, *The Tempest* envisages and discusses numerous utopias, and free speech is a central component of the ideology of the play—and of the politics of the day. Norbrook holds that the characters in the play show a ludic attitude to language itself and that this self-aware sense of rhetoric is a utopian experiment that happens outside of "existing codes and signs" (21). The meta-linguistic awareness that characters like Caliban but also Gonzalo and the Boatswain all display tests the boundaries of accepted utterance—think of the Boatswain's cursing, of Caliban's cursing Prospero's language itself, of Gonzalo's struggle to describe the utopian society in language that is nevertheless and quite ironically taken almost verbatim from Montaigne's "Of the Cannibals." At any rate, language here draws attention to itself as the conduit to understanding utopia. Also, the fact that each character's idea of the perfect society "come[s] up for ironic [linguistic and rhetorical] scrutiny" does not necessarily mean that it [the play] is "pessimistic" on behalf of those same ideas, as Norbrook usefully reminds us (25–26). And in spite of the comfortably safe rhetorical veil achieved at the start of his speech with the hypothetical "had I," Gonzalo's dream vision contributes in great measure to the *debate* over free speech via its radical *ésprit* and logical political implications—and nowhere is this speech more freely expressed than in the New World.

With an eye to classical American literature, of course, Gonzalo's vision is essentially a pre-Romantic idea of a utopian-anarchistic society where man lives in ignorant bliss. It will suffice here merely to mention the importance that untrammeled nature represents in the works of James Fenimore Cooper, in the poems of Walt Whitman, in the literature of the transcendentalists Ralph Waldo Emerson and Henry David Thoreau, in Herman Melville, and even in Nathaniel Hawthorne, authors who were (in varying degree, at given times) extremely self-conscious about their Americanness, which sense of blossoming nationhood and identity was shaped in the very highest degree by the natural forces that Leo Marx mentioned at the outset of this chapter. Shakespeare was of course in no position to invent Americanness, but I believe it is very plausible to assert that the play *prefigures* a sense of utopian American free speech and the European struggle to contain it in an eerily accurate fashion. *The Tempest,* I think, is a play that *feels* relevant to America like no other Shakespearean play, independent of red herrings like Caliban's Indianness.

There is a deep and paradoxical sense of *discontinuous continuity* between the Old World and the New World, and it is, of course, from this, in some ways, confining linguistic and cultural heritage and mindset (Caliban's plight) that Ralph Waldo Emerson tried to liberate himself with his *American Scholar* in 1837. (Of course, the New World, as evolving history has since shown us, bears the cultural and linguistic DNA of Europe and the Old World, as American place names like Alexandria, Athens, Florence, New York, New Orleans, Memphis, and many others usefully testify.) In many respects it is prudent for the purposes of free American speech here to look to the Puritans in New England. The Puritan experience was in many ways an "errand into the wilderness," as Perry Miller has argued so persuasively in his eponymous book: "Changes there had to be: adaptations to environment, expansion of the frontier, mansions constructed, commercial adventures undertaken. These activities were not specifically nominated in the bond Winthrop had framed. They were thrust upon the society by American experience" (Miller 9). In America the Puritans could come to form a new community of believers, a city on a hill that would shine as a beacon of light to the Old World—or so they hoped. This in many ways positive view, however, was tinged with fear of the Native Americans, of the dark forests, and of the diabolism they believed existed in them. And we see the same ideas expressed in Strachey's account from Bermuda and Virginia, a narrative on which *The Tempest* relies in large measure in its treatment of themes of the journey, the displacement, and the pioneering readiness and know-how shown first and foremost by Ferdinand. The difference between Prospero and Miranda and the Puritans of 1620—only nine years after the play was written—is that the old Duke of Milan has been overthrown and set out on the open sea to a most involuntary exile. Common to them both is their reliance on and longing for *muted* speech; indeed, Rachel Ingalls' novel *Mrs. Caliban* suggests that this tendency toward censorship and surveillance is "a Presbyterian dream come true—you know, God sees it all" (17).

Still, the very space Prospero fails to cover himself functions as an "American" locus and a(n) (ou-)topos of free speech insofar as immediate reaction and punishment under law is suspended here—as it also often was in the New World colonies. Thus, the island setting that the text goes to extraordinary lengths to befuddle as ultimately geographically, cartographically utopian is here nevertheless vested with a degree of *thematic* New World, proto-American utopianism. For the play comprises several interrelated ideologies that are unified in their generally benevolent and humanistic attitudes: it displays utopian longings, anarchical urges, and Christian-pastoral impulses, and importantly, these optimistic and life-affirming discourses seem to take precedence over the play's sterner practical-political concerns and come together to form the play's ludic and comic vision of *a* new world, one freer than the Old. The play frames a number of free discourses *inside* a muted speech self-referentially nodding in the direction of a *dramatic* structure that was subject to sometimes strict, other times lax censorship at the hands of Edmund Tilney, Master of Revels. Hence even though the play could be seen as silencing the frank sauciness of the Boatswain, the passionate protests of Caliban, and the vulgar desires of Stephano and Trinculo, their dangerous utterances are in fact given voice, are heard *if* dismissed, paid attention to if ultimately discarded—and I stress "if" because I don't think they ultimately are. Hence, the play incorporates a powerful and dangerously radical "American" discourse within its fragile official "European" framework of authority, an Old World-political construct that threatens to dismantle and crumble any minute, one that is under pressure, stretched, and challenged from several "Americanist" or New World angles. Thus, rhetorically-structurally speaking, the play posits a strong sense of utopian radicalism within the weak and ramshackle framework of an authoritarian dystopia, encapsulating tensions that cannot be reconciled within a structure that, in the course of time, will not hold.

Part IV

Post-Communist Topicalities

Toward a Post-1989 Reading of *The Tempest*

As the previous chapters have shown, political readings of *The Tempest* have become the established norm rather than the anomaly in the last sixty years, but the political interpretation has been a curiously one-sided affair. I have expressed concerns earlier about how much of this criticism has taken on a self-centered and emotional hue that produces analyses often glaringly at odds with the holistic text it purportedly seeks to address. This textual inaccuracy is often a weakness in otherwise pointed political criticism, as the chapters both on the island's setting and on Caliban demonstrate. Such readings are not textually weak somehow because of their historicist or presentist nature but rather on account of an active and sometimes entirely conscious misreading of narrow and limited textual passages. Post-colonial, New Historicist, Cultural Materialist, and presentist scholarship has brought much valuable attention to the political ways in which the play has been read through the ages. Yet it is as disappointing as it is unsurprising that political criticism of *The Tempest* has been so bafflingly uninterested in exploring presentist post-1989 angles that could tie the play's action and its invitingly open island setting to our own epoch, which is the purpose of this chapter.

Some will no doubt point out the obvious inconsistency in insisting upon a more textually faithful reading of Shakespeare while at the same time diving headlong into a presentist reading of *The Tempest* colored by 1989. Yet, as Grady and Hawkes remind us, "we can never . . . evade the present. And if it is always and only the present that makes the past speak, it speaks always and only to—and about—ourselves" (5). While such a phenomenological criticism has already been largely validated these last thirty years, Grady and Hawkes do well to stress that "the first duty of a credible presentist criticism must be to acknowledge that the questions we ask of any literary text will inevitably be shaped by our own concerns, even when these include what we call 'the past' " (5). Still, I will argue in this chapter that readings that manage to address and respect the primary text fully conscious of their presentist provenance as a necessarily intervening co-text are always going to be more convincing than those that let such both valuable and obstructive discourses eclipse it. Above all, I contend that the 1989 moment provides new, topically more resilient presentist parallels that also resonate better with Shakespeare's *The Tempest* than do, for example, most post-colonial readings that are by now firmly canonical.

But we also cannot know for sure—perhaps especially in relation to the reading I suggest in this chapter—whether 400 years of history does not, in fact, obstruct our understanding of the play's themes, despite Grady and Hawkes' otherwise useful validation of such a leap as an inevitable "irony which . . . constitutes . . . [an] inescapable aspect of any text's being" (5). One brief example will illustrate both the reality of such transhistorical "ironies" and the violence that such blithe "time travel" or translation might potentially do to the text: my book is, as far as I can see, perhaps the first to argue that Caliban is a cynical political schemer, an actor of many faces who, both skillfully and successfully enough for his purposes, tempts Stephano and Trinculo to assist him in his attempt on Prospero's life. Virtually all established criticism of *The Tempest* since 1945 has certainly understood it otherwise, namely that Caliban is taken advantage of by European hoi-polloi colonizers, that he is fed alcohol to dull his senses and resistance, that he is duped and regarded as a monster, that he suffers racism at the hands of all involved (Orkin, "Whose Thing" 153), that he is seen as a salable commodity, that he is, in short, the Colonial Victim. It has, in fact, become impossible to ignore the play's colonial elements, despite the fact that Prospero's project is anti-colonial in nature, as several scholars have by now begun to underline (Sokol 78–79). But Caliban's brief flirtation with alcohol, his savageness, and his general colonial victimization is woven into the (hi)stories we tell ourselves, our sensibilities, our very eyes and ears—we have great difficulty interpreting Caliban as anything else than a poor, alcoholic illiterate native the same way we find it impossible not seeing *The Merchant of Venice* as connected with the Holocaust. The anachronistically re-engineered figments of "Caliban," then, lead us away from Caliban's proper epistemological and textual being—the Old World-cynical Caliban who drinks and flatters primarily to deceive. Thus, one of the most interesting aspects of historicist and presentist interpretations of the play is found not so much in its parallels to historical and/or contemporary events as in those textual passages that it, for reasons to do with a political ideology that is too much with us, chooses to misread or elide.

My contention is that our failure to arrive at such a textually consistent interpretation—that we instead tend to inflate Prospero's colonial ambitions beyond any level that can reasonably be seen in the text—is a trend that is governed by an emotion-centered response to certain dark travel narratives from the age of discovery and by our understanding of *later* colonial strategies designed to suppress native or slave resistance by means of powder, alcohol, opium, and divide-and-conquer policies, strategies of which Shakespeare and England in 1611 were of course largely ignorant. Such readings seldom provide "the basis of the only effective purchase on Shakespeare" that Grady and Hawkes claim (5). Rather, for all our resurgent historicist and/or presentist criticism since 1980, few *Tempest* scholars have been able to articulate metareflectively why Caliban ought to be seen as a native colonial victim in the light of his drinking alcohol. Such common problems among aboriginal peoples such as rampant alcoholism and attendant health problems were to happen much later, which makes Leslie Fiedler's otherwise eccentrically outlandish claim that *The Tempest* is a play in which "the whole history of imperialist America" is "*prophetically* revealed to us" the more convincing in comparison (238–239, my emphasis).

In what follows, I suggest that a utopian reading of the text of *The Tempest* may potentially realign itself far more seamlessly with the moment of 1989. Whereas "early" scholars like Castells in 1995 (who speaks of Cuba) and very recent critics like Aviženis (who addresses the Baltic states) and Stavreva (Bulgaria) have done admirably in their very initial attempts to take new political ownership of the play, to nudge it away from the tried and tested post-colonial readings, focusing instead on how the play engages with post-communist understanding of both the past and the present, surprisingly few Western or even "third world" scholars have evinced much interest in seeing the play's evocative events as similar in nature to historical or literary exiles beyond the tried and tested discussions of pre-1989 post-colonial diasporas, suppressed indigenes, and victims of exclusively Western colonialism. The reason for this absence, one more than suspects, is political in nature. To the extent that 1989 has been seen as the ultimate victory for the Western political right, it would seem that the use of a 1989-specific lens perhaps tends to tilt the discourse in terms of political balance in a direction that is hard to swallow for post-colonial thinkers, Cultural Materialists, and New Historicist critics who have enjoyed a near-Prosperian hegemony over the play's interpretations these last four decades, as I mentioned in Chapter 1. Thus, the predominant recent discourse surrounding the play, the characters, and the themes have fed directly into the critics' own research interests in the very highest degree shaped by long-held political persuasions, but, with the tables turned by history: uncomfortable silence. For a particularly sore point for any serious post-colonial scholar ought to be those Soviet exiles and Cuban refugees, whose existence and suffering we now know much more about but whose examples Marxists, both reformed and unreformed, have been oblivious to or simply reluctant to raise to the critical center of a political discussion of *The Tempest*. Thus, the obvious weakness of much post-colonial criticism is that it is employing increasingly dated symbols of Calibanic victims at this revolutionary, pan-Arab "1989 redux," to the extent that *Tempest* criticism of Western colonialism, for instance, no matter how justified, offers little more than faint echoes of previous colonial battles, of very similar problems to do with discrimination and disparities, that have already been widely acknowledged, even championed in academia and in the Western media.

It is at this point, in 2011, 400 years after the play was written, and in the midst of the "Arab Spring," the second mass revolution in 22 short years, that it becomes tempting to furnish more relevant parallels to political exiles than those that have been suggested in the past. With regard to making *The Tempest* speak to newer, more pressing political and social problems than do both post-colonial scholars and the much more recent presentism called for by Grady and Hawkes, one such fresh, new take on the play's post-modern topicality was presented by London's Tara Arts Theatre's 2008 *Tempest*. Its program notes link Prospero to Ayman al-Zawahiri hiding in a cave in Afghanistan, fuming with rage over the decadence of his native Egypt. While this very topical and recent angle was mentioned in passing but, sadly, not really expounded upon in the production itself beyond costumes, its topical hints and thematic, presentist grounding still invites an important question: why have we not seen similar political references in cutting-edge scholarship? Is it too cynical a suspicion to hold that the current critical hegemony is not only unwilling to fully admit its own biases but in fact also reluctant to reflect on events in our own times?[1]

The Tempest is perhaps that one Shakespearean text that "speaks" best to our own epoch, perhaps the one text we most often rehearse politically, though often with little respect for its textual or even contextual integrity, a recent instance of which is found in Martin Orkin's shrill criticism in 1997 of textually faithful, "racist" productions that dare cast Caliban as the "deformed" monster the text stipulates ("Whose Thing" 153). In some ironic contrast, Orkin's own *Shakespeare against Apartheid* from 1987 presents a far more usable utopian (so it must have seemed at the time) reading that, post-1989, yearns for a critical paradigm shift while retaining textual sensitivity that this chapter calls for:

> At the same time though, such questions themselves relate to the context of their own production, confirming the truism that every age understands Shakespeare in its own way. We cannot escape our own mode of seeing or, some would have it, our own particular discourse.... The multiplicity of readings of Shakespeare that have occurred, since he wrote, in succeeding ages partly bears witness to the extent to which the product of one moment can be perceived only by means of rather than despite the discourses available at another. The indeterminacy of readings, for this and other reasons, has loomed large as an issue in recent critical writing. *We do need to respond to the text but the way in which we do this, some would say the way in which we appropriate it, will always be a vital issue.* And in South Africa, the attempt to read Shakespeare's plays, even in the last decades of the twentieth century, presents its own special difficulties. (*Shakespeare against Apartheid* 13–14, emphasis mine)

Much as Orkin's own interpretation credits readings from the early 1980s by Drakakis, Dollimore, Sinfield, and Greenblatt, I list his concerns here to suggest contiguity with a *post*-1989 and/or presentist understanding of *The Tempest* that naturally departs radically from the political context of 1987. I seek to move the discourse toward the 1989/post-1989 moments also in order to reinstate a vibrant utopian dimension to a critical tradition that for twenty-two years has been marching lemming-like away from unreconstructed Marxism in the face of authoritarian socialism's widely discredited ability to furnish a credible and desirable humanistic worldview—not to mention an aesthetic one. This utopian emphasis, I think, better enables us to address issues of aesthetic form, Shakespearean text, and the social, political, and interpretative matrices that form some of the factors that enable us to understand any text in *our* "present."

I do so for reasons to do with the sheer "presentist relevance" of current criticism, too. As David Schalkwyk writes,

> [i]nstead of wanting to speak to the dead—perhaps the most well-known dictum of the founder of the New Historicism—presentism wishes, with not a little self-righteousness, to speak to the living. Invoking the platitude that one can approach the past only with the preconceptions and the preoccupations of the present, the new presentism makes both the epistemological point that we can never recover the past or the phenomenology of past experience and the political point that our responsibilities lie towards the here and now, and the possibilities of the future. (3)

Still, it seems a reasonable expectation for presentism to be informed by the "present," by current events, and to be able to metareflect on the "past" events that midwifed the "now," whatever (or whenever) that "now" or "present" might be—and the only thing that seems truly meaningful in this discussion is that a multiplicity of such presents exist.

And instead of a utopian presentist impulse in *Tempest* scholarship colored by 1989, especially the years leading up to and following the quincentennial of Columbus's landing in 1492 witnessed a whole raft of starkly dystopian takes (what Bloom—perhaps just a touch resentfully—terms "the school of resentment") often directly, other times indirectly, inspired by Marxism. Cultural Materialism, New Historicism, feminism and ecocriticism, and various shades of post-colonialism have since continued to dominate *Tempest* studies with readings that propose historicist/presentist interpretations that are sometimes helplessly historically adrift, mired in the struggles of the 1960s and '70s. The paradox is thus obvious that the sum of the political concerns of such trends makes Shakespearean scholarship in general but *Tempest* criticism in particular less engaged with current issues but rather eschews presentist concerns for a backward-looking, nostalgic yearning for a distinctly Western-Eurocentric understanding of the mythopoesis of 1968. Until such glaring contradictions can be solved, much *Tempest* criticism finds itself not so much "on the wrong side of history" as stuck in the past shade of the present, threatened to be entangled by their own trans-historical "Heimlich manoeuvres."

True, it has been a good twenty-two years since 1989, but it is no exaggeration to claim that its moment was and still is inescapably "now," ideologically as well as causally convergent with the popular revolutions in Arab countries—movements that, until recently, would have seemed desperately utopian—that are happening all over again as one dictatorship after the other is falling. As I am writing this paragraph on January 31, 2011, there has been announced a million-man march in Alexandria, Egypt. Nobody knows what will happen—Hosni Mubarak's dictatorship might come to an end. Some claim he has already to fled to Sharm el-Sheikh, waiting out the future. The Tunisians have already ousted their own, European- and American-backed autocrat, confiscated his property, and sent his relatives to jail. Nobody knows if this moment is to be the same "1989" for the Middle East as it was for Eastern Europe, what will take the place of the *ancien regimes,* or if people will want "full, Western" democracy. But nobody knew in 1989, either—some urged calm and measured protest, a gradual disentanglement from old communist rule, while others wanted revolutions to have taken place as early as 1956, 1968, or 1982. What does seem hopeful for me today is that, after a (for many in the West) disappointing return to authoritarian rule in the ex-Soviet republics, 2011 could be democracy's greatest renaissance since 1989 and that this moment might improve the human rights situation, boost markets, change international policy, forge new political alliances, and create new ideological paradigms.

Perhaps it is true that one successful way of keeping *The Tempest* relevant is to seek new conflict rather than tacit resolution, which is why, perhaps, ever-changing post-colonial victims are usually preferred as Calibans—the Irish, as in Brown; the American natives in countless works *pace* Malone and Sidney Lee; the Africans in Cartelli; the Malagasy in Mannoni; the Irish again in Callahan; the myriad *peoples,* generally, once under especially English or French rule. Their topical relevance has been thematically clear as day and pathetically poignant for sixty years, now—and so they remain to many. But if we can accept that Caliban shares much (or rather little, as Chapter 3 argues) with the plight of native Americans and later post-colonial subjects, then we should also be able to see the modern Saidian link between Prospero and his daughter and those Arabs who were tossed out of Israel in 1948 and be able to appreciate Ricardo Castells' link to those Cubans who, in the small boats that give them the name *bolseros,* had to escape Fidel Castro's political persecutions and seek refuge in Florida (176–177).

I suggest that not only Caliban but the entire play be seen in light of the revolutions that took place in 1989 and their immediate aftermath, which is to say the time we live in right now. In so doing, I am greatly indebted to Howard Felperin's "Political Criticism at the Crossroads: The Utopian Historicism of *The Tempest*" from 1995, a work that seeks to reconcile the idealist and materialist schools of criticism by re-establishing a textually founded utopianism vis-à-vis *The Tempest.* I argue on the pages that follow that such a reading will form a natural continuum with the insights gained from post-colonial studies and also form a more convincingly textually faithful interpretation that can bridge the strictly textual with the "merely topical," to use Frank Kermode's eminently provocative phrase.

My argument is also that *The Tempest* should have seen an extremely natural and seamless continuation in theater and criticism from its brave new world of allegorical post-colonial-topical adaptations and appropriations. Instead, why this great rupture? Why this deafening silence? Now, in 2011, there are at least three extremely good reasons to pose these questions, the quadricentennial of the play itself being the first and most obvious, and the twenty years that have passed since the dissolution of the Soviet Union the other. The third reason has to do with the revolutions taking place in North Africa and the Middle East, a 1989-come-lately that brings back that year to the front of our minds and to the midst of our discourse. The point is that there is a veritable black hole in much literary scholarship with regard to the immense revolutions that happened in 1989 (Berlin and most of Eastern Europe), 1991 (the dissolution of the Soviet Union), and 1990–1994 (the gradual demise of Apartheid in South Africa)—which, for simplicity, I will refer to collectively as a catch-all "1989."

Much too little has been written on Shakespeare in light of 1989. A handful of East European scholars have made serious forays into theatrical performances (especially the Romanian and Bulgarian scholars Nicoleta Cinpoeş and Kirilka Stavreva, respectively) and Soviet interpretations in scholarship (by Irena Makaryk). Extremely little has otherwise been written in Western Europe or in America, however, as a reflection on how the great paradigm shifts that happened post-1989 (could/should have) altered how we read Shakespeare. The stark reason is, perhaps, that the manner in which we read Shakespeare has not changed at all, though certainly not for literary scholars' lack of political interest. But since an endlessly narcissistic and Western-obsessed, self-flagellant academe has simply not registered the most important events of our time, it seems that the debate I am attempting to kick off with this book is simply too important to be left to Shakespeareans alone. The fact that 1989 might be happening all over again should only serve to underscore how literary criticism failed to appreciate it the first time round—failed, that is, to understand and reflect upon how its own biases and prejudices are engendered by our own present and our recent history. In fact, post-colonial scholars, of all critics, should best be able to articulate what the 1989 moment of revolution meant then and means to us now. Thus, I call not for a break with the many worthwhile literary pursuits and wider political concerns of post-colonialism but rather a critique of its unprincipled practitioners for not having been willing to apply their significant critical apparatus to expose those colonial and imperial excesses and violations that haunted Eastern Europe, the Soviet Union, Cuba, Tibet, Burma, and Cambodia.

The earliest attention to studying Shakespeare through the lens of 1989 appeared already in 1991 at a conference that resulted in the collection of essays called *Shakespeare in the New Europe*. As the editors note, "with the collapse of totalitarian regimes in the East, it was inevitable to ask how those critical projects that had been based on what was understood as Marxism in both east and west would appear when the eastern versions of the socialist experiment had so obviously and catastrophically failed" (Hattaway, Sokolova, and Roper 18). As we shall see later, this very early yet timely and important inquiry into the by then unclear *gestalt* of still raw revolutionary aftermaths comes up for critical scrutiny in later works that, in comfortable retrospect, find fault with the book's alleged deprioritization and relegation of local and regional politics.

By 2000, however, Zdeněk Stříbrný's *Shakespeare and Eastern* Europe was in a position of a better historical purview and reflects on examples of the sort of theater productions one could perhaps expect to see in Berlin around 1989, commenting specifically on Heiner Müller's 1990 version of *Hamlet*:

> The totally disillusioned actor doing Hamlet refuses to play any more roles and, during an anti-communist insurrection, is swayed by divided loyalties between the rebels and the defenders of the state. He wants to become a machine without pain and thought. Finally, however, he puts on the armour of the Ghost representing "the beloved blood-thirsty dog" (Stalin) and splits the busts of Marx, Lenin, and Mao, throwing the world back into the Ice Age. (138)

Much as "Müller's *Hamlet/Maschine* could be received as a farewell to the Communist era in East Germany" and as "a warning vision of a brave new world," though, Stříbrný points out that it could also be seen as invested with "Brechtian touches of sarcastic humour and irony," resulting in "an artistic obituary stemming from the director's conviction that the German Democratic Republic was not so bad that it did not deserve a decent funeral" (139).[2] Thus buried along with the dead empire that supported it, communist aesthetics, often conservative in its tastes, received a quietus and a last oil of sorts from one of its own.

Alexander Shurbanov and Boika Sokolova's *Painting Shakespeare Red: An East-European Appropriation* from 2001 points out that as a result of the political and ideological sea change that took place "in the years since the fall of communism in 1989 ... [a]n important aspect of the new situation is the demonstratively individualist freedom of dealing with the text and its complex relationship to an emergent pluralistic society and its changing theater" (25). As a general tendency, the sense of textual and contextual elasticity and interaction was at the same time liberating and limiting to post-1989 theaters. The pitfalls of this "individualist freedom" as opposed to the relative comforts of the rigors of communist aesthetic conventions is that it runs the risk of individual narcissism. Making Shakespeare deal primarily with oneself, which has certainly been one of the dominant tendencies in *Tempest* appropriations since 1945, makes Shakespeare become interesting because he is not so much Jan Kott's "contemporary" but our proper selves, as we saw with regard to Caliban in Chapter 3.

Addressing precisely such a conflict between universalism and historically conditioned presentism, Terence Hawkes' excellent article "Band of

Brothers" in *Presentist Shakespeares* from 2007 is both entertaining and informative. Speaking of the historical groundedness of literature in opposition to a modern, facile, and bardolatrous vision of Shakespeare as a transcendent wisdom-dispenser fit "for all times," Hawkes' essay rails mercilessly against the Royal Shakespeare Company's "The Complete Works" Festival that put on all thirty-seven plays with a relentlessly multicultural, global, and topical appeal to a politically current sensibility, one of many triggers to which is found in the most recent war in Iraq:

> This is modern-dress boundary-blurring with a vengeance. Indeed, it's a prospect that's recently inspired the director of London's Globe Theatre to speak—with apparent seriousness—of a forthcoming "Shakespearetastic" year in which this non-specific, virtually non-terrestrial figure, will dominate the cultural horizon.... A theatre company consisting of homeless people called "The Cardboard Citizens" will stage [*Timon of Athens*] .... We'd be forgiven for thinking that the Bard had finally turned into Bob Geldof. (21)

While it is true that the brunt of Hawkes' criticism explicitly deals with a putatively unpolitical Shakespeare who somehow transcends all boundaries and like some black hole swallows up all meaningful difference round him, it is tempting to see Hawkes' scathingly sarcastic critique of our obsession with *ourselves* reflected *in* this eternal playwright-prophet as an overwhelming hindrance overall to making an "effective purchase on Shakespeare" that the book's introduction calls for—in defense of a presentism that "speaks always and only to—and about—ourselves" (5). This latter position not only seems overtly to contradict the former but also appears to brush aside some vital *tensions* that exist between primary text and presentist co-text. For instance, the fact that not even the most historically astute scholars are equipped to read 400-year-old works *perfectly* phenomenologically in the same spirit of the time when they were composed does not mean that attempts to appreciate problems to do with primary text as well as the archeology of their materialist moments are somehow futile.

But five years prior, in 2002, Hawkes made a different case for presentism, less cynically suggesting that

> there are two areas in which presentism seems particularly well suited to make a significant contribution to the study of Shakespeare.... The first concerns the recent development of "devolution" in British politics.... The whole process requires that the "Great Britain" project, chronicled and championed repeatedly in the Shakespearean canon, must henceforth be seen, not just as the opening of a new and apparently permanent world order,

but as the beginning of an enterprise that, after four hundred years, has now reached its conclusion. (4)

For all the value of such a "devolutionist" take in 2012, though, I again struggle to see that a reading that seeks to link Shakespeare to homelessness and the war in Iraq or Afghanistan is somehow less valid than one that attempts to make Shakespeare speak to present British devolution—unless such judgments are measured against a provable textual fidelity and hard and fast historical parallels to personages and events in *The Tempest*. To his credit, and unlike many scholars and teachers who shirk away from such arbitration for fear of being found dismissing and even undemocratic, Hawkes manages both to entertain and provoke with his penchant for the polemically excessive turn of phrase. However, as I mentioned in Chapter 1, extremely few scholars—for reasons to do with a modern democratic acceptance of a multiplicity of readings—venture into such splenetic judgments as "chilling" theater adaptations and a "sinister" interpretation of Shakespeare's global preeminence that is tantamount "blood-money-cannibalism" (*Presentist Shakespeares* 21).

A spurious and blithely simplistic, exploitative adaptation of *The Tempest* and of Shakespeare in the light of 1989 (for example, in the immediate aftermath of the fall of the Berlin Wall) might admittedly have invited similar criticism, though in principle I suspect that most serious scholars will be hard pressed to distinguish between a reading where Shakespeare "reaches into" the lives of his future readers (as in the case of *King Lear* and the process of British devolution) and the more humanistic interpretation that Shakespeare's oeuvre is of such thematic magnitude and elasticity that it transcends its historical and materialist moment and "speaks to" homeless Gulf War veteran soldiers or "deals with" the problems faced by Japanese schoolchildren. The criteria for judging such transhistorical and transcultural leaps are presumably found in the quality of the performance or in its thematic convincingness, seen against the "text itself." Shakespeare post-1989, as we will discover, finds especially relevant and meaningful resonances in *The Tempest*.

Nicoleta Cinpoeş' " 'Lose the name of action': Stillness in Post-1989 Romanian *Hamlets*" from 2007 makes the useful point that, "during communist oppression, *Hamlet* functioned as a dissident play; the story of a director . . . who could finally speak freely" (71). Cinpoeş also mentions in a note that,

[a]s in every country in the Soviet sphere of influence, *Hamlet* was ousted from Romanian repertoires after World War II: it was one of the foreign plays

openly vetoed by Stalin. In 1959, when it finally returned to the Romanian stage, *Hamlet* began to play a double political game. It served as an explicit anti-Soviet protest that celebrated the end of Russia's supra-national domination in the Eastern Bloc. (80)

However, Cinpoeş explains that *Hamlet* saw a long Romanian hiatus "after the final Bulandra performance in 1992," that the main reasons for its "delay was that it took *Hamlet* longer than most plays to shed the particular political significance it had acquired before 1989," and that "Romanian theater went through successive stages of taking liberties with language and the body, as it experimented with Western theatrical innovations and entered a veritable technological orgy" (63). As a result of these and other factors, "a detachment from political immediacy came only years later when the 1989 revolution had become assimilated as history, and when the euphoria and hysteria" had abated (63). Cinpoeş further refers to *Hamlet* as "the ventriloquist of local histories" during a repressive censorship in communist Romania (and Eastern Europe in general) and to how Gabor Tompa's 1997 production—eight years after the revolution—"used this strategy to double effect: by exposing Shakespeare's *Hamlet* as an undercover agent, he enabled both the audience and Hamlet to leave the past behind—a ghost laid to rest" (66).

Similarly to the Tompa production, Ion Sapdaru's 1998 version "also wanted a text free from political association, which meant it could not recycle a translation used on stage in the past half of the century" (73). The Romanian problems with a politicized *Hamlet* that could never escape its pre-1989 contextual grounding interestingly correspond with seemingly apolitical *Tempests* in Bulgaria, as we will see later. Cinpoeş further notes that "with a lean text in hand [because] *Hamlet*'s Romanian textual ghosts (anti-communist tongue, academic discourse, and linguistic obsolescence) banished, this production could focus on the story" (73). The significant violations done to Shakespeare's text were primarily a Brechtian strategy of "vandalism" so as to do away with "the actors' and audience's almost automatic tendency to identify *Hamlet* with Romania's dissident history under communism" (74). Still, the politics of the present were impossible to avoid:

[S]hock-therapy for everybody involved was *Hamlet*'s and theatre's *modus vivendi* in post-1989 Romania: it satisfied the need to expose the communist past and its enormities; in so doing, it both exorcized its ghosts and exercised the free mechanisms of an uncensored theatre.... Both *Hamlet* and Romania needed to move on and move away into democracy, which could neither be sustained nor advanced by wallowing in a theatrical self-referentiality recognizable only to a very cultured elite. (78–79)

It was perhaps a mature decision of theater-loving Romanians to put *Hamlet* aside until its moment was ripe for something new, something "rich and strange." Romanian theaters clearly needed to engage with the moment of 1989, but at the same time there is a sense in which certain play-texts were simply not ready for the audience's sensibilities without doing violence to the specific ideas that the moment demanded. But we cannot know whether this was a wise move, whether theaters effectively communicated an emotionally necessary new version of *Hamlet* expunged of its anti-communist residue, or whether this was an opportunity lost to chase away the ghosts of communism in a different, more public form of political catharsis.

The transition from a traditionally East European-communist, de-politicized aesthetics in vogue with apparatchiks in the 1960s have since given way to more political translations of the text of *The Tempest*, too, as has been ably demonstrated by Madalaina Nicolaescu's "Reframing Shakespeare in Recent Translations of *The Tempest*" from 2010. Nicolaescu's work analyzes two fresh translations of *The Tempest* expressions of the sort of Romanian yearning for pan-Europeanism and hopeful new identities that other East European critics—specifically Stavreva and Kostihová—criticize as simplistic and sentimental, if not occluding, obfuscating, and downright dangerous. Nicolaescu nevertheless claims that the contrast between the archaic and Slavonic-inflected translation of Leon Levitchi from 1964 and the far more irreverent recent work by Ioana Ieronim and Cristi Juncu lies in the "challenge to and contestation of the canonical socialist Shakespeare" (36). For while the notion of a "canonical socialist Shakespeare" might seem like a contradiction to most readers in the West, "doctrinaire Marxist view[s] on Shakespeare" very much ruled the East European day in the 1960s (Nicolaescu 38) but was ironically diametrically opposed to the sort of Marxist readings "against the grain" that were done in the West in the 1970s and '80s: "From the perspective of party officials, a Shakespeare distanced from the present was obviously politically safer than a Shakespeare projected as 'our contemporary' " (38–39). For, as Nicolaescu points out, Levitchi's older translation both de-situated and de-politicized Shakespeare's terms "with archaic words of Slav origin that have lost their political resonance to modern audiences" (40) so as to be able less problematically to present a Prospero who is "the humanistic magus or the enlightened leader 'close to his people', as doctrinaire Marxist propaganda described progressive historical leaders" (41). In contradistinction to Levitchi's translation,

> Ieronim's and Juncu's "post-integration" policy (that is, after the integration of Romania to the EU) rejects the previous radical localization of

Shakespeare with its assertion of "authentic" Romanian values, set up as different from those of modern Western culture. The 2009 translations are keen to identify links and continuities with Western culture without being either imitative or derivative. (44)

If we can accept that Nicolaescu offers an accurate description of these translations as "conducive to the construction of a European identity" that is both "post-national" and "cosmopolitan," then local voices in other East European countries form a diametrically opposed view that creates tensions both in the political sense and in the theatrical struggles over the meanings of *The Tempest* in post-1989 Europe.

Kirilka Stavreva's "Dream Loops and Short-Circuited Nightmares: Post-Brechtian *Tempests* in Post-Communist Bulgaria" of 2008 is preoccupied with appropriation and Brechtian "creative vandalism" (6) done to the Shakespearean text, a strategy that has clear strengths as well as weaknesses, as we shall see. Stavreva's essay does well to anticipate the link between post-1989 and post-colonial studies but points out that "the politics of post-communist and post-colonial Shakespearean appropriations are markedly different" (3). Furthermore, the essay seems determined to avoid any sense of nostalgia for the moment that was 1989:

> Given the reputation of *The Tempest* as a play of forgiveness and redemption, it is tempting to speculate that its productions in Bulgaria's post-communist era . . . would be likely to develop what Susan Bennett would label a "nostalgic" vision of the play. "Nostalgia," Bennett explains, is the representation "of a past which forms a continuous trajectory into the present and through into the future"—in other words, a false dialectic of the past and the present in which the critical tension of conceptualizing difference has been eliminated. . . . Profoundly conservative, "collective nostalgia can promote a feeling of community which works to downplay or (even if only temporarily) disregard divisive positionalities (class, race, gender, and so on); when nostalgia is produced and experienced collectively, then it can promote a false and likely dangerous sense of 'we.' " . . . The immediate, personal connection that theater establishes between its humanly embodied stage narratives and live audiences, makes it an especially effective tool for inculcating collective nostalgia. (6–7)

Stavreva first conceives of *The Tempest* (the play that Shakespeare wrote, that is) as particularly fitting for a post-1989 Bulgarian understanding in terms of "forgiveness and redemption," both important *Tempestian* themes. It is a highly interesting observation because the entire moment that was (and still is) 1989 and/or post-1989 is one that would in many meaningful ways be the natural continuation of post-colonial scholars' concerns with *The Tempest.*

Equally puzzling, though, is her seeming urgency to pigeonhole such a hypothetical production (and/or critical interpretation?) as one too "nostalgic" for the "dangerous" throngs of "we" who would witness the theatrical spectacle. It is perhaps most disappointing that her article does *not* fall for the "tempt[ation] to speculate" (6–7) on how such stagings and readings would form a perfect continuum with the post-colonial readings and liberationist appropriations Stavreva acknowledges at the very outset of her essay (3). Instead of exploring critically this "tempting" avatar seriously, the essay instead falls for the temptation to dismiss it as "nostalgic" and as a

> production of *The Tempest* for Bulgarian audiences around the turn of the millennium, [that] would smooth over the gaps and tensions in the play's narrative to endorse Prospero's dream .... It would indulge in the play's promise of freedom regained by Ariel and even (implicitly) by Caliban. It would resort to seamless characterization, celebrating the restoration of Prospero's benevolent idealism and the age-wise love of Milan's future young rulers .... [S]uch a production would showcase its representational value as an elaborate allegory of the redemption of the abhorred communist past of secret informers, abrogation of individual freedoms .... The past would be forgiven, if not forgotten .... Such a staging of the play would certainly provide emotional gratification to audiences by fitting recent Bulgarian history into the master narrative of a continually revitalized Western History periodically cleansed of the sins of the past. (7)

That somewhat moralizing and heavy-handed warning seemingly necessitates the following clarification: "Let me be clear: Euro-nostalgia is *not* among the intertexts merging Shakespeare's play text and the cultural narratives of the post-communist experience in these dialectical theater productions" (7).

It is Stavreva's argument's weakness that it does not spend any time explaining why such an essentially utopian reading of Shakespeare's text would be insufficient or less valid than the three productions it praises for sometimes dystopian and cynical political Bulgarian contextualization. The article speaks approvingly, for instance, of Petar Pashov's *The Tempest*'s ability to raise both mundane and serious local political and ecological problems:

> The experience of a grand, but barely controllable, experiment underway in this small place of beauty is of course painfully familiar to the play's spectators, young and old. Parents and grandparents would have remembered only

too well the failed social experiment of communism, which among other things redrew the navigable outlines of the scenic Varna bay. Both young and adult audiences would have witnessed the recent frantic construction of imposing, bold-colored hotels and homes carried out in ecologically vulnerable locations. Most of the adults would be too familiar with the mad rush to seize the mirage of business opportunity as the country transitioned from the government-run communist economy to a free-market economy. (10)

It is in fact such pessimistic local regional resonances that Stavreva's essay spends most time elucidating. If the three Bulgarian productions that the essay involves are any reflection of a national or even regional atmosphere, it is a decidedly skeptical, pessimistic, suspicious, and dystopian one. The "false" sense of *The Tempest*'s pan-European optimism that Stavreva's essay fears might run away with the appropriations does at any rate not materialize on stage, and the political angles explored are far less obvious, at the same time localized but also hinting at several much larger politically sensitive problems peculiar to country, region, and continent:

In Pashov's production, when Emilia Petkova's Ariel breaks through the membrane of Prospero's magical island, having served for twelve years as the living cornerstone for Prospero's civilization, the audience witnesses the implosion of the "pure race" Balkan myth. Earlier, Prospero's characterization had satirized the Western myth of the multi-talented Renaissance Man of towering ambition wielding magical control over his life-story and of his world. The production, then, juxtaposes and finds wanting both the myth of the civilizing and conquering Western Humanism and the Balkan myth of a polity built on pure eternal brotherhood. Furthermore, since the "hero" in both of these identity-constitutive mythic narratives is Prospero, the outcome of the production compels audiences to deconstruct the very dichotomy of the metropolitan West and its Balkan fringe. (12)

Stavreva locates the three appropriations as firmly within the "revisionist tradition" that post-colonial productions made use of "to confront the oppression of the subaltern in various colonial and post-colonial settings" (23). Yet, "their focus is not Caliban . . . . Embedded within the Bulgarian post-communist cultural context, *The Tempest* remains Prospero's play, though it is by no means a nostalgic celebration of the enlightened and compassionate ruler" (23).

Stavreva's essay concludes by seeking to redefine what Bulgarian political theater means after 1989:

Unlike Brecht, most Bulgarian theater professionals would hasten to declare that theirs is no political theater, for it offers neither political nor moral alternatives to the fallen idols and their value systems. It is worth questioning, however, whether the cognitive and ethical questions raised in these experimental, intellectually engaging productions do not constitute the kind of dialectical contradiction that provides a much needed corrective to the concept of the political. (24)

The most telling aspect about the essay's conclusion, I think, is that it calls for a "corrective" to an understanding of the (non-existing?) limits of the political with reference to a play that has seen little but heavily politicized criticism these last forty or fifty years. It is peculiar, as well, that the increased political interpretation that the essay otherwise seems to endorse and encourage should need to be expunged of "nostalgic" pitfalls that hypothetical stagings (and perhaps also critical readings?) might fall into—whatever form such "nostalgia" might assume.

If the decidedly utopian reading of *The Tempest* that my book calls for—and that this chapter in particular tries to see in some basic phenomenological contextuality with post-1989 paradigm shifts—can be said to qualify as nostalgic, it is an oddly "prophetic" sort of nostalgia that yearns for a moment that has heretofore remained unacknowledged in *Tempest* scholarship, as Marcela Kostihová's *Shakespeare in Transition: Political Appropriations in the Postcommunist Czech Republic* from 2010 certainly attests. Kostihová's book is important insofar as it sketches out a way in which Shakespeare is interpreted through the lens of EU skepticism in Central and Eastern Europe. She, like Hawkes, seeks to move away from the idea that Shakespeare is somehow just a permanent, unpolitical gnome who dispenses "truth" and "wisdom" about a permanent human nature. Yet, Kostihová defends her country's engagement with Shakespeare as a way of forming a proper identity, so important in the wake of the vacuum that also was 1989: "That Shakespeare could be involved in the sociopolitical discourse of postcommunist countries should not come as a surprise, considering the engagements of Shakespeare's texts in nation-building (and nation-bashing) processes around the globe" (30). Further, "[i]ndeed, thanks to four centuries of colonial domination by three distinct empires, the Czechs have gathered extensive experience in subversive resistance well-covered with surface compliance" (7). However, Kostihová warns that the danger of positioning Shakespeare as what Jonathan Bale called "The Dead White Male in chief" and Terence Hawkes recently labelled the "industrial-strength insect-repellent" lies in the use of Shakespeare as an extendable arm of exploitive Western practices, ranging from the classical colonial regimes of the eighteenth and nineteenth century to current neoliberal practices. (31)

Kostihová's critique of Western neoliberal exploitation is different from the warning against sentimentality and nostalgia issued above by Stavreva but shares its dystopian cynicism. It is a political skepticism that the book finds wanting in Hattaway, Sokolova, and Roper's 1994 *Shakespeare in the New Europe:*

> A defining characteristic of the [essays included in *Shakespeare in the New Europe*] is a staunch denial of the political dimensions of postcommunist Shakespeare. Despite Shakespeare's explicit involvement in postcommunist cultural redefinition parallel to political and economic reconstruction ... most of the authors maintained that postcommunist Shakespearean production has lost its political edge.... The consensus seems to be that once the revolutionary dust settles, Shakespeare will be safely relegated to the realm of pure culture, no longer tainted by the polluted sphere of public politics. *It is ultimately this desire to cleanse culture of politics* that articulates the hope that the [Central and Eastern European] Shakespeareans held for the upcoming Westernizing process: *the submersion of political commentary in Shakespearean scholarship and production during communism had been a thing of necessity,* utilized in response to restrictions on free speech in the public sphere; the hope for working democracy promised to remove this necessity, *leaving Shakespeare to soar freely towards politically-untainted heights.* (39–40, my italics)

This analysis is interesting, as it addresses a highly palpable sense of a post-communist critical paradigm shift that led critics to break out of the Marxist straitjacket. After only five years that had passed since 1989, then, the tendency in 1994 was supposedly apolitical, a reflection of a new critical climate that was no longer bound up in for-the-time-being widely discredited Marxist modes of analysis but sought to find eternal values, universalism, humanism, artistic transcendence, aesthetics, and so on.

Yet the political insights that Kostihová's 2010 book enjoys over the 1994 *Shakespeare in the New Europe* has the significant benefit of sixteen years of hindsight. A strength as well as weakness with Kostihová's book is its dystopian angle, one that axiomatically results from its critical affiliation as Cultural Materialist. Its overt and sharp critique against the European Union, against neoliberalism, post-communism, and economic globalization, grounds it in a critical tradition that has not always been able to distinguish the Shakespearean text from an often imagined and even more often very "narrow," selectively chosen, "overread" context of "colonial evocations" (Felperin 50). In the case of *The Tempest,* the vast majority of New Historicist critics and post-colonial scholars have by and large been unwilling or unable to interpret Prospero's Christian-utopian relinquishing of power as anything else than Machiavellian un-Christian cementation of power.[3] In such a view, vitally important utopian passages in the text are dismissed as a confirmation of their opposite nature, which makes any dystopian or anti-nostalgic "purchase" on the text insufficient, to say the least.

Kostihová's book is also concerned much less with the Shakespearean texts than with demonstrating "that postcommunist Czech Shakespeare has begun to serve as a newly emerging site of resistance to neoliberal practices of the neo-imperial West" (17). In fact, the first specific textual passage mentioned occurs on page 106 (a reference to *The Taming of the Shrew* in Michal Dočekal's production), and hence the book fails to point to sufficient textual proof that persuades us to accept these attacks as grounded in Shakespeare's texts or in a radical rewriting of the same. And that is perhaps the book's unarticulated modus operandi, for Kostihová's book's understanding of Shakespeare relies seemingly not so much on text as on Czech reception and reaction, which makes its attack on "conservative" reactions so needlessly feeble, failing to provide almost any specific, concrete details from the plays or sonnets that can demonstrate how invalid or insufficient or skewed interpretations are that do not arrive at conclusions espoused by Cultural Materialist critics, feminists, or post-colonialists. The book also fails to make more than one passing mention of *The Tempest,* which is a great shame, as one does not have to be a bardolatrous "presentist" to claim that the play speaks to and problematizes shell-setting utopian events and moments like 1989 in a way that still speaks louder and more meaningfully than do most critics of the same.

In short, *Shakespeare in Transition* is a work that deals with politics— Shakespeare is merely an afterthought, one whose texts are hidden away to make room for the cultural image of Shakespeare, the fawning and backward-looking, nostalgic vision that the Central and Eastern European have adopted from a victorious West. Although such criticism is pointed and relevant with regard to the sometimes uncritical intoxication over Shakespeare (or indeed over the poetics of 1989 narratives in themselves), it is not entirely clear how Shakespeare's texts figure into this criticism of (the notion of) a permanent human nature, of universal values, or of the lemming march toward pan-Europeanization, globalization, and an "end of history" that, for a time, left many post-communist citizens disappointed and financially worse off.

My own reading of both *The Tempest* and the wake of 1989 are markedly different: I see the 1989 moment as one of exactly the sort of revolutionary utopias that Prospero's reclaiming and relinquishing of power provides (no matter how short-lived) in the play. In other words, whereas Kostihová focuses on the dystopian disappointments that came after 1989, I am concerned with the utopianness and promise of the moment itself and, by extension, the climax of the play rather than the perhaps inevitable hangover of having to deal with Machiavellian schemers like Caliban, Antonio, and Sebastian. In contrast, the Eastern European critiques dealt with above seem bent on reading into the different versions of the theatrical adaptations a set of localized, Euro-skeptical, anti-globalist, and affirmative action politics that may be found in the productions themselves but which, in said readings, registers little to no contact with the Shakespearean texts. In general, one misses a greater reflection, too, of the otherness that Shakespearean outsiders like Othello, Aaron the Moor, and Shylock represent to post-colonial scholars—not to mention the towering *Tempestian* characters Prospero, Caliban, Ferdinand, Miranda, Gonzalo, and Ariel, so compelling to any Shakespearean scholar interested in identity, nationhood, language, power, and the vacuum that comes in its wake. Leaving out such characters of discussions over post-communism and post-1989 post-coloniality might be an indication of a tacit critical acceptance that Caribbean, South American, and African claims to "Calibanismo" have told their own versions of the play and that those versions constitute some Fukuyaman "end of history," when in fact there is a great contiguity between these two forms of post-coloniality.

This post-colonial continuum is elegantly articulated in the 2006 essay collection *Baltic Postcolonialism,* edited by Violeta Kelertas. Kelertas claims that "it is still unusual to see or hear the term 'postcolonial' applied to the Baltic States" and that "resistance to the application of [post-colonial] terms overlooks the facts that Russia and/or the Soviet Union were colonial empires" (Kelertas 1). In the same volume, Karl E. Jirgens also acknowledges that "the applicability of postcolonial perspectives on contemporary Baltic culture has become a contentious subject of debate" (45). Jirgens notes that "some critics challenge the validity of postcolonial analyses of the Baltic states purportedly because the 'postcolonial' approach should be restricted to capitalist, not socialist occupations" (Jirgens 46). Furthermore, since, in the words of David Chioni Moore, "many postcolonialist scholars, in the United States and elsewhere, have been Marxist or strongly on the left ... [they] have therefore been absurdly reluctant to make the Soviet Union a colonial villain on the scale of France or Britain" (Moore 20). Jirgens laments that "it was not until after the atrocities of the Gulag became painfully obvious to the world that thinkers such as Michel Foucault raised both the Soviet and the Gulag question" (Jirgens 46).

It is in the specific political context of the collection that Jūra Avižienis ventures into a post-colonial understanding of Siberian labor camp imprisonment and exile that uses *The Tempest* as an important metaphor, seen clearly in her essay's title, "Learning to Curse in Russian: Mimicry in Siberian Exile." Caliban's (meta)linguistic rebellion, she writes,

> can also be read as an affront—he is throwing Miranda's gift back in her face by using language, that "perfect instrument of empire," to demonstrate the instrument's—and the empire's—true nature. Several centuries later, *an entire colony of Baltic Calibans, isolated from the rest of the world not by sea, but by barbed wire, makes a similar gesture* .... By forcing middle-class, in large part urban, educated Lithuanians, Latvians, Estonians, and Finns to learn to survive and adapt to inhumane conditions in the camps, a new subject was created: *homo sovieticus,* a Soviet man/woman—not as s/he was defined by Communist Party propaganda—but as the product of "a flawed colonial mimesis." (Avižienis 187, my emphasis)

One is starkly reminded by Avižienis's lines of not only the keen sense of "Calibanismo" of this particular experience but, for my own part, to a much greater extent of Aleksandr Solzhenitsyn's *A Day in the Life of Ivan Denisovich,* of Stalinist excesses, of concentration camps formed in the name of revolution and liberation, of rampant Russification, of Soviet expansionism, paranoia, Kafkaesque trials, and Arielic dreams of escape.

And one might also be reminded of South Africa during and immediately after Apartheid. Marinus van Niekerk problematizes how extremely complicated reading the co-texts of oneself and one's own culture and historical experience can be when such a reading is applied to an equally dizzying primary text like *The Tempest:*

> I read *The Tempest* as my biography to express the singularity of my experience. I am the bilingual Caliban who has only one language, I am the monolingual Prospero whose language (a language which is both for the other and closes it off) is and is not the language of the oppressor, is not his. I read in this representative way precisely to also avoid representativity: I am not the postcolonial experience nor the postmodern experience nor the post-apartheid experience, though my experience may be a postmodern, postcolonial, post-apartheid one. I read in this way so that I cannot, through Shakespeare, teach about humanity, here, now, in South Africa, even as I do teach in this way, or at least attempt to say something useful. (119)

While van Niekerk does well to illustrate the postmodern ambivalence to both Shakespearean text and identity as part of a set of meanings that undercut their own validity—the Caliban who curses at the Prospero inside himself in a language that is only partly his own but fully Shakespeare, South Africa's uninvited guest—the sense of paradox also illustrates how multivalency and openness can both reveal and conceal thematic parallels found in the text that to Martin Orkin pose a clear-cut "relevance" to South African "resistance" in light of "April 1994" ("Whose Thing of Darkness" 143, 142, 144). Orkin's concerns are anti-canonical and reader-responsive-specific to the end of Apartheid and calls for a revaluation of "the perfect imperialist" interpretations "perhaps found in Kermode's renowned edition" (150). The strengths of Orkin's reading lies in its clarity of political identification with Caliban and its call for a revised understanding of the racial undertones of central words like "savage" and "slave" as these are applied to Caliban, an interpretation that aligns itself with a more presentist sensibility. With particular regard to the latter, the relative weakness of both these South African readings of the play is their failure to reflect over how, in presentist hindsight, the text itself more obviously lends itself to an interpretation that sees the country's greatest hero, Nelson Mandela, in terms of a Prosperian exile. Indeed, the fairy-tale ending to Nelson Mandela's tribulations, his return from Robben Island to the mainland of free men, black as well as white, soon-to-be president rather than political prisoner, surely poses a perfectly textually consistent Shakespearean-*Tempestian* triumph to a potentially tragic fate. Mandela's successful and bloodless takeover in power certainly seems textually far more faithful in hindsight to *The Tempest*'s dénouement than does Retamar's widely read essay "Caliban," a Cuban-Caribbean political reading that Ricardo Castells has faulted on the grounds that the Soviet-inspired Retamar was complicit in "rigorous [Revolutionary Government] suppression" (Castells 178).

It is partly therefore that I feel the need to call for a change in the way we read, in light of 1989 and 2011, perhaps as a start by a rehabilitation of previously muted voices whose long silence—and subsequently unacknowledged relevance to *Tempest* themes—was due not so much to their own lack of eloquence or topical convincingness as to the oppressive nature of the society they were at one point against. I have neither the desire nor, obviously, the ability and credibility somehow to voice the interpretations—and even less so the experiences that shape them—of people who never had the chance to speak out themselves. Yet it is suitably within the scope and purpose of this work to call for a critical *space* that can facilitate discussions of literature in general but Shakespeare's dramatic literature in particular in light of the moment that was and, hopefully, is again 1989.

It is also the *Tempest*-specific purpose of this chapter and my book in general to suggest that more thematically recent historical personages, some heroic, others deeply human—I'm thinking (rather impression-istically) of Nelson Mandela, of Desmond Tutu, of Steven Biko, of Václav Havel, Lech Walesa, and in particular of the exiled Aleksandr Solzhenitsyn—more relevantly, more hauntingly, more textually faithfully illustrate and align with *The Tempest*'s utopian themes of exile, impris-onment, escape, forgiveness, and triumph. Such recent historical figures are not by any means the only meaningful or evocative parallels to the play, but perhaps the most recently critically neglected instance in the play itself—that which pertains to Prospero's forgiveness—finds human flaws as well as heroic utopian echoes of a Nelson Mandela renouncing revenge: "You, brother mine, that entertain'd ambition, / Expell'd remorse and nature, whom, with Sebastian / (Whose inward pinches therefore are most strong), / Would here have kill'd your king, I do forgive thee, / Unnat-ural though thou art" (V.i.75–79). Furthermore, in the Epilogue, when Prospero addresses the world at large, an entity of whom the old magus has seemed most conscious also as a character throughout the play, the request for a better forgiveness than he himself has been able to muster is in itself a confirmation of such a utopian yearning: "Let me not, / Since I have my dukedom got, / And pardon'd the deceiver, dwell / In this bare island by your spell, / But release me from my bands" (Epilogue 9).

Such a "sentimental" reading would be simplistically naïve, though, not to consider the immense power such forgiveness demands, and Prospero, his ultimate designs to powerlessness and divine pardon notwithstanding, provides little in the way of solace and salvation to the minds of a modern audience in his display of a dictatorial "mercy" toward an anxious Caliban that is brief enough to be seen as an arrogant afterthought: "Go, sirrah, to my cell; / Take with you your companions. As you look / To have my pardon, trim it handsomely" (V.i.292–294). Caliban's emotional and polit-ical rebellion has just been publicly humiliated, and the dramatic situation demands it of him that he grovels here: "Ay, that I will; and I'll be wise hereafter, / And seek for grace. What a thrice-double ass / Was I to take this drunkard for a god, / And worship this dull fool" (V.i.295–298). The lines that Caliban here speaks indicate a sense of guilt and gratefulness that in the face of the very real threat of a Renaissance absolutist ruler's tor-ture is hardly rational: "I shall be pinch'd to death" (V.i.276). Hence, rather than take his words at face value in this moment of great stress, modern readers post-1989 might better apprize the levity that Caliban experiences for this stinting, brief, and conditional forgiveness in relation to that sense of momentary and schizophrenic effusiveness often experienced by polit-ical prisoners who, seemingly by some divine intervention, escaped their confinement by the "grace" and "mercy" of their captors—who would no doubt still be scrutinizing the transgressor's future conduct extremely closely.

Ariel's service is one based on a traumatic background that has instilled a fairly similar kind of irrational gratitude made possible by the release from the terror of one despot for the relative lack of discomfort of serving another in offices ranging from surveillance and intelligence gathering to bringer of potions and "dew" for magical concoctions. More complex than Aimé Césaire's facile Uncle Tom/Martin Luther King figure, Ariel could presently bear upon willing collaborators in crimes against democratic rule, as bureaucratic serfs or freewheeling *eminences grises* in totalitarian employ. Ariel, who was at one stage in unnatural bondage to Caliban's mother, Sycorax, now poses as Prospero's secret police, a crypto-bourgeois cog in the wheel of an absolutist system that coldly understands and weighs his personal urges for freedom against his continued servitude, a tension successfully prolonged by repeated promises of individual freedom's imminent fulfillment. Such Ariels will of course find myriad new parallels with every reading, yet at the risk of parroting too closely Retamar's and Marquez's absolute claims to Calibanismo: who better poses *The Tempest*'s Ariel of today if not the deeply human and flawed Stasi agent Gerd Wiesler spying on the playwright Georg Dreyman in Florian Henckel von Donnersmarck's 2006 film *The Lives of Others*?

Ferdinand and Miranda's own wish for freedom *within* the Prosperian system as the beneficiaries of a privilege that is not democratically sanctioned similarly poses a presentist irony that should not be lost on modern critics. Ferdinand plays a sycophant to Prospero's old-order system so patiently and so successfully that the young prince's character metamorphosis and subsequent plot development almost get ahead of the old magus's control. It is much to his credit as a growing politician that Ferdinand's futile initial resistance to Prospero's enslavement (I.ii.465–467)—an example of a futile mediaeval bravado that poses swords against Renaissance magic, demonology, and Machiavellianism—is swiftly left behind for more subtle modes of influence. Yet modern sensibilities will find it hard to square Ferdinand and Miranda's inherited privilege and present and future complicity in political suppression with democratic principles. The fact that both are young and likable characters who have so far found themselves entirely without power of course smooths over such concerns in much the same way Prospero's own relinquishing of power could well be said to euphemize his own rule's imperfections, exemplified by his enslavement of Ariel, Caliban, and—briefly—Ferdinand. Whereas his swift and bloodless strike-down of Stephano, Trinculo, and Caliban's rebellion is both comical and in some sense justified, his class's dismissal of their right to be heard is equally problematic for a democratic audience, especially in 2011, as we have seen.

For it is equally true that the play in its tone seems well at ease with, in fact condoning, Prosperian surveillance and his secret police Ariel. Previous scholarship has established that, for his purported similarity to Renaissance *conquistadores* and other later imperialists, Prospero cannot be trusted. Yet it is perhaps time to acknowledge the clear similarities between the play's omnipotent magus and *several* inhumane and authoritarian regimes that (like Prospero and Miranda) prescribed language, (like Prospero) governed work, allowed and disallowed creative pursuits like writing and publication, censored radio, film, television, newspapers, journals, periodicals, and theater, and imprisoned and punished the opposition. Yet despite all these uncomfortable parallels, the Erich Honeckers and Nicolae Ceauşescus of 1989 are not best associated so much with the Prospero of Shakespeare's play (though admittedly even less so with Caliban) as with Antonio and perhaps Sebastian. Prospero, in his own witness, makes the vital politically explicit point that Antonio is an illegitimate usurper of a power that belongs to, if not the people or a democratically elected representative during the Age of Absolutism, then at least to one who enjoyed "so dear the love [his] people bore [him]" as one important claim of legitimacy (I.ii.141). In fact, this democratic or meritocratic quality was the sole reason why Antonio and his co-conspirators "durst not" kill the rightful Duke and his daughter (I.ii.140).

The Polish scholar Jan Kott could claim at the chilliest time of the Cold War—to wide acceptance, much later resistance, but generally to unanimous interest and debate in the West—that Shakespeare was indeed our contemporary. As Elsom points out,

> *Shakespeare Our Contemporary* opened the floodgates to political metaphor. Connections tumbled through, some far-fetched, others closer to home. At a time when the rigours of Stalinist censorship could be felt through Eastern Europe, Shakespearean productions became a way of commenting on political events without running the risk of banning or imprisonment. Some plays, it is true, were discouraged by the authorities (such as *The Merchant of Venice* in the German Democratic Republic), but Ministries of Culture were reluctant to take arms against the work of a playwright so central to European drama. They would have made themselves look ridiculous. (2)

It is interesting to reflect on the fact that whereas there were Trojan horse productions of Shakespeare's *Richard III* in communist Eastern Europe where "Richard III limped around the stage under the weight not just of his humpback but of his Uncle Joe moustache" (Elsom 2), "[in the West] *The Tempest* became a tract against colonialism, with Caliban as an oppressed black" (3). It is both interesting and important to ponder what social and historical forces nudged the play into the service of a political cause that among intellectuals and radicals in both Europes took on such diametrically opposed views. If it is true that Shakespeare is popular worldwide because he is always our contemporary; if we can accept that his texts will necessarily be interpreted in reaction to the people, to the time and place that reacts; and if we ought to seek to make political sense of both *The Tempest* and the important events in our own times, then 1989 must be acknowledged during a time of similar upheaval in 2011.

The truth is that post-colonial critics of the play have failed to problematize these tensions. Frantz Fanon, George Lamming, or Aimé Césaire were of course in no position to assess the relevance of 1989, to some extent also of communist imperialism, but recent post-colonial scholarship has been unable or has willfully neglected to re-contextualize Shakespeare's most post-colonial-topical play with regard to those millions of people who suffered under communism, and its proponents have barely acknowledged the post-1989 moment. It is on the basis of this fact that Peter Hulme's (2000) otherwise well-intentioned panegyric on George Lamming's *Pleasures of Exile* is in dire need of updating. For where are the Prosperian parallels, in *Tempest* criticism, to a jaded and disillusioned Ivan Denisovich in his cell in the Stalinist Siberian Gulag? Why has Mandela's glorious return to the mainland not been mentioned in relation to the play? What has prevented critics from acknowledging the velvet revolutions inspired by the playwright Václav Havel? Where and when—and why not?—the fall of the Berlin Wall or the brutal massacre at Tiananmen Square and their important aftermath?

Post-colonial authors were at one stage distinctly ahead of their time. Now it seems many post-colonial critics are not even *behind* their time if that entails a certain belated acceptance of a seminal historical moment that changed paradigms. It is both imprecise and toxically polemical to speak of literary critics "being on the wrong side of history," a phrase that has become ubiquitously applied to various dictators during the Arab Spring of 2011. But in their dithering and petty hesitance to acknowledging 1989 as a post-colonial moment, many critics of Shakespeare and especially *The Tempest* run the risk of sailing adrift of a recent historical development that could resituate and recontextualize their own concerns. What I have tried to argue for in this chapter is in other words partly to call for a more *relevant* political interpretation, for a paradigm shift in terms of making use of more updated symbols and heroes. For can there be any greater triumph than 1989–1991 and 1994 for post-colonial scholars' myriad concerns over language, empowerment, return from exile, and end of imperialism and political oppression? And can there be any more interesting site of these benign impulses than the primary Shakespearean text that brings them to life when considered against its more sinister tendencies?

Conclusion: Readers vs. Text in the Age of Democracy: *The* Formalist *Tempest* or Presentist *"Tempests"*?

Reader-response critics and reception aesthetes like Wolfgang Iser have been successful in stressing that most, if not all, textual meaning resides somewhere *between* the text and the reader's mind and experience. The general tendency has been (perhaps more so among reader-response critics than with Iser) to privilege the reception and experience rather than the author or on the active making of art. However, such a readjusted focus on the beholder rather than on the artist is of course not tantamount to insisting that reading is a process independent of that which is, after all, being read, namely the text. Still, however fashionable it has become among recent scholars to point out that New Critics got carried away with their idea of the autotelic and hermetic text, the reader-response critic Stanley Fish warns against a "kind of criticism" that "practitioners of cultural studies or cultural materialism" uphold as morally superior on the basis that a "rejection of formalist criticism is a political act that demonstrates their political virtue" (9). Less kindly, perhaps, "[i]f you can link the so-called literary work with revolutionary sentiments, or with the crisis of the nation state, or with the emancipation of the liberal subject from the hegemony of religion and political tyranny, you're doing the Lord's, or rather the proletariat's, work" (10). While Fish must stand by his own Clintonism that, among several competing texts, contexts, and co-texts, "It's the poetry, stupid' " (10), my own position is also that the foremost locus of interpretative breadth and depth is the text itself—but it clearly isn't the only one. Evocative textual snippets should be—and often were, in varying degrees—read in the light of other texts by Shakespeare and viewed in fruitful relation to sources and intertexts by other authors of the Renaissance. Also, the social, historic, and cultural-material forces that helped produce these texts were widely taken into account to illuminate the work in question when the text, author, and intertexts themselves were silent or ambiguous.

As we find in *The Tempest*, a densely layered text where text, context, and co-text are frequently difficult to establish and privilege, each reader must find a reasonable balance or compromise between the textual and contextual strands of approach. The text itself is, of course, traditionally seen as more immediately relevant to meaning (i.e., quality), but this meaning, depth, or quality clearly cannot exist without breadth, quantity, discourse, history, or life itself, for that matter—not to mention an active reader. The complex nature of a text like *The Tempest*, then, makes it a very demanding play to teach—moving away from the "inner sanctum" that is the text itself often both clarifies and muddles the issues. Problematically, of course, the terms "text," "context," "co-text," and so on are themselves concepts whose relative importance to the play varies in great degree with different critics. Hence, we run the risk of a *sense* of linguistic nihilism by exhibiting the same caution and skepticism that post-structuralists as well as Marxists have traditionally done, when the terms "history" and "ideology" suffer the same postmodern fate as the "texts" or "authors" that recent criticism has sought to deconstruct. In other words, *the* Author is dead, but so are necessarily also *the* History, Ideology, and Discourses that were, supposedly, midwives to *The Tempest*.

The ultimate logical consequence of such rampant deconstruction is that authoritative meaning lies at full fathom five, and the very "words" and "concepts" of "literature" and "criticism" glide in and out of one another in a breathtakingly confusing and playful fashion. The idea of clearly delineated and defined fields like "literature," "history," and "criticism" is in other words *simply no more* since it hinges on fickle designations. In such a semiotic chaos—for so it must surely appear to many readers—few fixed truths remain. All that remains is half-told tales, slant-told "truths," and (hi)stories obscured by subjectively added color. On such wobbly ground only the text and the Noble Savage stand tall. And I would like to suggest that this *critical ground zero* is perhaps our best starting point for how to approach literature. With all questioned authorities and even disciplines under fire from a Babel-like cacophony of critical voices, in the undergraduate classroom less is necessarily more.

For in a post-postmodern and post-chaotic world, it becomes necessary to start the world all over again, in the spirit of Gonzalo's dream. In this sense it becomes meaningful to *wish* to read Adamically, to want to engage in an extremely individualistic interpretation, independently of all critical traps and theories. An Adamic reading that entails one heroic reader's unprejudiced and untainted encounter with the text in a pure and individual effort of communication is indeed how many undergraduate readers like to *think* they read. This way of reading (and way of interpreting the act of reading), even if it is naïve in the extreme with its stress on an impossible insularity and exaggerated sense of individuality, can nevertheless be enormously appealing to many. Reading Adamically over time, however, logically prevents any communication between readers and also presupposes no contact between potential readers to have taken place in the past. This extremely circumscribing attitude toward the social act of interpretation is patently not a tenable position for scholars and teachers entirely dependent on interpersonal communication.

But the desire to read "individualistically" and "in an unprejudiced fashion"—nihilistic quotation marks notwithstanding—is a valuable impulse and purpose with regard to any fresh interpretation of *The Tempest* in the sense that it forces us to invent criticism all over again. In many ways, of course, this same desire to turn back the clock to a critical ground zero is the independent impulse that has led critics to read "against the grain" and against the literary canon. The fact that we dismantle and tear down critical traditions when we are so clearly standing on the shoulders of those who came before us represents another ironic sense of discontinuous continuity. Importantly, of course, this highly schizophrenic bent has always been at the very center of the Hegelian dialectical progression of spirit and history more broadly considered. Also, in the case of *Tempest* criticism and literary criticism more generally, we have seen how scholarship is able to move forward by posing theses against antitheses, and the synthesis that ideally follows is a natural result and progression of this dialectic.

Any search for a fresh reading, for an original interpretation, for new *meaning* in a thoroughly canonical play like *The Tempest* necessarily often becomes the painstaking search for a very slim niche within existing methodologies, for instance by unearthing some previously unknown documents, tracts, pamphlets, or sermons that can speak about, question, and re-illuminate texts and past critical authorities. Few "schools" or sustained impulses in literary and cultural scholarship have been more successful in these latter attempts than have the practitioners of New Historicism vis-à-vis Shakespeare's last unassisted play. Cultural Materialist scholarship, too, has done extremely well to argue the case that a(n) (in)visible censorship has often been politically at work in a tradition that claimed to operate beyond politics—and to identify, move, and overstep the accepted boundaries of interpretations that the latter have managed to establish. These struggles are in many ways a fight over intellectual hegemony, accepted meaning, and institutionalized opinion that in the Renaissance saw its natural culmination with the schism caused by Martin Luther's Reformation. Thus, as theologians have interpreted Scriptures, as historians have (re)written the texts of history to fit their own (or their patrons') political agendas, so also practitioners of literary criticism have sought to establish accepted interpretations of canonical texts, readings that align themselves with certain political expediencies, whether these be nationalism, communism, crypto-capitalistic bardolatry and neo-colonial tourism, or modern multiculturalism. For their part, the most valuable ways in which New Historicism and Cultural Materialism have redefined what was perceived as an intellectually closed literary scholarship forward lie in their refusal to treat texts as hermetic and autotelic, independent artifacts that somehow ought to be studied in isolation from the forces that clearly helped shape them.

Still, however useful such textual and cultural archeology is to our understanding of the complex forces that go into the production of text, its weakness with regard to *The Tempest* lies not so much in its willingness and tendency to venture outside of traditionally understood textual scholarship but rather in its choosing to downplay those primary-textual tensions that, for 400 years, have yet to be satisfactorily resolved. For by moving outside of the text, by shifting the focus away from the Shakespearean text, one runs the perhaps unintended risk of presuming that closer methods of analysis have already been exhausted and found wanting, that the textual point of departure or "springboard" is a settled matter. To the extent that this book employs original modes of reading, they lie in a fusion of presentism, historicism, and a formalism that in concert can reveal, as I have hoped to demonstrate, some textual and cultural problems that are now seldom treated as such—the island's geographical anti-setting and Caliban's political scheming, to mention just two. An abandonment of either method—close reading, historicist archeology, or attention to our current cultural co-text—would not yield the same finds. It is for this reason increased study of a sometimes neglected primary text is paramount.

Such an emphasis seems especially justified in light of the great desire to set the record straight that is at the core of the political branch of literary and cultural theory, which moreover often serves a clearly leftist political agenda, typically taking the form of anti-colonial and post-colonial analyses of *The Tempest*'s assumed involvement in New World history. Here, both the text and its author have become vulnerable to unconvincing accusations of the arrogance, racism, imperialism, and inhumanity displayed in the European colonies at the time the play was written. Not only does the political thrust of such discussions seem curiously tainted with

an anachronistic bias, but presenting—indeed *presentizing*—the historical conditions of Renaissance England and colonial Virginia as the *real* or
dominant concerns of *The Tempest* often requires a sense of textual elasticity that borders on taking fictional liberties with regard to both literature
and history. As B. J. Sokol has remarked,

> [i]t is very important to differentiate artistic re-writings or renditions from
> scholarly and critical interpretations. There is nothing wrong—and quite a
> lot that is interesting—in the many post-colonial appropriations of *The Tem-
> pest* that have re-written the play to reach conclusions dictated by latter-day
> "moral and sociopolitical agendas"; however, logical difficulties arise when
> such agendas direct literary scholarship which lays claim to an historical
> grasp. The trouble is not that moral outrage anachronistically mis-targets
> supposed offenders or cultural productions; this kind of condemnation can
> be answered on the basis of historical evidence, or even sometimes internal
> evidence.... The greater problem is that an emphasis on anachronistic con-
> cerns (or the need to retort to this emphasis) interferes with needed analysis
> of the subtle interactions of literary and historical matters. (79)

The fertile ground and "interaction" that ideally exists between history and
literature is nevertheless often tilted toward recent interpretations where,
for example, several textual passages from the play might clearly suggest
a Mediterranean sphere for the play's setting but where more credence is
given to the one passage that might suggest an American-Atlantic geography or culture for setting. Thus, selective and partial bits and pieces are
taken out of con-*text* and measured for quality or meaning with an imprecise and subjectively fickle scale. In other words, the individual critic's
ability to find a plausible historical or discursive parallel to the *single passage* rather than to the *totality* of the text decides its significance, Eric
Cheyfitz's blanket identification of Caliban as a Native American being
one example where "subtle interactions" between "literary and historical
matters" are actually prevented from taking place.

These creative adaptations and critical readings have at any rate managed to ground *The Tempest* as perhaps Shakespeare's most political play.
Yet there are sound reasons to question the *extent* to which the play can
be said to be involved in what is traditionally understood as politics.
For instance, rather than political creatures, Gonzalo, Ariel, Ferdinand,
Miranda, and the repentant Alonso are presented as primarily *ethical*
beings, and their desires are religious, pastoral, and freedom-seeking in
nature. The play also puts great emphasis on the moral regeneration of
Prospero, who is able to extend his forgiveness to his usurping brother
Antonio in the end as well as to the other political conspirators. The cynics

are defeated, order and some degree of liberty and attendant responsibility are restored, and all is seemingly peaceably settled by Prospero's pardon. His Christian act of forgiveness, then, combined with a cunning, almost Machiavellian scheme to regain the power that enables him to forgive in the first place, forms an acceptable ending to a political struggle that is counterpointed at various stages with radical visions, culminating in a happy union of marriage where the innocent characters Miranda and Ferdinand are also reunited with their parents. To some, of course, a critical stress on this perhaps too tidy and sugary ending might be the very manifestation of "Ben Jonson's monstrous vision: an eternally relevant Shakespeare for all time, bloated by the gassy values he is presumed to endorse, and blandly ballooning above the world's disparate cultures to dispense, as Superbard, some universal industrial-strength unction for the soul. Love, usually" (Hawkes, "No escaping" 2). But with its primarily cheery and quite often utopian tone and atmosphere, the play clearly owes a debt to the genre of the romance and is also heavily influenced by Christian-pastoral motifs that see Christ as the ultimate shepherd of men. Christ is of course absent from the play, but *The Tempest* displays a spirit that is benevolently Christian-humanist in its stress on practical generosity, compassion, love, and forgiveness. Also, the utopian dimensions of the play here stress the personal relationships that already existed and the relationships that are being formed and strengthened in a manner that puts the emphasis on familial love and friendship. In this sense, of course, the seemingly miraculous familial unions and reunions that Prospero *politically* as well as psychologically orchestrates engender feelings of profound relief and happiness in a way that develops from the political sphere into a much more complex familial and emotional dimension.

While it is true that such a ploy to move his own "play's" concerns away from politics might be seen as the ultimately Machiavellian move that cements Prospero's power, the play importantly seems convergent with Prospero's vision by fusing pastoral impulses with religious virtues in a way that allows us to see them as part of the same utopian yearning for a better world. The problem is that the play does not do so without giving voice to radical passages and explicitly radical utopian material that it does not fully manage to contain or reconcile. Such passages are interspersed and convergent with motifs that envision an anarchical sense of freedom. Much of *this* impulse, in turn, has to do with setting. For the freedom of expression that characters like Gonzalo, Caliban, Stephano, and Trinculo experience in the play is a direct result of the sense of free pastoral nature that the setting affords. As Julie Robin Solomon has argued in her article on absolutism and movement in *The Tempest*, "an analysis of movement's significance may be the best way to apprehend the play's intervention into the increasingly conflicted discourse of monarchical sovereignty in early-seventeenth-century England" (4). Furthermore, to Solomon, "travel replaces the Jacobean metaphor of magic as the trope which best delineates the process by which human beings empower themselves through knowing" (12). On the island, when spatially removed from the rulers of Milan, Naples, and Tunis, authority in its conventional and civilized form ceases to exist, and the resultant vacuum in power furnishes a space in which speech is not censored but empowered. In a place that exists almost totally outside of censorship, the characters in the play experiment with freedom of speech in a way that might be seen as analogous to the way Hamlet explores the same issue in his play-within-the-play. As such, it is possible to see *The Tempest*'s stress on freedom and frank expression as a veiled political commentary against censorship per se. *The Tempest* can thus be said to deal with the power to speak and the power to disobey in a way that is both a subversive and an important part of the play's utopian ethos.

We also see in both the play and in its adaptations and criticism that the act, or *art*, of reading is not only a desire to hear and listen in peace and quiet, but also a sometimes unarticulated wish to *be* heard, a wish to share, a longing for good company, social acceptance, respect, love— a greater sense of existential meaning. In other words, reading is a social activity, as active as it is passive. And it is in this activity that one finds the frequent wish to *speak back* to the medium itself, which we see so clearly in Caliban's frustrated attack on Prospero's language. I see Caliban's anger as part of a more universal human desire to re-inscribe the text, history, the past, and present, with *new* meaning, new dialogue, to intervene to become part of the work of literature oneself, and ultimately change it in one's own image. Nowhere can this longing be seen more clearly than in Gonzalo, in Aimé Césaire, and in George Lamming. The act of reading, in this light, is in many ways a question of power, the power to leave one's mark on the world, to be heard, understood, and respected. This wish comes not without its attendant ironies. Note, for example, Antonio's and Sebastian's saucy remarks about the thinly disguised tyranny in Gonzalo's reverie: he wants to do away with a structure of power that stifles rather than encourages free interpretation and expression. But Gonzalo's initially positive attitude to free speech can best be seen in relief with his exchange with the seemingly death-bound Boatswain in the play's opening storm scene. Here, the Boatswain fails to observe good taste and class decorum when he defiantly berates the noblemen for their unnecessary interruptions: "What cares these roarers for the name of king? To cabin! silence! trouble us not" (I.i.16–18). In other words, the sailor implies that the elements are stronger than whatever kings might be aboard the ship—and for this he is chastised by the self-same Gonzalo. Hence, in light of Gonzalo's insistence on courtly decorum, the irony later becomes apparent, and Antonio and Sebastian's cynical interjections into his utopian passage are thus validated. For Gonzalo's search for a new and freer society is undercut by his chastisement (humorous or otherwise) of the foulmouthed Boatswain.

As regards Stephano and Trinculo, they have little occasion to air their views—such Shakespearean privileges seem to be the time-and-place-conditional prerogative of theater-obsessed princes, desperate sailors, cross-dressing noblewomen, and court jesters only. And for Stephano and Trinculo free speech was never anything but a mirage, an alcohol-induced and delirious fantasy for which they pay by being soaked in urine in the horse-pond. But even though the issue of free speech is fraught with pointed ironies here, the play's utopian thrust (of which freedom of motion and expression form an important part) is best illustrated by Gonzalo's admittedly schizophrenic position and Caliban's dearly bought license to curse. Both Caliban and Gonzalo (and we as critical readers, too, perhaps) feel a great urge to rearrange the world according to their own design, but it is of course not in their power to do so. In Peter Greenaway's film adaptation *Prospero's Books,* it is instead Prospero alone who wields this total power, obviously playing on the idea of the omnipotent Author, very probably gesturing toward Shakespeare himself. And in a climate that prizes books and the printed word above the might of dukedoms (for so Prospero once thought) and where words of poetry immortalize and almost raise people from the dead (cf. Shakespeare's Sonnets 73 and 74), this power is vitally important in *The Tempest.* We note with interest, for example, that Prospero's magical prowess seems to reside in printed form, as words in books, and that his powers are broken as soon as these printed works are drowned. But most vitally, the right and the freedom to speak is an issue that forms an essential part of the utopian ideology found in the play. This freedom is in turn greatly dependent on the relative emptiness and vastness of the setting, which in its pastoral nature furnishes a set of religious, spiritual, and cultural discourses that are also highly relevant to later New World history and American literature. For this reason, rather than on the grounds of physical and geographical setting, we may say that *The Tempest* displays an American ethos, and hence the play's sense of utopian Americanness comments in an intersecting way on its ever-ambiguous setting.

Much as utopian modes of approach can be linked to the New World in the historical light of 1611, their presentist complexion 400 years later will be colored by different symbols and metaphors, most fruitfully, as I have suggested, by the revolutions of 1989 and 2011. I was an impressionable Western European youth of fifteen when the Berlin Wall came down, and hence the "Meaning of 1989" (or its problematic—in the case of Yugoslavia, cataclysmic—aftermath) is hardly a history that I am most credibly equipped to understand or write. Still, I call for a revised understanding of *The Tempest* in light of this moment because Shakespeare criticism in general has not sufficiently recognized the epoch as one of positive progression and potential. In its wake, we have seen the emergence of eco-criticism, a strengthened queer theory, some reformed but waning offshoots of Marxism, and various forms of liberal feminism and post-colonialism. These are general trends that in sum make Shakespearean scholarship strengthened and more engaged with contemporary problems, dovetailing the presentism that Grady and Hawkes' 2007 book *Presentist Shakespeares* calls for. Yet the marked tendency of such critical strands toward a backward-looking, nostalgic yearning for a distinctly Western-Eurocentric understanding of the moment that was 1968 is due for revision. In light of the staggering political upheavals of 2011, a post-1989 utopian prism is one possible and useful way of discovering *new* dimensions that this previous and, quite paradoxically, dystopian mode has allowed, perhaps especially if such a presentist "purchase on Shakespeare"—Cultural Materialist, New Historicist, post-colonial, reader responsive—manages to fuse its various worthwhile social and political concerns with a credible sense of textualism.

Notes

Introduction

1. Graham Bradshaw had castigated critics like Greenblatt, Fieldler, Traversi, Sinfield, and Dollimore two years earlier, in 1993, for the same tendency. See Graham Bradshaw, *Misrepresentations: Shakespeare and the Materialists* (London: Cornell University Press, 1995), especially 1–33.
2. Citations will be to the Riverside edition (1997) unless otherwise specified.
3. In order to arrive at some explanation of this seemingly self-contradictory stance it is in many ways tempting to conduct one's own informal "new historicist" (and to some extent also a "cultural materialist") analysis of the phenomenon that is New Historicism (and, of course, Cultural Materialism). The language and terminology, the ideological zeal, the issues at hand—in other words, the historical "discourse"—is prime New Historicist "evidence" that the tenor of their arguments coincide with some larger political project around the time most of the articles were written. These articles are in other words a reflection of the scholars' training in academia in the 1960s and 1970s (and, in Europe, until the fall of the Berlin Wall)—an institution that was thrown into a process of upheaval of old traditions, rapidly forming revolutionary ideas and ideological bases from which to interpret texts—and these are bases that correspond quite well with the political-ideological thrust of many New Historicist and Cultural Materialist stances vis-à-vis *The Tempest*. Whether it be focus on revolutions in third world countries, the ousting of old colonialist powers, redefinition and hybridization of indigenous cultures, or simply polemical articles over the perceived racism in the play, one would be hard-pressed to find no more than a handful of issues dealt with academically that were not, at the same time in history, addressing a trademark leftist political argument. Hence, it makes as much sense to see the issues that these critics have raised over the text in light of their own historical moment as it does to see the text of the play in light of the colonial and imperial issues they so readily point to as a valuable backdrop to *The Tempest*. It is this particular lack of self-insight that Ivo Kamps has recently argued is the main weakness in New Historicist critics like Stephen Greenblatt. See Ivo Kamps, "New Historicizing the New Historicism; or, Did Stephen Greenblatt Watch the Evening News in 1968?" *Historicizing Theory*, ed. Peter C. Herman (Albany, NY: University of New York Press, 2004), 159–189.

Chapter 1

1. Translation from Danish is mine.
2. Graff and Phelan do not openly declare an affiliation with new historians or with post-colonialism but somewhat densely hint that readers should easily find out where they stand. An (imaginary) splenetic male "traditionalist" professor of a certain age not wanting to engage in an open discussion at all with the students about post-colonial issues that he has no time for himself hints that position away, however. An interesting side question to this humorous portrayal is whether it is an acceptable premise that those professors who espouse post-colonial theories are somehow less absolutist, more musically attuned to the students' youthful and open sensibilities. Graff and Phelan's contribution nevertheless feels post-political and post-partisan— although it remains an open question how *un*political a work can be that fails to challenge or even question the hegemonic paradigms. For all that, their book remains the preeminent source for those interested in *Tempestian* pedagogy.

Chapter 2

1. I am indebted here to Marjorie Levinson, who writes of "reinstat[ing] close reading both at the curricular center of our discipline and as the opening move, preliminary to any kind of critical consideration" (560). Marjorie Levinson, "What Is New Formalism?," PMLA 122.2 (March 2007): 558–569.
2. I shall be assuming throughout that Italian really is "my/our language," as the nominal Italians Ferdinand, Trinculo, and Stephano all put it.
3. In his 1987 Signet edition of the play, Robert Langbaum glosses Sycorax's name as a Greek composite: "*Sycorax* (name not found elsewhere; probably derived from Greek *sys*, 'sow,' and *korax*, which means both 'raven'—see line 322—and 'hook'—hence perhaps 'hoop')." William Shakespeare, *The Tempest*, ed. Robert Langbaum (New York: Signet Penguin, 1987) 51.
4. In Ronald Herder's Dover edition, Setebos is glossed as "the greatest of the devils in Patagonian worship (from an early account of Magellan's voyage)." William Shakespeare, *The Tempest*, ed. Ronald Herder (Mineola, NY: Dover Publications, 1999) 14.
5. The Riverside edition explains the reference as "the legendary harp of Amphion, which raised the walls of Thebes. Gonzalo's error has created whole new city." William Shakespeare, *The Riverside Shakespeare, The Tempest* (Boston: Houghton Mifflin Company, 1997) 1669.
6. Philip Whitefield, *The Simon and Schuster Encyclopedia of Animals* (New York: Simon & Schuster, 1998).
7. 2 *Macmillan Encyclopedia* 1996, ed. Alan Isaacs. (Aylesbury, England: Market House Books, 1995).

8. John Gillies, however, citing Sidney Lee, claims that the word "fish-dams" is a particularly American or Virginian term, as English colonizers often admired the ability of the Indians to catch fish, and realized that they relied in a great degree on fish for their own survival. See "The Figure of the New World in *The Tempest*," in *The Tempest and Its Travels*, 198.

9. These are in many ways a problematic couple of lines, since Ariel, who speaks them, is lying to the Milanese and Neapolitan officials. He does so in order not to reveal Prospero's grand master plan and reconfirms the shipwrecked party's initial supposition—and that of the play's header—that the island is uninhabited. Hence, it might not have much credibility vis-à-vis the physical setting, even though it clearly does on the textual and dramatic levels. See also Smith, who claims that a similar sloppiness can be detected in the reference to the "filthy-mantled pool near Prospero's cell that is indubitably a horse-pond (IV.i.182, 200) yet no horses are in evidence" (6–7).

Chapter 3

1. The latest trend in this undertaking has been argued by Terence Hawkes and Hugh Grady in their *Presentist Shakespeares*, a work that sets out to relativize our understanding of the past—and especially literature written in a distant past—as inevitably colored by our present assumptions. Texts like Shakespeare's are accordingly changed, altered, and modified by our own involvement and sensibilities, but this involvement is fruitful because, according to Hawkes and Grady, it is the only one we can possibly make.

2. This is a recent tendency that several critics note: see, for example, Hamlin 20.

3. We know next to nothing about how Renaissance productions of *The Tempest* presented Caliban—the earliest review of Caliban's theatrical appearance, based on the influential Dryden-Davenant production *The Tempest; Or, The Enchanted Island*, an adaptation that would dominate the theater for the next 150 years, dates from Samuel Pepys' diary on May 11, 1668. According to Pepys, Caliban was simply cast as a "monster," with no further description given (the Vaughans, *Caliban* 174).

4. Caliban's mother's eyes, it should be noted, could be seen also as "ringed and bagged in blue," which Fiedler mentions, and not blue "like those of some fair girl." Thus, he takes this as evidence that, "on his mother's side, [Caliban] was an African" (205). Leah Marcus questions whether the modern critical tendency that consistently denies that Sycorax' "blew" eyes mean that she is "a blue-eyed Algerian" is perpetuated because "blue eyes . . . are associated with the Anglo-American imperialist . . . rather than with the colonized peoples" (5–17).

5. For a discussion on New World discourse in the play, see also Baldo 138–139.

6. It is important to remember that this "formula" also applies to countries like Canada, New Zealand, and Australia, which are both the victims and

perpetrators of international and intranational colonization, respectively. Brydon holds that in Canada, there has been a marked tendency to see Canada and Canadians through the lens of *The Tempest* as obedient Mirandas rather than rebellious Calibans. This preference, Brydon claims, is a reflection of a national character and history peculiar to Canadians, who are "reluctant to deal openly with Caliban," on the basis, she feels, that Canada has a history of racism and colonization of its own (87).

7. Interestingly, the Vaughans speaks of a "thirty-year gap" between scholarly articles and theatrical productions, in the sense that it took the theaters an extra thirty years to cast Caliban as a black man after the interpretation was commonplace with critics. In other words, the theater can be seen as either more conservative or more democratic than critical views, since it represents Caliban "more clearly how he was conceived by each generation as a whole, not just by editors and scholars" (173). However, Caliban's topical reign supreme may now be a thing of the past; in the program for London's Tara Arts Theatre production of the play in January 2008, director Jatinder Verma's focus is firmly on Prospero, linking him to Ayman al-Zawahiri, "Bin Laden's right-hand man, a learned doctor confined in a cave somewhere in the desolate border between north-west Pakistan and Afghanistan, plotting vengeance on the West to 'recover the purity' of his homeland, Egypt" (n.p.).

8. See Cheyfitz 89.

9. That is to say, derived from *pathos,* emotion.

10. The term was coined by the Franco-Argentine author Paul Groussac during a speech in Buenos Aires in 1898, reacting against the Spanish-American War.

11. See Jonathan Gil Harris for a critique on how historicizing criticism fails to historicize itself and admit its own prejudices.

12. For excellent discussions on Christianity in the play, cf. John D. Cox and Robert Grams Hunter.

13. Caliban calls Stephano a "god" and his liquor "celestial" (II.ii.117), though Caliban treats the alcohol more than Stephano as godly but always with a political aim—he is the one in control of the situation.

14. Because of the passage's harshness, many believe that the lines are intended to be delivered by Prospero.

15. As early as in 1885, F. W. Fairholt noted that gabardines "were peculiarly indicative of Jews, when that persecuted people were obliged to wear a distinctive dress, principally of that and the tall yellow cap" (176).

16. It is in this textually defined and *con*fined sense Frank Kermode was right when he made his by now infamous claim that "[t]here is nothing in *The Tempest* fundamental to its structure of ideas which could not have existed had America remained undiscovered and the Bermuda voyage never taken place" (xxxiv).

17. "Hag," according to the *American Heritage Dictionary,* is derived from the Old English word "*hægtesse,*" meaning "1. An ugly old woman. 2. A witch; sorceress." "Hag," *American Heritage Dictionary,* 1994 ed. It may have come from the

Scandinavian "*haugtuss(a)*," which literally means "(the) troll of the hills." The word "whelp" is defined as "1. A young offspring of an animal, such as a dog or wolf. 2. An impudent youth." "Whelp." Caliban is certainly impudent, and the sense of animality is only emphasized by the connotation/denotation to a dog. Also this word has an Old English origin—"*hwelp*"—as well as a Nordic homophone and parallel in "*valp*," or puppy dog. The Old English-Scandnavian link is important in the sense that Caliban's name, which may very well be an anagram of "*Can(n)ibal*" or version of "*Carib[be]an*," may help establish his geographical origin, as we saw in the second chapter. The distinctly Northern European words that describe Caliban here—as opposed to, for example, "canis," "vulpus," or Sycorax as a "furia"—could possibly hint that Caliban should be initially seen in an English folkloric context, and perhaps also in light of neighbouring locales.

18. This point has been noted by many scholars—see, for example, Vaughan and Vaughan's *Caliban* (10).

19. Barbara Baert calls for a redefining our narrowly understood "wild man" into a broader and more detailed concept that extends outside literature. Baert stresses that there are myriad sources for the "wild man": (1) Pliny's *Historia Naturalis* from 77 B.C.; (2) Solinus's *Collectanea Rerum Memorabilium* from the fifth century A.D.; and (3) Nymphs, satyrs, mermaids, and mermen who are usually either Indo-Germanic or Indo-European in origin. Among the latter group, the Wodewose and the Green Man of the forests thus belong to the Indo-Germanic realm, while the hairy and animal-like creature belongs to the Indo-European tradition (45–46). Caliban's "bestial lusts" lust naturally affirm him as a wild man (49) but owes much to both the Wodewose of the Forest as well as to the animal-like Indo-European variant.

20. See also Sir Arthur Quiller-Couch for a discussion of this particular cross—in a proto-Kristevan exercise in intertextual criticism, Quiller-Couch was quick to point out that especially folkloric and theatrical sources are a fleeting and indefinable factor in determining a play's intellectual origin in Europe, since the countries, even in 1610–11, were so closely connected and interdependent. Hence, he makes a credible case for England when he claims that the (ur-)play might as well have been introduced the other way round, from England to Germany (14–15).

21. Cf. Tom McAlindon's excellent article on the discourse of cursing and blessing in *The Tempest*. McAlindon also suggests that Caliban's name be seen as Greek in etymology, especially when Caliban screams out his song of "freedom" where he plays on the rhythm of his own name by singing it as "'Ban, 'Ban, Ca-Caliban," which in Greek translates as "bad" as well as giving stress to the English word "ban" ("to curse") (137–149).

22. John Cox has done well to stress the role of religion in *The Tempest*, especially Prospero's eventual forgiveness. Robert Grams Hunter makes the useful point that Prospero's court masque is essentially like the Holy Communion, where Alonso can go to and eat and be forgiven for his past transgressions.

23. Another reading that has been suggested by Terence Hawkes argues that the relationships between the diverse characters in the play "find their nourishment in the ancient home-grown European relationships of master and servant, landlord and tenant." Delabatista holds that Hawkes feels such readings "cannot be divorced from the discursive field of the enclosure movement which was in full swing in Shakespeare's very own Warwickshire during the play's composition" (Delabatista 6). However, in cases of anachronistic readings of *The Tempest*, "Caliban then becomes a mere emblem of the interpreter's own situation" (6).

24. In this increasingly democratic hermeneutic environment, it seems almost curious that Caliban has not yet been presented as a Viking, despite the fact that he clearly fits the ticket as an uncouth and illiterate would-be rapist with a hefty appetite for alcohol, a wild man possessing great physical strength and good survival skills. The pagan Vikings also kept thralls, much like Prospero keeps Ariel and Caliban in service for a limited time. If Shakespeare had read or at least heard about the early Viking raids on the monastery at Lindisfarne and later on coastal villages in Northeastern England, we might suggest with a far less peripheral geographical "match" vis-à-vis the core that, from this possible biographical and discursive detail, Caliban might indeed be seen as a marauding Norseman and that the play's setting should therefore be reconsidered and read in the context of North Sea pillage, trade, and late pagan tradition of the Middle Ages rather than the Mediterranean of the Italian city-states or the Atlantic Ocean of the English Renaissance.

25. Malone links Caliban to Robin Goodfellow (Vol. XV, 11–14).

26. Paul Franssen addresses exactly this sense of locating one's own self in Caliban: Shakespeare's "salvage and deformed slave" becomes a "dark mirror" or a "walking screen for projection" (23–42).

27. Cf. James W. Coleman's *Black male fiction and the legacy of Caliban*, which operates with an idea of "Calibanic discourse" as a term to account for the ills of African American society in general and males in particular, as they are manifested in both real life and black male novels.

Chapter 4

1. In an article published in 1995, Asselin Charles claims that "Marxism challenged the very foundation of colonialism to the extent that it targeted the very economic system, capitalism, responsible for colonial exploitation" (148). Charles reads Shakespeare's *The Tempest* and Césaire's *Une Tempête* through this particular ideological lens and goes on to say that, in spite of a "chorus of freedom fighters and spokesmen for the colonized, which include such towering figures of our times as Frantz Fanon, Fidel Castro, Che Guevara, Ho Chi Minh, Mao Zedong, Patrice Lumumba, Malcolm X, Julius Nyerere," the third world countries are still "replete with Ariels at the service of Western Prosperos, speaking for and from the standpoint of their masters" (150). Asselin Charles, "Colonial

Discourse Since Christopher Columbus," *Journal of Black Studies* 26.2 (1995): 134–152.

2. Jonathan Hart repeats Gordon Brotherston's argument that questions the historically accepted notion that the natives of the New World "had no writing" (60). It is Brotherston's contention that Europeans tried to neglect or "eradicate" cases of literacy among the natives "because it posed a threat to the Scripture (the Bible) they brought with them" (60). Jonathan Hart, "Images of the Native in Renaissance Encounter Narratives," *ARIEL: A Review of International English Literature* 25.4 (1994): 55–76.

Chapter 5

1. We predictably find myriad examples of this traditional sense of manhood in Castiglione, Spenser, Sidney, Jonson, Marlowe, and Wyatt, for instance. While our own critical preoccupations tend to incline us toward a study of how manliness in literature can be negotiated, earned, increased, or decreased, it is worth keeping in mind that male characters in Renaissance literature very often *do* behave in a conventionally understood masculine way. For an excellent discussion of how masculinities are manifested and refined by tears and grief in a fluid social process in a wide range of Renaissance literary selections, please consult Jennifer Vaught, *Masculinity and Emotion in Early Modern English Literature* (Aldershot, England: Ashgate, 2008).

2. Miranda has also been interpreted as displaying a particular mentality that one may find in, for example, Canada, New Zealand, and Australia, countries that are both the victims and perpetrators of international and intranational colonization, respectively. Diana Brydon, "Re-Writing *The Tempest*," *World Literature Written in English* 23, 1 (1984): 75–88. Brydon mentions that in Canada, there has been a marked tendency among writers like Gottlieb, Laurence, and Charles G. D. Roberts, to see Canada and Canadians through the lens of *The Tempest* as obedient Mirandas rather than rebellious Calibans. This preference, Brydon claims, is a reflection of a national character and history peculiar to Canadians, who are "reluctant to deal openly with Caliban," (87) on the basis, she feels, that Canada has a history of racism and colonization of its own.

3. Please see note 8.

4. The parallels that Miranda in her isolation poses to tragic present-day cases of enforced enclosement like Josef Fritzl's recent atrocities are topically tempting to us, yet feminists and psychoanalytic critics would be well advised to survey the psychic territory that these sorts of parallels pose to Miranda's education with a clear separation between case and text, not always a strength in recent critical discourse on the play. Most feminist critics have nevertheless done well to discuss how Miranda has been raised and educated to be a wife to any politically advantageous suitor, her sense of individuality firmly controlled by Prospero.

5. Much though I am indebted to Eric Cheyfitz, his book fails to recognize or even discuss Ferdinand as a possible Shakespearean New World avatar of Edgar Rice

Burroughs's Anglo-African lord: the nobleman who thrives better in a primitive setting, the one whose innate nobility is enabled only by his encounters with primitive tribes and wild animals. Eric Cheyfitz, *The Poetics of Imperialism: Translation and Colonization from The Tempest to Tarzan* (Philadelphia: University of Pennsylvania Press, 1997).

6. The Vaughans mention that in 1974, "Denis Quilley's Caliban at London's National Theatre was likened by reviewers to James Fenimore Cooper's Chingachgook," but importantly as a hybrid creature comprising two sides, one of which was a "noble savage," the other an "ugly deformed monster" (Vaughan and Vaughan, *Caliban* 192). This observation is as important here as it is with a view to Caliban's origin and the play's location, since the politically motivated tendency to confuse Gonzalo's dream with Caliban's characteristics often identifies Caliban as *the* New World *topos* of the play, a very common red herring in much recent scholarship. See Frank W. Brevik, "Calibans Anonymous: The Journey from Text to Self in Modern Interpretations of *The Tempest*," *Authority of Expression in Early Modern England,* ed. Nely Keinänen and Maria Salenius (Newcastle-upon-Tyne: Cambridge Scholars Publishing, 2009), especially 188.

7. And yet, as David Scott Wilson-Okamura reminds us, Prospero, unlike Ferdinand, but "like Gonzalo . . . exhibits a marked aversion to manual labor" (725). Clearly, though, Prospero's settler attitude and Gonzalo's utopian speech set them apart as American Adams but in different ways from Ferdinand's experience. In other words, as the American experience is a many-faceted phenomenon, so *The Tempest* draws on situations that might or might not be termed American situations with equally liberal definitions in mind. David Scott Wilson-Okamura, "Virgilian Models of Colonization in Shakespeare's *Tempest,*" *ELH* 70 (2003): 709–737.

8. Related to power and the naming of such "potencies," there is also great confusion involved in that, for the entire play the key word "master" can mean at least four things: the ship master, who has conveniently exited just previous to this scene; God; the sea itself, nature, part of God's creation; or either King Alonso of Naples or the Duke of Milan, Antonio. This is a frenetic passage where references go unaddressed, misaddressed, and seem to give us a foretaste of what is to come with regard to the play's ludic and postmodern use of geography. See also Tom MacAlindon's wonderful work on the discourse of prayer in *The Tempest:* Tom MacAlindon, *Shakespeare Minus "Theory"* (Aldershot: Ashgate, 2004).

Chapter 6

1. Of course, Dover Wilson neglects the important interdiction against mentioning the names of God and Christ in the theaters. Instead, their omnipotent counterparts—where they could be found—were sought in figures like Zeus and Jupiter in Greek and Roman mythology instead. But Dover Wilson's argument stands, since such surrogate deities are also conspicuously otiose in the play.

2. The "Indians," of course, were not from India and not at all "American" in any meaningful sense until Amerigo Vespucci had returned to have the entire continent named after him, which provides a good example of the sort of cultural, linguistic, and anthropological mazy paradoxes the New World-Old World duality comprises.

Chapter 7

1. See Kamps, 159–181.
2. See also Werner Habicht, 172.
3. John Cox's article's title speaks volumes: "Recovering Something Christian about *The Tempest.*" *Christianity and Literature* 50.1 (2000): 31–51.

Works Cited

Abrahams, Roger D. "Folklore and Literature as Performance." *Journal of the Folklore Institute* 9 (1972): 75–94.

Aercke, Kristiaan P. " 'An Odd Angle of the Isle': Teaching the Courtly Art of *The Tempest.*" *Approaches to Teaching Shakespeare's the Tempest and Other Late Romances.* Ed. Maurice Hunt. New York: Modern Language Association of America, 1992. 146–52.

Amanda Bailey and Roze Hentschell, *Masculinity and the Metropolis of Vice.* New York: Palgrave Macmillan, 2010.

Arnold, A. James. "Césaire and Shakespeare: Two *Tempests.*" *Comparative Literature* 30 (1978): 236–48. *Academic Search Premier.* U of Louisiana at Lafayette Edith Garland Dupré Library. 28 Apr. 2005 <http://search.epnet.com/>.

Avižienis, Jūra. "Learning to Curse in Russian: Mimicry in Siberian Exile." *Baltic Postcolonialism.* Ed. Violeta Kelertas. Amsterdam: Rodopi, 2006. 187–202.

Baert, Barbara. "Caliban as a Wild Man: An Iconographical Approach." *Constellation Caliban: Figurations of a Character.* Amsterdam: Rodopi BV, 1997.

Bach, Rebecca Ann. "*Mrs. Caliban*: A Feminist Postmodernist *Tempest?*" *Critique: Studies in Contemporary Fiction* 41.4 (2000): 391–402.

Baldo, Jonathan. "Exporting Oblivion in *The Tempest.*" *Modern Language Quarterly* 56.2 (1995): 111–45.

Baker, David J. "Where Is Ireland in *the Tempest?*" *Shakespeare and Ireland.* London: Macmillan, 1997. 68–88.

Barker, Francis and Peter Hulme. "*The Tempest* and Oppression." *The Tempest: A Casebook.* Ed. D.J. Palmer. London: Macmillan, 1988.

Bartolovich, Crystal. " 'Baseless Fabric': London as a 'World City.' " *The Tempest and Its Travels.* Ed. Peter Hulme and William H. Sherman. Philadelphia, PA: U of Pennsylvania P, 2000. 13–26.

Belsey, Catherine. "Historicizing New Historicism." *Presentist Shakespeares.* Ed. Hugh Grady and Terence Hawkes. Abingdon, Oxon.: Routledge, 2007.

Berger, Harry. "Introduction to *The Shepheardes Calender.*" *Edmund Spenser's Poetry.* 3rd ed. Ed. Hugh Maclean and Anne Lake Prescott. New York: Norton, 1993.

Bloom, Harold. *The Invention of the Human.* New York: Riverhead Books, 1998.

——. *The Western Canon.* London: Papermac Macmillan, 1995.

Boelhower, William. " 'I'll Teach You How to Flow': On Figuring out Atlantic Studies." *Atlantic Studies* 1.1 (2004): 28–48.

Bradshaw, Graham. *Misrepresentations: Shakespeare and the Materialists.* London: Cornell UP, 1995.

Breen, T.H., Robert A. Divine, et al. *America Past and Present.* 5th ed. Vol. I New York: Longman, 1999.

Brevik, Frank W. "Calibans Anonymous: The Journey from Text to Self in Modern Interpretations of *The Tempest.*" *Authority of Expression in Early Modern England.* Ed. Nely Keinänen and Maria Salenius. Newcastle-upon-Tyne: Cambridge Scholars Publishing, 2009. 181–201.

Brotton, Jerry. "'This Tunis, Sir, was Carthage': Contesting Colonialism in *The Tempest.*" *Post-colonial Shakespeares.* Ed. Ania Loomba and Martin Orkin. London: Routledge, 1998. 23–42.

———. "Carthage and Tunis, *The Tempest* and Tapestries." *The Tempest and Its Travels.* Ed. Peter Hulme and William H. Sherman. Philadelphia, PA: U of Pennsylvania P, 2000. 132–7.

Brown, Paul. " 'This Thing of Darkness I Acknowledge Mine': *The Tempest* and the Discourse of Colonialism." *Political Shakespeare.* Ed. Jonathan Dollimore and Alan Sinfield. Manchester: Manchester UP, 1985. 48–71.

Brydon, Diana. "Re-Writing *The Tempest.*" *World Literature Written in English* 23.1 (1984): 75–88.

Bullough, Geoffrey. *Narrative and Dramatic Sources of Shakespeare.* Vol. VIII. London: Routledge and Kegan Paul, 1957. 75.

Burke, Kenneth. *Kenneth Burke on Shakespeare.* Edited with an Introduction by Scott L. Newstok. West Lafayette, IN: Parlor Press, 2007.

Cartelli, Thomas. "Prospero in Africa: The Tempest as Colonialist Text and Pretext." *Shakespeare Reproduced.* Ed. Jean E. Howard and Marion O'Connor. New York: Methuen, 1987. 105–07.

Castells, Ricardo. "Fernández Retamar's '*The Tempest*' in a Cafetera: From Ariel to Mariel." *Cuban Studies* 25 (1995): 165–82.

Césaire, Aimé. *Discours Sur Le Colonialisme.* 6th ed. Paris: Présence Africaine, 1955.

Cefalu, Paul A. "Rethinking the Discourse of Colonialism in Economic Terms: Shakespeare's *The Tempest,* Captain John Smith's Virginia Narratives, and the English Response to Vagrancy." *Shakespeare Studies* 28 (2000): 85–119.

Charles, Asselin "Colonial Discourse Since Christopher Columbus." *Journal of Black Studies* 26 (1995): 134–52. JSTOR. U of Louisiana at Lafayette Edith Garland Dupré Library. 28 Apr. 2005. <http://www.jstor.org/>.

Cheyfitz, Eric. *The Poetics of Imperialism: Translation and Colonization from The Tempest to Tarzan.* Philadelphia, PA: U of Pennsylvania P, 1997.

Cinpoeş, Nicoleta. " 'Lose the Name of Action': Stillness in Post-1989 Romanian *Hamlets.*" *Shakespeare Bulletin* 25.1 (Spring 2007): 61–85.

Coleman, James W. *Black Male Fiction and the Legacy of Caliban.* Lexington: UP of Kentucky, 2001.

Columbus, Christopher. *Travellers' Tales*. Ed. Jay Du Bois. New York: Everybody's Vacation Publishing Co., n.d. 44–50.

——. "The Letter of Christopher Columbus to Luis de Santángel." *Travel Narratives from The Age of Discovery: An Anthology*. Ed. Peter Mancall. New York: Oxford UP, 2006. 207–13.

Coursen, Herbert. "Using Film and Television to Teach *The Winter's Tale* and *The Tempest*." *Approaches to Teaching Shakespeare's The Tempest and Other Late Romances*. Ed. Maurice Hunt. New York: Modern Language Association of America, 1992. 117–24.

Cox, John D. "Recovering Something Christian about *The Tempest*." *Christianity and Literature* 50.1 (2000): 31–51. *Literature Resource Center*. U of Louisiana at Lafayette Edith Garland Dupré Library. 21 Oct. 2003. <http://galenet.galegroup.com/>.

Cullen, Patrick. *Spenser, Marvell, and Renaissance Pastoral*. Cambridge, MA: Harvard UP, 1970.

Danielsen, Eric. *Vygotsky: Psykologiens Mozart*. Copenhagen: Dansk psykologisk forlag, 1996.

Delabatista, Dirk. "Caliban's Afterlife: Reading Shakespearean Readings." *Constellation Caliban: Figurations of a Character*. Ed. Nadia Lee. Amsterdam: Rodopi B.V., 1997. 1–22.

Desmet, Christy, and Roger Bailey. "The Shakespeare Dialogues: (Re)producing *The Tempest* in Secondary and University Education." *College Literature*. 36.1 (Winter 2009). 121–40.

Devereaux, E.J. "Sacramental Imagery in *The Tempest*." *Shakespeare's Christian Dimension*. Ed. Roy Battenhouse Bloomington & Indianapolis, IN: Indiana UP, 1994. 254–57.

Drake, Sir Francis "Drake's Famous Voyage—1577–1580." *Travellers' Tales*. Ed. Jay du Bois. New York: Everybody's Vacation Publishing Co., n.d. 153–66.

Duplessis-Hay, Michèle. " 'Th'indias of Spice and Mine': An Overview of the Poetic Plundering of New Worlds by Shakespeare and His Contemporaries." *Shakespeare in Southern Africa* 15 (2003): 1–10.

Elsom, John. *Is Shakespeare Still Our Contemporary?* London: Routledge, 1989.

Fairholt, F. W. *Costume in England: A History of Dress to the End of the Eighteenth Century*. Ed. H. A. Dillon. 3rd ed. London: George Bell and Sons, 1885.

Felperin, Howard. "Political Criticism at the Crossroads: The Utopian Historicism of *The Tempest*." *The Tempest*. Ed. Nigel Wood. Buckingham, England: Open UP, 1995.

Fiedler, Leslie A. *The Stranger in Shakespeare*. London: Croom Helm, 1973.

"Filberts." *Macmillan Encyclopedia 1996*. Ed. Alan Isaacs. Aylesbury, England: Market House Books, 1995.

Fish, Stanley. "Why Milton Matters; Or, Against Historicism." *Milton Studies* 44 (2004): 1–12.

Fitzmaurice, Andrew. *Humanism and America: An Intellectual History of English Colonisation, 1500–1625*. Cambridge: Cambridge UP, 2003.

Fleissner, Robert. "Caliban's Name and the 'Brave New World.'" *Names: A Journal of Onomastics* 40.4 (1992): 295–8.

Franklin, John Hope. *From Slavery to Freedom*. 3rd ed. New York: Vintage Books, 1969.

Franssen, Paul. "A Muddy Mirror." *Constellation Caliban: Figurations of a Character*. Amsterdam: Rodopi B.V., 1997. 23–43.

Frassinelli, Pier Paolo. "Shakespeare and Transculturation: Aimé Césaire's *A Tempest*." *Native Shakespeares: Indigenous Appropriations on a Global Stage*. Ed. Craig Dionne and Parmita Kapadia. Aldershot, England: Ashgate, 2008. 173–186.

Frey, Charles. "*The Tempest* and the New World." *Shakespeare Quarterly* 30.1 (1979): 29–41.

Gillies, John. "The Figure of the New World in *The Tempest*." *The Tempest and Its Travels*. Ed. Peter Hulme and William H. Sherman. Philadelphia, PA: U of Pennsylvania P, 2000. 180–200.

"Gorse." *The Oxford English Dictionary*. 4 Apr. 2006. www.oed.com

"Goss." *The American Heritage Dictionary*. 3rd ed. 1994.

Grady, Hugh, and Terence Hawkes. *Presentist Shakespeares*. London: Routledge, 2007.

Graff, Gerald, and James Phelan. *William Shakespeare's The Tempest: A Case Study in Critical Controversy*. 2nd ed. New York: Bedford/St. Martin's, 2000.

Grams Hunter, Robert. "The Regeneration of Alonso." *Shakespeare's Christian Dimension*. Ed. Roy Battenhouse. Bloomington & Indianapolis, IN: Indiana UP, 1994. 263–7.

Greenblatt, Stephen. *Marvelous Possessions: The Wonder of the New World*. Chicago: U of Chicago P, 1991.

——. *Learning to Curse: Essays in Early Modern Culture*. London: Routledge, 1990.

——. "The Best Way to Kill Our Literary Inheritance Is to Turn It into a Decorous Celebration of the New World Order." *The Tempest: A Case Study in Critical Controversy*. 2nd ed. Ed. Gerald Graff and James Phelan. Boston: Bedford/St. Martin's, 113–5.

Griffiths, Trevor. " 'This Island's Mine': Caliban and Colonialism." *Yearbook of English Studies* 13 (1983): 159–80.

Habicht, Werner. "Shakespeare and the Berlin Wall." *Shakespeare in the Worlds of Communism and Socialism*. Ed. Irena Makaryk and Joseph G. Price. Toronto: U of Toronto P, 2006.

"Hag." *the American Heritage Dictionary*. 3rd ed. 1994.

Hale, John. "Ferdinand as 'Log-Man' in *The Tempest*." *The Shakespeare Newsletter* 50.1 (2000): 31.

Hamilton, Donna. *Virgil and the Tempest: The Politics of Imitation*. Columbus, OH: Ohio State UP, 1990.

——. "Shakespeare's Romances and Jacobean Political Discourse." *Approaches to Teaching Shakespeare's The Tempest and Other Late Romances*. Ed. Maurice Hunt. New York: Modern Language Association of America, 1992. 66–77.

Hamlin, William M. "Men of Inde: Renaissance Ethnography and *The Tempest.*" *Shakespeare Studies* 22 (1994): 15–44.

Hariot, Sir Thomas. *A Brief and True Report of the New Found Land of Virginia.* New York: The History Book Club, Inc., 1951.

Harris, J.G. "Historicizing Greenblatt's Contrainment. *Critical Self-Fashioning: Stephen Greenblatt and the New Historicism.* Ed. Jürgen Pieters. Frankfurt: Peter Lang Verlag, 1999. 150–73.

Hart, Jonathan. *Columbus, Shakespeare, and the Interpretation of the New World.* New York: Palgrave Macmillan, 2003.

———. "Images of the Native in Renaissance Encounter Narratives." *ARIEL: A Review of International English Literature* 25.4 (1994): 55–76.

———. "Redeeming *The Tempest*: Romance and Politics." *Cahiers Elisabéthains: Late Medieval and Renaissance Studies* 49 (1996): 23–28.

Hassan, Ihab. *Radical Innocence: Studies in the Contemporary American Novel.* Princeton, NJ: Princeton UP, 1961.

Hawkes, Terence. *Shakespeare in the Present.* London: Routledge, 2002.

———. "Band of Brothers." *Presentist Shakespeares.* Abingdon, Oxon.: Routledge, 2007. 6–26.

———. "Swisser-Swatter: The Making of a Man of English Letters." *Alternative Shakespeares.* Ed. John Drakakis. London: Methuen, 1985.

Headlam Wells, Robin. *Shakespeare on Masculinity.* Cambridge: Cambridge UP, 2000.

Hess, Andrew. "The Mediterranean and Shakespeare's Geopolitical Imagination." *The Tempest and Its Travels.* Ed. Peter Hulme and William H. Sherman. Philadelphia, PA: U of Pennsylvania P, 2000. 121–30.

Holy Bible. *Authorized King James Version.* Brussels: Thomas Nelson, Inc., 2001.

Hopkins, Lisa. *Shakespeare's The Tempest: The Relationship Between Text and Film.* London: Methuen, 2008.

Hulme, Peter. *Colonial Encounters.* London: Routledge, 1986.

———. "Hurricanes in the Caribbees: The Consititution of the Discourse of English colonialism." *1642: Literature and Power in the Seventeenth Century.* Ed. Francis Barker, et al. Colchester, England: University of Essex, 1981. 55–83.

———. "Reading from Elsewhere: George Lamming and the Paradox of Exile." *The Tempest and Its Travels.* Ed. Peter Hulme and William H. Sherman. Philadelphia, PA: U of Pennsylvania P, 2000. 220–35.

Hunt, Maurice. *Approaches to Teaching Shakespeare's the Tempest and Other Late Romances.* Ed. Maurice Hunt. New York: Modern Language Association of America, 1992.

"Jays." *Macmillan Encyclopedia 1996.* Ed. Alan Isaacs. Aylesbury, England: Market House Books, 1995.

Jirgens, Karl E. "Fusions of Discourse: Postcolonial/Postmodern Horizons in Baltic Culture. *Baltic Postcolonialism.* Ed. Violeta Kelertas. Amsterdam: Rodopi, 2006. 45–80.

Jourdain, Sylvester. "A Discovery of the Bermudas, Otherwise Called the Isle of Devils." *A Voyage to Virginia in 1609*. Ed. Louis B. Wright. Charlottesville, VA: UP of Virginia, 1964.

Kamps, Ivo. "New Historicizing the New Historicism; or, Did Stephen Greenblatt Watch the Evening News in 1968?" *Historicizing Theory*. Ed. Peter C. Herman. Albany, NY: U of New York P, 2004. 159–89.

Kelertas, Violeta. "Introduction: Baltic Postcolonialism and Its Critics." *Baltic Postcolonialism*. Ed. Violeta Kelertas. Amsterdam: Rodopi, 2006. 1–10.

Kingsley-Smith, J. "*The Tempest*'s Forgotten Exile." *Shakespeare Survey: An Annual Survey of Shakespeare Studies and Production* 54 (2001): 223–33.

Knapp, Jeffrey. *An Empire Nowhere: England, America, and Literature from Utopia to The Tempest*. Berkeley, CA: U of California P, 1992.

Knox, Bernard. " '*The Tempest*' and the Ancient Comic Tradition." *The Tempest*. Ed. Robert Langbaum. New York: Signet Penguin, 1987. 163–81.

Kostihová, M. *Shakespeare in Transition: Political Appropriations in the Postcommunist Czech Republic*. Basingstoke, England: Palgrave, 2010.

Lamming, George. *Pleasures of Exile*. Paperback ed. Ann Arbor, MI: U of Michigan P, 1999.

La Grand, Virginia, and Craig Mattson. "Brave New Performance Space: Castaway Pedagogy in the Age of Caliban." *Christian Scholar's Review*. XXXV.4 (Summer 2006): 471–91.

Lee, Sidney. *A Life of William Shakespeare*. London: Smith, Elder, 1898.

Leggatt, Alexander. *Shakespeare's Political Drama*. London: Routledge, 1988.

Levinson, Marjorie. "What Is New Formalism?" *PMLA* 122.2 (March 2007): 558–69.

Lewis, R.W.B. *The American Adam: Innocence, Tragedy, and Tradition in the Nineteenth Century*. Chicago: U of Chicago P, 1955.

Linton, Joan Pong. *The Romance of the New World: Gender and the Literary Formations of English Colonialism. New York: Cambridge UP, 2005.The Literature of Renaissance England*. Ed. John Hollander and Frank Kermode. London: Oxford UP, 1973.

Loomba, Ania. *Shakespeare, Race, and Colonialism*. New York: Oxford UP, 2002.

———. Excerpts from *Gender, Race, Renaissance Drama*. *The Tempest: A Case Study in Critical Controversy*. Ed. Gerald Graff and James Phelan. Boston: Bedford/St. Martin's, 2009. 389–401.

MacIntyre, Jean. "Enchanted Islands Floating on the Foam of a Perilous Sea." *Quidditas* 26 & 27 (2005–2006): 78–89.

Macmillan Encyclopedia 1996. Ed. Alan Isaacs. Aylesbury, England: Market House Books, 1995.

Malone, Edmond. *An Account of the Indicents, Form Which the Title and Part of the Story of Shakespeare's Tempest Were Derived; and Its True Date Ascertained*. London: C. & R. Baldwin, 1808.

———. *The Plays and Poems of William Shakespeare*. Ed. Edmond Malone. Vol. XV. London: F.C. & J. Rivingston et al., 1821.

Mannoni, Octave. *Prospero and Caliban; the Psychology of Colonization.* London: Methuen, 1956.

Marcus, Leah. *Unediting the Renaissance: Shakespeare, Marlowe, Milton.* London: Routledge, 1996.

"Marmazet." *Macmillan Encyclopedia* 1996. Ed. Alan Isaacs. Aylesbury, England: Market House Books, 1995.

Márquez, Robert. "Foreword." *The Massachusetts Review* XV (1973–1974): 6.

Marx, Leo. *The Machine in the Garden.* London: Oxford UP, 1964.

McAlindon, Tom. *Shakespeare Minus "Theory."* Aldershot, England: Ashgate, 2004.

McNee, Lisa. "Teaching in the Multicultural Tempest." *College Literature* 3/1.19/20 (1993): 195–202.

Montaigne, Michel de. "Of the Canniballes." *The Essayes of Michel Lord of Montaigne.* Trans. John Florio. Ed. Henry Morley. London: George Routledge and Sons, 1885. 92–99.

Moore, David Chioni. "Is the Post- in Postcolonial the Post- in Post-Soviet? Towards a Global Postcolonial Critique." *Baltic Postcolonialism.* Ed. Violeta Kelertas. Amsterdam: Rodopi, 2006. 11–43.

Miller, Perry. *Errand into the Wilderness.* New York: Harper & Row, 1964.

Nicolaescu, Madalina. "Reframing Shakespeare in Recent Translations of *The Tempest." EMCO* (2010/2011): 35–47.

Niekerk, Marinus van. "*The Tempest* in South Africa: Multilingualism and Our Profit On't." *The English Academy Review* 23 (2006): 114–21.

Norbrook, David. " 'What Cares These Roarers for the Name of King?': Language and Utopia in *The Tempest." The Politics of Tragicomedy.* Ed. Jonathan Hope and Gordon McMulland. London: Routledge, 1992.

Orkin, Martin. "Whose Thing of Darkness? Reading/Representing *The Tempest* in South Africa after April 1994." *Shakespeare and National Culture.* Ed. John J. Joughin. Manchester: Manchester UP, 1997. 142–69.

Percy, George. History Channel; ABC Clio. *The Jamestown Colony.* 27 Jan. 2008. <http://209.85.165.104/search?q=cache:Fn3GDD1x83QJ:www.jamestown.abc-clio.com>.

Prospero's Books. Dir. Peter Greenaway. Perf. Sir John Gielgud, Michael Clark, and Michel Blanc. Allarts, 1991.

Quiller-Couch, Sir Arthur. "*The Tempest." Twentieth Century Interpretations of The Tempest.* Ed. Hallett Smith. Englewood Cliffs, NJ: Prentice Hall, 1969.

Radice, Betty. *Who's Who in the Ancient World.* London: Penguin, 1973.

Raleigh, Sir Walter. "The Discoverie of Guiana." *Travellers' Tales.* Ed. Jay du Bois. New York: Everybody's Vacation Publishing Co., n.d. 197–226.

———. "A Brief and True Report of the New Found Land of Virginia." *Travellers' Tales.* Ed. Jay du Bois. New York: Everybody's Vacation Publishing Co., n.d. 167–175.

———. "The Discovery of the Large, Rich, and Bewtiful Empyre of Guiana." *Travel Narratives from The Age of Discovery: An Anthology.* Ed. Peter Mancall. New York: Oxford UP, 2006. 332–7.

Retamar, Roberto Fernando. *Caliban and Other Essays*. Minneapolis/St. Paul: U of Minnesota P, 1989.

Richmond, Hugh M. "Teaching *The Tempest* and the Late Plays by Performance." *Approaches to Teaching Shakespeare's The Tempest and Other Late Romances*. Ed. Maurice Hunt. New York: Modern Language Association of America, 1992. 125–32.

Sanchez, Melissa E. "Seduction and Service in *The Tempest*." *Studies in Philology* 105.1 (2008): 50–82

"Scamels"/"Seamews." *Macmillan Encyclopedia 1996*. Ed. Alan Isaacs. Aylesbury, England: Market House Books, 1995.

Schalkwyk, David. "Between Historicism and Presentism: Love and Service in *Antony and Cleopatra* and *The Tempest*." *Shakespeare in Southern Africa* 17 (2005): 1–17

Schneider, Ben Ross. " 'Are We Being Historical Yet?': Colonialist Interpretations of Shakespeare's *The Tempest*." *Shakespeare Studies* 23 (1995): 120–45.

Scott-Wilson Okamura, David. "Virgilian Models of Colonization in Shakespeare's *Tempest*." *ELH* 70 (2003): 709–37.

Shakespeare, William. *The Tempest*. *The Riverside Shakespeare*. Boston: Houghton Mifflin Company, 1997.

——. *The Tempest*. Ed. Ronald Herder. Mineola, NY: Dover Publications, 1999.

——. *The Tempest*. Ed. Robert Langbaum. New York: Signet Penguin, 1987.

——. *The Tempest*. Ed. Stephen Orgel. Oxford: Oxford UP, 1987.

——. *The Tempest*. *The Literature of Renaissance England*. Ed. John Hollander and Frank Kermode. New York: Oxford UP, 1973.

——. *The Tempest*. Ed. Frank Kermode. London: Methuen, 1954.

——. *The Tempest*. Jatinder Verma. Tara Arts Theatre, London. 17 Jan. 2008.

——. *Antony and Cleopatra*. *The Riverside Shakespeare*. Boston: Houghton Mifflin Company, 1997.

——. *Othello*. *The Riverside Shakespeare*. Boston: Houghton Mifflin Company, 1997.

——. *Hamlet*. *The Riverside Shakespeare*. Boston: Houghton Mifflin Company, 1997.

——. *As You Like It*. *The Riverside Shakespeare*. Boston: Houghton Mifflin Company, 1997.

Shakespeare in the New Europe. Ed. Michael Hattaway, Boika Sokolova, and Derek Roper. Sheffield: Sheffield Academic Press, 1994.

Shurbanov, Alexander and Sokolova, Boika. *Painting Shakespeare Red: An East-European Appropriation*. Newark, NJ: University of Delaware Press, 2001.

Sillars, Stuart. *Painting Shakespeare: The Artist as Critic, 1720–1820*. Cambridge: Cambridge UP, 2006.

Smith, Hallett. "The Tempest as Kaleidoscope." *Twentieth Century Interpretations of the Tempest*. Ed. Hallett Smith. Englewood Cliffs, NJ: Prentice Hall, 1969.

Sokol, B.J. *A Brave New World of Knowledge: Shakespeare's The Tempest and Early Modern Epistemology*. London: Associated UP, 2003.

Sousa, Geraldo de. *Shakespeare's Cross-Cultural Encounters*. London: Macmillan, 1999.

——. "Alien Habitats in *The Tempest*." *The Tempest: Critical Essays*. Ed. Patrick M. Murphy. New York: Routledge, 2001.

Skura, Meredith Anne. "Discourse and the Individual: The Case of Colonialism in *The Tempest*." *Shakespeare Quarterly* 40 (1989): 42–69.

Solomon, Julie Robin. "Going Places: Absolutism and Movement in Shakespeare's *The Tempest*." *Renaissance Drama* 22 (1991): 3–45.

Stavreva, Kirilka. "Dream Loops and Short-Circuited Nightmares: Post-Brechtian *Tempests* in Post-Communist Bulgaria." *Borrowers and Lenders: The Journal of Shakespeare and Appropriation*. III.2 (Spring 2008): n.p.

Stoll, E.E. "*The Tempest*": *Twentieth Century Interpretations of The Tempest*. Ed. Hallett Smith. Englewood Cliffs, NJ: Prentice Hall, 1969.

Strachey, William. "A True Reportery of the Wreck and Redemption of Sir Thomas Gates, Knight." *A Voyage to Virginia in 1609*. Ed. Louis B. Wright. Charlottesville, VA: UP of Virginia, 1964. 1–102.

Stříbrný, Zdeněk. *Shakespeare and Eastern Europe*. New York: Oxford UP, 2000.

Taylor, Gary. *Reinventing Shakespeare: A Cultural History from the Restoration to the Present*. New York: Oxford UP, 1989.

Thomson, Ann. " 'Miranda, Where's Your Sister?': Reading Shakespeare *The Tempest*." *The Tempest: A Case Study in Critical Controversy*. Eds. Gerald Graff and James Phelan. Boston: Bedford/St. Martin's, 2009. 402–12.

Tillyard, E.M.W. *The Elizabethan World Picture*. London: Penguin, 1990.

——. *Shakespeare's Last Plays*. London: Chatto and Windus, 1951.

Traversi, Derek. *An Approach to Shakespeare 2: Troilus and Cressida to The Tempest*. 3rd ed. London: Hollis and Carter, 1969.

Vargas Llosa, Mario. *The Storyteller*. Trans. Helen Lane. New York: Penguin, 1989.

Vaughan, Alden T. and Vaughan, Virginia Mason. *Shakespeare's Caliban: A Cultural History*. Cambridge, England: Cambridge UP, 1991.

Vaughan, Alden T., "Shakespeare's Indian: The Americanization of Caliban."*Shakespeare Quarterly* 39 (1988): 139–153.

——. "Trinculo's Indian: American Natives in Shakespeare's England." *The Tempest and Its Travels*. Ed. Peter Hulme and William H. Sherman. Philadelphia, PA: U of Pennsylvania P, 2000. 49–59.

——. "Caliban in the Third World: Shakespeare's Savage as Sociopolitical Symbol." *Massachusetts Review* 29 (1988): 289–313.

——. *American Genesis: Captain John Smith and the Founding of Virginia*. Boston: Little, Brown, and Company, 1975.

Vaught, Jennifer C. *Masculinity and Emotion in Early Modern English Literature*. Aldershot, England: Ashgate, 2008.

Walch, Gunter. " 'What's Past is Prologue': Metatheatrical Memory and Transculturation in '*The Tempest*.' " *Travel and Drama in Shakespeare's Time*. Ed. Jean-Pierre Maquerlot and Michele Willems. Cambridge, England: Cambridge UP, 1996.

White, Jessica L. "*The Tempest*: A Warning against Colonization." Term paper. LaGrange College, 2009.

Whitefield, Philip. *The Simon and Schuster Encyclopedia of Animals.* New York: Simon & Schuster Editions, 1998.

Wilson, John Dover. "The Enchanted Island." *Twentieth Century Interpretations of The Tempest.* Ed. Hallett Smith. Englewood Cliffs, NJ: Prentice Hall, 1969.

Wylie, John. "New and Old Worlds: *The Tempest* and Early Colonial Discourse." *Social and Cultural Geography* 1.1 (2000): 45–63. *JSTOR*. Web. 12 Nov. 2009.

Index

Absolutism, 155, 164
Adam, American, 15, 105, 106, 176
Adamic readers, 7, 14, 15–16, 18, 22–3,
    26, 160–1
African-American, 3, 55, 61–2, 65, 120,
    174
Alcohol, 68, 110, 132–3, 166, 172, 174
America, 3, 4, 5, 8, 9, 10, 13, 15, 21–2,
    25–6, 39, 42, 43, 47, 50–1, 53, 55,
    57–8, 59, 61, 62–3, 65, 74–5, 76,
    79, 86, 89–90, 91–2, 99–101,
    104–6, 114, 118–2, 133, 136–8,
    163, 166, 171, 172, 174, 176, 177
America; as setting for *The Tempest*,
    51–4, 56–60, 62, 64, 65, 74,
    99–100, 114, 119, 120, 163–4
Anarchy, 105–6, 117–19, 120, 121, 123,
    125–6, 128, 164
    Christian pacifism as anarchy,
        117–19
    as voluntary order, 117–19
Antigone, 61
Antony and Cleopatra, 35, 87
Apartheid, 134–5, 138, 151–2
Arab Spring, 134, 137, 156
Atlantic, 39, 41, 42, 45, 47, 50, 53, 62,
    65, 114, 163, 174
Atlantis, 49–50, 114
Aurelius, Marcus, 103, 110
Australia, 25, 171, 175

Bach, Rebecca Ann, 71, 97–8
Beowulf, 67, 100
Berlin Wall, 138, 139, 141, 156, 167,
    169

Bermuda, 8, 16, 30, 36–7, 41, 43, 45,
    49, 51–2, 63–4, 172
Bible, 49, 67, 81, 84, 86, 88
Bloom, Harold, 24, 136
Burma, 95, 138

Caliban, 3, 4, 5, 7, 8, 9, 10, 11, 16, 17,
    18, 22, 23, 26, 28, 29, 30, 31, 40–1,
    42, 44, 46–7, 50, 51, 54, 55–68, 72,
    73, 74, 76, 77, 78, 79, 80, 81, 84–5,
    86, 88, 89, 90, 94, 96, 98, 100, 107,
    108, 110, 113, 115, 120–4, 125,
    126, 127, 128, 131, 132, 133, 134,
    137, 139, 145, 146, 150–2, 153–5,
    156, 162, 163–6, 171, 172, 173,
    174, 175, 176
Calibanismo, 16, 22, 59, 68, 150, 151
Callahan, Dympna, 137
Cambodia, 138
Capitalism, 75, 120–1, 150, 162, 174
Caribbean, 7, 11, 18, 46, 57, 60, 62, 64,
    74, 150, 152
Castro, Fidel, 137, 174
Ceausescu, Nicolae, 155
Césaire, Aimé, 5, 9, 22, 56, 62, 72, 73–5,
    80, 89, 120, 154, 156, 165, 174
China, 156, 174
Christianity, 6, 25, 84, 172
Christian pacifism, 117
Class, 25, 37, 74–5, 76, 80, 95, 124, 144,
    151, 155, 165
Climate, 8, 42, 43
Colonialism, 3, 5, 6, 7, 8, 24–5, 39, 41,
    42, 72–8, 82, 87, 90, 96, 119, 120,
    133–4, 136, 156, 167, 174

Columbus, Christopher, 39, 43, 62–3, 93, 107, 136
Communion, 173
Communism, 5, 11, 78–9, 133, 136, 139, 141–3, 144–7, 148–9, 151, 155, 156, 162
Conquistadors, 155
Cooper, James Fenimore, 105, 127, 176
Cuba, 11, 58, 133–4, 137, 138, 152
Cultural materialism, 5, 8–9, 14, 36, 41, 68, 131, 133, 136, 148, 149, 159, 161, 162, 167, 169

Derrida, Jacques, 40
Dystopia, 6, 9, 75, 105, 128, 136, 145–6, 148–9, 167

Elizabeth I, 102
Emerson, Ralph Waldo, 126–7
England, 36, 39, 50–1, 53, 62, 67, 76, 96, 102, 106, 133, 163, 165, 173, 174
Eutopia, 85
Exile, 11, 36–7, 39, 41, 44, 45, 46, 61, 74, 92, 98, 105, 121, 122, 128, 133, 134, 150–1, 152, 153, 157
Soviet exiles, 134, 150–1

Fanon, Frantz, 9, 75, 120, 156, 174
Feminist scholarship on *The Tempest*, 10, 71, 91, 95–8, 102, 136, 149, 167, 175
Ferdinand, 4, 10, 47–8, 66, 72, 86, 90, 91, 95, 98–111, 114, 125, 127, 150, 154, 163–4, 170, 175, 176
Fish, Stanley, 159
Folklore, Old World, 65, 73, 90
Foucault, Michel, 150
France, 150
Fukuyama, Francis, 150

Geography, 7–10, 19, 35–56, 58, 60, 62, 65, 74, 76, 90, 100, 102, 109, 114, 119–20, 128, 162, 163, 166, 173, 174, 176

German Democratic Republic, 139, 155
Germany, 55, 66, 139, 155, 173
Globe Theatre, 50–1, 107, 140
Graff, Gerald, 19–21, 170
Greece, 38, 65
Greenblatt, Stephen, 24, 63, 87, 135, 169
Grendel, 67

Hablador, El, see Storyteller, The
Hamlet, 28, 53, 106, 110, 139, 141–3, 165
Hassan, Ihab, 105–6
Headlam Wells, Robin, 98–9, 103
Hegel, Georg Wilhelm Friedrich, 161
Herrick, Robert, 117
Historicism, 5, 7, 9, 14, 17, 20, 24, 26–7, 36, 39, 41, 68, 96, 131, 132, 133, 135, 136, 137, 148, 161–2, 167, 169
Hitler, Adolf, 73
Hobbes, Thomas, 117–18
Honecher, Erich, 155
Hulme, Peter, 5, 7, 37, 60, 66, 120, 156
Human rights, 10, 25, 61, 83–4, 122, 125, 126, 137, 155, 166

India, 25, 177
Indians, *see* Native Americans
Ireland, 67, 76–7, 86
Irish, 55, 67, 76–7, 137
Iser, Wolfgang, 159
Israel, 85, 137
Italian, 36, 44, 47–8, 170
Italy, 38–9, 41, 44, 48, 58, 117, 174

James I, 102
Jarman, Derek, 31
Jesus Christ, 102, 107, 164, 176
Jewish, 68, 72, 81, 85, 87, 172
Jourdain, Sylvester, 107, 118

Kenya, 22, 58–9
Kermode, Frank, 37, 65, 66, 82, 115, 121, 137, 152, 172

King, Dr. Martin Luther, 154
Kott, Jan, 37, 139, 155

Lamming, George, 5, 18, 22, 23, 26, 41,
    60–2, 72, 74, 75, 80, 120, 156, 165
Laputa, 7, 37, 56
Lee, Sidney, 3, 57, 59, 137, 171
Lewis, R.W.B., 15, 105
London, 8, 50–1, 102, 134, 140
Loomba, Ania, 5, 95–6

Machiavellianism, 105, 124, 148, 150,
    154, 164
Machiguenga, 72, 81–2, 84–9
Malone, Edmond, 3, 59, 137, 174
Mandela, Nelson, 10, 152–3, 156
Marlowe, Christopher, 49, 92, 175
Marxist criticism, 6, 8, 72, 134, 136,
    138, 143, 148, 150, 160, 167, 174
Marx, Leo, 10, 36, 96, 99–100, 103, 118,
    119–20, 127
Miranda, 57, 63, 66, 72, 79, 80–1, 83,
    84, 85, 86, 91, 95, 96, 98, 103–4,
    108, 110, 114, 121, 124, 127,
    150–1, 154, 155, 163, 164, 172, 175
Missionaries, 79, 83, 84–9
More, Thomas, 53, 65, 114, 117, 118
Mubarak, Hosni, 136
Myanmar, see Burma

Native Americans, 14, 20, 37, 69, 73,
    75, 132, 175
New criticism, 7, 26, 171
New historicism, see Historicism
Ngugi wā Thiong'o, 22, 58
Non-violence, see Pacifism

Orgel, Stephen, 47, 96, 97
Orkin, Martin, 10, 132, 134–5, 152

Pacifism, 117
Paul of Tarsus, 86, 117
Phelan, James, 19–21, 170
Phenomenology, 131, 135, 140, 147
Pocahontas, 47–8

Post-colonialist criticism, 4, 5, 9, 10,
    13, 16, 17, 18, 19, 20–1, 23, 24, 26,
    36, 57, 68, 71, 73, 95, 98, 120,
    131–2, 133–4, 136, 144–5, 148,
    150, 156, 157, 162, 167, 170
Prospero, 4, 5, 6, 11, 17, 18, 23, 25, 26,
    29, 30, 31, 38, 40–1, 43, 44, 45–7,
    48, 51, 56–7, 58–9, 61, 63, 64–8,
    72, 73–5, 76, 77, 78–9, 84–5, 86,
    89, 91, 95–103, 105–6, 108,
    109–10, 114, 115–16, 119, 121–2,
    124–5, 126, 127–8, 132, 133, 134,
    137, 143, 145–6, 148, 149–50, 151,
    153, 154–5, 163–5, 166, 171, 172,
    173, 174, 175, 176
Puritans, 10, 49, 106, 118, 127, 172

Quiller-Couch, Arthur, 35, 173

Ralegh, Walter, 94
Reader-Response theory, 14, 17, 22,
    159
Revolutions of 1989, 4–5, 10–11, 95,
    129–57, 167
Romania, 138, 141–4

Said, Edward, 42, 137
Shakespeare, William; plays by:
    1 Henry IV, 68
    Antony and Cleopatra, 35, 87–8
    Hamlet, 28, 53, 106, 110, 139, 141–3
    King Lear, 68, 141
    Macbeth, 28, 67–8
    Merchant of Venice, 16, 22, 68, 96,
        132, 155
    Othello, 16, 28, 46, 68, 92, 93, 96,
        110, 150
    Pericles, 35
    Titus Andronicus, 16
    Winter's Tale, 28, 35
    As You Like It, 116, 126
Skura, Meredith Anne, 5–6, 42, 63
Solzhynetsin, Alexandr, 151, 153
Soviet Union, 10, 134, 137–8, 141–2,
    150–1, 152

Stalin, Joseph, 139, 142, 151
Stoicism, 98, 103
Storyteller, The, 20, 83–4, 92–3, 99, 101–2
Strachey, William, 16, 22, 30, 36, 37, 39, 41, 62, 63, 92, 93, 107, 110, 118, 127

Thoreau, Henry David, 105, 126–7
Tillyard, E.M.W., 124

Uncle Tom's Cabin, 154
Utopia, 53, 65, 114, 117, 118

Vargas Llosa, Mario, 9, 71–90
Vaughan, Alden T., 7, 30, 47, 50, 55, 58, 59, 62, 172, 173, 176
Vaughan, Virginia Mason, 7, 30, 47, 55, 58, 59, 62, 172, 173, 176
Vaught, Jennifer, ix, 99, 104, 175
von Donnersmark, Florian Henckel, 154

Walesa, Lech, 153
White, Jessica, ix, 13, 20–7, 28–32
Whitman, Walt, 101, 127

Zuratas, Saul, 72–3, 81, 82, 83, 85–8